THE POWER OF FUN

THE POWER OF FUN

Why fun is the key to a happy
and healthy life

CATHERINE PRICE

PENGUIN BOOKS

TRANSWORLD PUBLISHERS
Penguin Random House, One Embassy Gardens,
8 Viaduct Gardens, London SW11 7BW
www.penguin.co.uk

Transworld is part of the Penguin Random House group of companies
whose addresses can be found at global.penguinrandomhouse.com

First published in Great Britain in 2021 by Bantam Press
an imprint of Transworld Publishers
Penguin paperback edition published 2023

A CIP catalogue record for this book
is available from the British Library.

ISBN
9781529176810

Typeset in Dante MT Pro by Jouve (UK), Milton Keynes.
Printed and bound in Great Britain by Clays Ltd, Elcograf S.p.A.

The authorized representative in the EEA is Penguin Random House Ireland,
Morrison Chambers, 32 Nassau Street, Dublin D02 YH68.

Penguin Random House is committed to a sustainable
future for our business, our readers and our planet. This book
is made from Forest Stewardship Council® certified paper.

To all my Fun Squads, past, present, and future:
Thank you for helping me feel alive.

"If you get in the habit of your life being fun, if you move through life believing it's supposed to be that way, you'll notice when it's not. I've been making life fun for so long I can't imagine putting up with no fun. But the inverse is true, too. If you get in the habit of life not being fun, you start to not even notice, because that's what you're used to."

—MICHAEL LEWIS

CONTENTS

CONTENTS

THE POWER OF FUN

PROLOGUE

WHEN IS THE LAST TIME YOU HAD FUN?

I'm serious. Think about it. When's the last time you felt exhilarated and lighthearted? When's the last time you didn't feel judged, by yourself or other people? When's the last time you were engaged, focused, and completely present, undistracted by thoughts about the future or the past? When's the last time you felt free? When's the last time you felt alive?

Maybe you were laughing with a friend. Maybe you were exploring a new place. Maybe you were being slightly rebellious. Maybe you were trying something for the first time. Maybe you felt an unexpected sense of connection. Regardless of the activity, the result was the same: You laughed and smiled. You felt liberated from your responsibilities. When it was over, the experience left you energized, nourished, and refreshed.

If you are having trouble thinking of a recent moment that fits that description, I hear you. Until recently, I didn't feel like I was having much fun myself.

And then two things happened that transformed me.

The first occurred as a result of the birth of my daughter. After years of debating whether to have a child, followed by more than a year of trying, I became pregnant in the middle of 2014. Instead of expressing our nesting instincts through reasonable, small-scale projects, like closet organization or rethinking our spice rack, my husband and I decided that my pregnancy would be the ideal time to embark upon a full kitchen renovation—as in, one that involved ripping the room down to the studs and removing the back wall of our house in the middle of an East Coast January.

With a shared love of creative projects (and control), we also decided to design it ourselves. In my husband's case, this resulted in him spending hours researching kitchen faucets. In my case, it meant figuring out how to incorporate salvaged architectural elements into the kitchen, such as a mirrored Victorian armoire front that I had found in a dead neighbor's basement (long story) that I decided would make a perfect façade for a cookbook case and pull-out pantry.

I also spent hours on eBay searching for interesting details that we could add to the kitchen, a quest that left my search history littered with entries such as "vintage drawer pull" and "antique Eastlake door hinge 3x3." (Even today, my eBay watch list still includes items such as "Victorian Fancy Stick and Ball Oak Fretwork or Gingerbread—original finish" and "Old Chrome Art-Deco Vacant Engaged Toilet Bathroom Lock Bolt Indicator Door.")

As my belly grew bigger and our house colder, we had a running joke with our contractors—who by that point had become friends—about which project would be finished first, the kitchen or my pregnancy. It turned out that I won that contest, not because they were slow, but because I had an emergency C-section five and a half weeks before my due date. Eventually the kitchen renovation was finished, the armoire front became the pantry façade of my dreams, and I could finally stop my eBay searches.

Except I didn't stop. Even though I no longer had any plausible excuse for spending thirty minutes at a time trawling through listings for antique door hardware, I still found myself picking up my phone and opening eBay on autopilot, often during middle-of-the-night feeding sessions with my daughter. I'd cuddle her in one arm and hold my phone with the other, using my thumb to scroll. It didn't matter that all of the doors in our house already had knobs and hinges. I was searching for architectural salvage in the same way that other people consume social media: eyes glazed, hypnotized by the stream of images on my screen. The photos were less glamorous, but the compulsion was the same.

And then one night, while I was in the midst of yet another session, I looked away from my screen for a moment and caught my daughter's eye. She was staring up at me, her tiny face illuminated by my phone's blue light.

This must have happened countless times before, given how often newborns eat and the fact that at that point in my life, my phone was basically an appendage. But for some reason—maybe the fact that I have a background in mindfulness, maybe delirium caused by sleep deprivation—this time was different. I saw the scene from the outside, as if I were floating above my body, watching what was happening in the room. There was a baby, gazing up at her mother. And there was her mother, looking down at her phone.

I felt gutted.

The image hovered in my mind like a photograph of a crime scene. How had this happened? After all the work I'd done to cultivate self-awareness, how had I become a zombie so mesmerized by images on my phone (of door hardware, mind you!) that I was ignoring the baby—*my* baby—cradled in my arms?

This was not the impression I wanted my daughter to have of a relationship, let alone her relationship with her mother. And I didn't want this to be the way I experienced motherhood—or my own life.

In that moment, I realized that—without my awareness or consent—my phone had begun to control me. It was the first thing

I reached for in the morning and the last thing I looked at before bed. Any time I had a moment of stillness, it appeared in my hand. On the bus, in the elevator, in the bed, I always had my phone.

I noticed other changes, too, that, when I took the time to think about them, seemed like they also might be linked to my phone. My attention span was shot; I couldn't remember the last time I'd made it through even a magazine article without feeling a compulsion to pick up my phone to check for something (really, *anything*). I was spending much more time texting with friends than talking with them, and was doing things that objectively made no sense, such as checking and rechecking the news even though I knew doing so made me feel bad, or searching for new real estate listings even though we had no intention of moving.

Hours that I might previously have devoted to *doing* things, like playing music, learning a new skill, or interacting with my husband (as opposed to sitting in the same room together, parallel-scrolling) increasingly were spent staring at a screen. I'd morphed from an interesting, interested, independent-minded person into someone who had been hypnotized by a small rectangular object—an object whose apps were programmed by people working for giant companies that stood to profit from getting me to waste my time.

I'm not saying that technology is evil and that we should throw our phones and tablets into a river. Some of our screen time is productive, essential, and/or enjoyable. Some of it provides relaxation or escape. But it's also gotten out of control. I've become convinced that our phones and other wireless mobile devices (which are sometimes referred to as "WMDs"—weapons of mass distraction) are pulling our internal compasses seriously offtrack, insinuating themselves into our lives in ways that aren't just scattering our attention; they're changing the core of who we actually *are*.

And now my phone had infiltrated one of the most sacred spaces of all: my relationship with my daughter. This was not okay. As my husband would attest, I am so primed toward poignancy that I can become nostalgic for an experience while I am in the midst of having it—a character trait that having a child has only made worse. Life is short; kids grow up so quickly. I didn't want to coast through my days distracted and only half-present.

I wanted to *live*. And that meant I needed to change, fast.

I have a longstanding habit of turning my personal issues into professional projects, and it occurred to me that my husband and I were hardly the only people who were losing ourselves to our phones; it was just that, at that point, very few people were paying attention to what was happening. In fact, the more I looked up from my phone and observed the world around me, the more concerned I became. (If you try it yourself, you will, too.)

I saw people texting while driving seventy miles an hour on the highway, or crossing busy streets. I noticed whole families out to eat at restaurants, with each person's nose buried in a different device. I observed my own interactions with friends and family members, where inevitably one of us would whip out a phone and stroke its screen, almost as a tic, before slipping it back into a pocket or putting it back on the table. I felt like I was caught in a modern, real-life version of "The Emperor's New Clothes": I could see that all of us were acting like addicts, but since *everyone* was afflicted, we were deluding ourselves into thinking that our behaviors were normal and okay.

I also realized that, while there were a number of books that sounded the alarm about the possible negative mental and physical effects of spending hours each day exposing our brains to the non-stop stimulation of the internet (and consuming content that polarizes and divides us), there weren't any that offered a solution. So, shortly after my soul-searching moment with my daughter, I started working on a book called *How to Break Up With Your Phone* about how we can (and why we should) create healthier relationships with technology. I wrote it because I wanted to wrest back control from my devices—and to help other people do the same—so that I could get back to actually *living*.

By the end of the process, I had created a plan for how we can have healthier, more sustainable long-term relationships with our phones, and I had followed it myself. The result was not perfection (it's impossible to have a perfect relationship with anything, let alone a device that's designed to addict you), but the effects were transformative. I got my attention span back. I felt more creative and less stressed. I became more present with my husband and daughter. By helping me to reclaim my own time, creating better boundaries with technology had given me an opportunity to take back my life.

And that led to the second event that inspired this book.

As part of my research for *How to Break Up With Your Phone,* my husband and I had been taking regular twenty-four-hour breaks from all screens, usually from Friday to Saturday nights. We thought of these breaks as digital sabbaths and were continually amazed by their effects on time—both in terms of the sheer amount that opened up, and in the way that avoiding screens made our perception of time slow down. Instead of allowing our time to *be* filled, we now were in charge of how *we* wanted to fill it. Without apps to distract us, we found ourselves with more hours in the day—hours that we were free to use on things that we truly enjoyed.

There was just one problem: I no longer knew what I enjoyed. It turned out that, for all of its benefits, "breaking up" with my phone was only the first step. If I *really* wanted to reclaim my life, I needed to remember how to live.

This came to a head one cold Saturday afternoon in early 2017, in the midst of a digital sabbath, when I found myself on our living room couch as our daughter took a nap and my husband ran some errands. This should have been a blissful moment in early parenting: I was alone, it was quiet, and I had at least an hour in front of me that I could spend however I liked. But when I tried to think of an offline activity that I wanted to do, I couldn't come up with anything. I didn't feel like reading a book; I wasn't hungry; there wasn't anyone to talk to. My mind was drawing a blank.

Oh my God, I thought to myself as I indulged in one of my favorite pastimes: catastrophic thinking. *I'm just sitting here, waiting for time to pass till dinner. Which really means that I'm just waiting to die.*

Around the same time, I had been reading a book called *Designing Your Life*, in which two Stanford professors use design principles to help people build "well-lived, joyful lives." In it, I'd come across an exercise that had primed me for this particular descent into despair.

The exercise asks you to decide how full your "tanks" are in four areas—love, work, health, and play—so that you can identify the parts of your life that need attention.

A diligent student of anything involving self-improvement, I had immediately pulled out a pen. Love, health, and work were all close to full. But play? Or, as the authors put it, "activity that brings you joy just for the pure sake of doing it"? I could hardly think of anything that would qualify.

One of the many great things about taking breaks from screens and devices is that it forces you to be still. This stillness can be very uncomfortable, but it also gives your brain a chance to breathe—and to come up with new ideas. As I sat there, contemplating my empty play tank and my inevitable march toward death, I asked myself a question that I'd been posing to people while researching *How to Break Up With Your Phone*: What is something you've always said you wanted to do but that you supposedly don't have time for? The idea is that you probably have more time for it than you realize; you just need to reclaim some of the minutes and hours you're spending on your phone.

The first answer that came to my mind was "learn to play the guitar." I have played piano since I was five, and during college my grandmother (with whom I was very close, and who played guitar herself) had given me money to buy one for my birthday. A friend had taught me a few chords, but it had been years since I'd taken it out of its case; it had spent almost two decades in a closet, attracting dust and guilt.

Then a related memory popped into my head: a flier I'd seen for a music studio.

Technically, the flier had been for a *children*'s music studio—it was advertising a class called "Baby Beyoncé." But this had sparked my curiosity to the point that I had looked up the studio online, and had learned that it was run by a guy known as Mister John, who has a devoted following among Philadelphia parents due to the fact that instead of traditional children's music fare like "Wheels on the Bus," he features artists of the week such as Alicia Keys and David Bowie (and, yes, Beyoncé). While poking around on the site, I'd seen a tab on his website for Grown-Up Fun and had learned that he also ran a beginner's guitar class for adults. This had intrigued me but I hadn't taken any action on it. (I'd probably gotten distracted by whatever website was open in the neighboring browser tab.) But existential malaise can be very motivating. The next day, when I was back on-line, I signed up.

I was nervous—I was joining the class midsession, with my knowledge of the guitar limited to about three chords. But it turned out that the class, which met on Wednesday nights, was low-stakes and BYOB; my fellow students were mostly other parents who seemed to value having an hour and a half to hang out with other adults, without babies, as much as they did the music instruction itself.

With that said, we legitimately learned to play the guitar; before long, I felt capable of holding my own at any campfire singalong. Thanks to the class, I had found a new hobby that I enjoyed, and I was regularly experiencing the satisfaction that comes from acquiring a new skill. I also had made progress on the second half of my problem: now, when I found myself with a pocket of free time, I was much less likely to waste it on my phone or tumble into an existential spiral of despair. Instead, I pulled out my guitar and practiced.

These changes were more than enough to make the class worthwhile, but it didn't take me long to notice that there was something much bigger going on. When I was at the studio, I felt engaged and energized in a way that, during my workdays in particular, I normally did not. The time seemed to fly by; every week I looked up at the clock and couldn't imagine how ninety minutes had already passed. It was an hour and a half in which I was totally free from my responsibilities, with no one to take care of but myself. As a rule-following, conscientious adult, this liberation almost felt rebellious.

During class, my shoulders were looser. My breathing was easier. My mind felt stimulated but also relaxed. At that point I didn't know the other students well—in fact, I only learned what their professions were when we started going out for drinks—and yet when we were in class together, I felt oddly connected with them, as if we had created our own private community, separate from the outside world. And unlike nearly everything else I did with my time, the class had no specific *goal*; our purpose, both literally and metaphorically, was simply to *play*.

The feeling was intoxicating—and puzzling. Whatever satisfaction I was deriving from learning barre chords could not explain how much I loved going to class, let alone the buzz I felt afterward. Every time I went, I came home feeling rejuvenated and refreshed. Wednesday nights quickly became a highlight of my week.

Even more intriguingly, the class infused me with an exuberance that buoyed me for days. I was more playful around my husband. I was more present with our daughter. I felt less resentful of my obligations and less burdened by my lists of to-dos. Sure, it was nice to have a new hobby, but I also felt like I had a new source of *energy*. Something inside of me had been ignited that I hadn't even realized had gone dark. The more of this energy I experienced, the more ravenous for it I became.

What *was* this feeling? It was deeply familiar, but I couldn't put my finger on what to call it.

And then one day, it hit me: I was having *fun*.

But not "fun" in the mild, casual sense in which we often employ the term. This wasn't the feeling of doing something "fun" for yourself, like getting a pedicure, or buying a new TV. It wasn't the "fun" that we try to portray on social media, or the "fun" people seek by getting hammered at a bar.

This was something different, something much more powerful and life-affirming. I decided to call the feeling *"True* Fun" to distinguish it from these other uses, and I became obsessed with figuring out how to have more of it. My hope was that if I could identify the factors that had generated it, I could transform True Fun—the deficit of which, I now realized, had led to my existential moment on the couch—from an occasional serendipitous occurrence to something that I could seek out and create.

I started by thinking of other times in my life when I'd experienced the feeling I now called True Fun.

There was the ride home from a wedding where my husband and I had packed our car with friends and spent the trip belting "Bohemian Rhapsody" at the top of our lungs.

There was the swing-dancing camp in New Hampshire that we'd attended—five straight days of music and dancing, starting in the morning and continuing till the wee hours. I love how dancing transports me out of my head and into my body, and while I am usually asleep by 10:30 P.M., I'd felt so exhilarated that I stayed up well past midnight each night of the camp; on the last day, I didn't get to bed until after 4 A.M.

There was the cross-country bicycle trip I did right after college, on which I spent sixty-three spandex-clad days pedaling from Connecticut to San Francisco with a group of classmates. Every day, we biked from sixty to more than a hundred miles; we slept on floors; we often got up before 5 A.M. to beat the summer heat. The trip was physically grueling; there's nothing quite like staring up at the Rockies and realizing that you're going to have to cross them on a bicycle.

But the trip also served as an opportunity to spend two full months hanging out with some of my closest friends. It took place before smartphones, so we spent our free time making our own entertainment—joking around with one another, playing games we'd created, and visiting county fairs. I laughed, *hard*, every single day. Despite its challenges, that summer was one of the peak experiences of my life.

As I kept thinking, more memories like this came to mind, with different people and in different contexts. In each case, the sensation of True Fun had been unmistakable: it felt like a powerful form of energy had been unleashed, as if there had been an electric current in the air that—much like lightning—revealed itself when a particular confluence of factors drew it to one spot. When I was having True Fun, this energy rushed through me like a spark.

True Fun, I realized, is the feeling of being fully present and engaged, free from self-criticism and judgment. It is the thrill of losing ourselves in what we're doing and not caring about the outcome. It is laughter. It is playful rebellion. It is euphoric connection. It is the bliss that comes from letting go. When we are truly having fun, we are not lonely. We are not anxious or stressed. We are not consumed by self-doubt or existential malaise. There is a reason that our moments of True Fun stand out in our memories: True Fun makes us feel alive.

I was thrilled to have given language to my experience, but as soon as I labeled the feeling from my guitar class as True Fun, more questions emerged. For example, was True Fun dependent on certain people or contexts? It didn't seem like it. My husband and I had experienced True Fun together more times than I could count, and I had dear friends with whom it occurred quite often—but we didn't *always* have True Fun when we were together. Intimacy didn't seem to be a prerequisite, either: I'd had True Fun with strangers, and there were some acquaintances with whom it also seemed to regularly pop up. And while certain settings seemed particularly conducive to it, it wasn't limited by location.

Nor was True Fun dependent on (or guaranteed to be produced by) activities themselves. This surprised me, because I had initially assumed that the experience of True Fun must have been the result of what I was *doing* at the time. I *like* playing the guitar and dancing and singing and biking—which suggested that the secret to having more fun was to add more of these activities to my schedule.

But that idea felt exhausting. And besides, I could think of situations in which I had participated in the same activities but had *not* experienced that euphoric feeling. I didn't feel it when I played music alone or took a solitary bike ride. I had attended lots of dance classes that felt stilted and awkward. I'd had plenty of car rides—even car rides that involved singing—that didn't make me laugh until my face hurt. While there were definitely particular activities, people, and settings that seemed to act like *magnets* for True Fun, that outcome was far from guaranteed.

On the flip side, I'd had experiences that on the surface were uncomfortable or unremarkable, but that stood out in my mind as treasured memories precisely because they had generated True Fun—like that post-college bike trip, for example, or getting stranded with some friends on a day off when I was a camp counselor and having to sleep on the ground in a town square, or moments when I was teaching middle school math and my students did something that made me laugh out loud.

The more I thought about True Fun, the more I realized that, despite years spent reading and writing about happiness and mindfulness, I'd never thought specifically about fun at all—let alone thought to ask questions that might help me experience it more often. What was the difference between "fun" in the everyday sense of the word and True Fun? Why did some activities—often anything involving the internet or my phone—start off feeling sort of "fun" (with heavy air quotes) but leave me drained? How—and why—did it vary so much in intensity and duration? What were the factors that needed to be present in order for True Fun to emerge? And, most importantly, how could I have more of it?

These questions have led me on an adventure that has changed my life—and I want you to join me.

Before we dive in, it's important to acknowledge that we can only focus on True Fun if our basic needs are taken care of—food, shelter, adequate rest, and physical safety are definitely prerequisites, and there are many situations that can make it difficult, if not impossible, to focus on fun, such as poverty, sickness, abuse, trauma, and job insecurity. But with that major caveat aside, I've come to realize that we have multiple misunderstandings about fun, and that many of our arguments against making it a priority don't stand up to scrutiny.

For example, I've had people tell me point-blank that they are not "fun people." (One person told me he was so incapable of having fun that a former girlfriend referred to him as "Nuf"—fun, backward.) But provided that the prerequisites mentioned above have been met, there is no rule saying that only certain types of people get to have fun (or be considered "fun people"). Nor do we need to compete with each other for it; True Fun is not a scarce resource, accessible only to an elite few. And while it's easy to get caught up in materialistic striving and be tricked into believing that if you were richer, you'd be having more fun, that's not true, either; sure, money can be helpful, but True Fun doesn't require wealth. While some of the changes I've made are things I've had to pay for (e.g., guitar class), many of them have been free, and some have actually *saved* me money. Once you realize that accumulating possessions doesn't lead to fun, you buy fewer things.

Some people think that they're not capable of having True Fun because they're anxious and depressed. This is a growing problem:

the past decade has seen huge increases in rates of depression and anxiety among people around the world, and Americans in particular. Even if we haven't received an official diagnosis, many of us are suffering from emptiness, loneliness, boredom, and a general sense of languishing.

But I would argue that in many cases, we are mixing up the cause and the effect: we are suffering from these afflictions *because we are not having enough fun.** True Fun isn't just a *result of* happiness, in other words; it's a *cause*.

A lot of people claim not to have *time* for fun. But fun does not necessarily require us to become busier, or to add more activities to our already full schedules. Instead, the first step in having more True Fun is to create space by doing *fewer* things, so that you can take advantage of opportunities for True Fun in your life that already exist and spend your free time in more targeted ways.

On the flip side, there are folks who push back against putting more energy into fun because they think they are *already* having enough of it. In some instances, they may be right—in which case I encourage them to teach others their secrets. But for many of us, a lot of what we do "for fun" isn't fun at all. Instead, we spend much of our leisure time on "Fake Fun," a term I use to describe activities and possessions that are marketed to us as fun, that we work long hours to be able to afford, but that are ultimately meaningless or a waste of time—such as binge-watching shows to the point that our eyes glaze over, buying things we don't need, or mindlessly scrolling through social media for hours at a time. Fake Fun is numbing and

* I don't mean to minimize the experiences of those suffering from severe anxiety or depression, in which cases mental health care is imperative, but I do see fun as a tool that can counter milder forms, as well as everyday languishing and ennui. In fact, there is a cognitive behavioral therapy technique called "behavioral activation," used for treating depression, that specifically focuses on incorporating more meaningful and enjoyable activities into your life. As a psychiatrist friend of mine tells his patients, "Depression tries to trick you into thinking that you can't do the things you enjoy because you're depressed, but it's actually the exact opposite: you're depressed because you're not doing the things that you enjoy."

leaves us empty when we're done. True Fun, on the other hand, makes us feel nourished and refreshed.

One of the foundational issues we face, when it comes to making True Fun a priority, is that we've been conditioned to believe that the pursuit of fun—particularly *our own* fun—is frivolous, selfish, and self-indulgent, even immature and childish. (That is, if we think about it at all.) We think that if we're focused on fun, we're not paying enough attention to the world's problems or doing enough to help other people. As for our own *self*-improvement, we tend to focus our efforts on seeking "loftier" and more "serious" goals, such as achieving happiness, wealth, long-term health, and a sense of meaning and purpose in our lives. We pursue these goals doggedly, reading self-help books, seeing therapists, taking antidepressants, sweating through workouts. When you add in the time that's required to fulfill the obligations of adult life—going to work, doing your taxes, cleaning the house, raising kids—it's understandable that fun ends up as an afterthought. We enjoy it when we experience it, but when it comes to our priorities, it's often at the very end of the list.

But what we don't realize is that, far from being frivolous or self-ish, the pursuit of fun will help us achieve all of these goals. Life is not a zero-sum equation: we can care about fun *and* be conscientious citizens who are committed to improving the world—indeed, fun can give us more energy with which to do so. And if we want our own lives to be satisfying and joyful, True Fun isn't optional. It shouldn't be an afterthought. It should be our guiding star.

Even if you do buy into the idea that True Fun is important and decide that you want to have more of it, it can be hard to know how to start. Part of the challenge of having more True Fun is that its occurrence can feel so random; we've all been forced to do things "for fun" that were anything but. (Think of awkward icebreakers, or any situation in which people seem to be trying too hard.) We've also all had experiences where True Fun has popped up in everyday, seemingly boring situations—the times you find yourself laughing hysterically with a friend in a diner about nothing at all, or the moments that you try to describe to people afterward, only to find yourself saying, "I guess you had to be there." When True Fun happens, it can feel like magic. And to a certain degree, it *is* magic; True Fun cannot be forced.

But I've discovered that provided our basic needs have been met, we each have the power to have more fun. Unlike other elusive positive states, such as joy or rapture or even happiness, True Fun is approachable and down-to-earth—it *wants* to be invited to hop off its pedestal and play with us in the dirt. We have more control over fun than we realize; we just need to better understand the factors that generate it for us personally, and design (and put ourselves in) more situations in which these factors are present.

It is worth the effort.

Once we understand what True Fun is and what it feels like—and make it a priority—not only will we find it easier to make wiser decisions about how to spend our time and attention in the moment, but the long-term effects will be life-changing.

True Fun is restorative. It increases resilience and empathy. It creates community. It reduces resentment. True Fun does wonders for our emotional well-being by empowering us to connect with other people, escape from self-judgment, and be fully present. Orienting our lives around True Fun will boost our creativity and productivity. It will make us better—and happier—partners, parents, workers, citizens, and friends.

True Fun is good for our health. It gets us up from our desks, out of our heads, and into the world. Having more True Fun lowers our stress levels, and over time, that will likely lower our risks for all the health problems that are triggered or exacerbated by stress, such as heart attacks, strokes, obesity, type 2 diabetes, and dementia.

The pursuit of True Fun helps us stay true to our authentic selves, with less time spent on mindless distraction and empty pursuits and more time devoted to people, experiences, and activities that bring us a sense of meaning and joy.

Best of all, orienting our lives around True Fun is, well, *fun*! Unlike most self-improvement projects, which require us to exercise willpower and self-restraint in hopes of achieving some future goal, prioritizing fun will make our existence more invigorating and enjoyable in the moment. It's like going on a diet that requires you to eat *more* foods that you love.

I've now spent several years figuring out specific steps each of us can take to manufacture more of the magic that is True Fun—and I want to teach you what I've learned. We'll start by talking about what True Fun actually *is*, so that we're on the same page about its definition. Next, we'll explore why it can be so hard for us to recall a recent time in which we had True Fun—which is a nice way of saying that we're going to discuss why we feel dead inside. Just when I've taken you to the brink of despair, we'll do an abrupt pivot and delve into the surprising science of why True Fun is so astoundingly *good* for us—not just for our mood in the moment but for our long-term emotional and physical health and our ability to flourish.

And then comes the *fun* part: after I've made the case for True Fun, we'll discuss how to have more of it. I'll explain how to identify True Fun when it's happening—and how to distinguish it from its evil alter ego, Fake Fun—so that you can do an audit of how much True Fun you're currently having and home in on your personal fun magnets and fun factors—that is, the people, activities, and settings (and the *characteristics* of these things) that are the most likely to attract True Fun for you. We'll use an acronym I developed, called SPARK, to experiment with practical, hands-on techniques that will enable you to invite more fun into your everyday life, and we'll develop a long-term, sustainable plan for how to continue to prioritize fun in the future.

I'm not saying that if you follow my advice your life will become a nonstop stream of fun, or even suggesting that that should be the goal—even the most fun-filled life isn't *always* filled with fun. But with True Fun as your compass, you will be happier, you will be healthier, and you will be better able to shoulder whatever life throws your way. You will laugh more, you will smile more, and you will feel more alive.

And that, at its core, is what this book is about: feeling alive.

It's about how we can harness the power of fun to make us awake and fully present for our brief moment on this planet. My goal is to use what I've learned to help you build a life that is so rich, so engaged, so bursting with True Fun, that if I were to ask you to share with me a recent experience in which you had fun, I wouldn't be able to get you to stop talking.

PART I

Fun, Seriously

CHAPTER 1

WHAT *IS* FUN?

"Conceptualizing fun is not straightforward."
—I. C. McManus and Adrian Furnham

WHEN I STARTED THINKING ABOUT TRUE FUN AND HOW
I could have more of it, the first challenge I ran into was defining
what it actually *is*. I was confident that "fun" was the best word to
describe the powerful feeling I had tapped into as a result of my guitar classes, but I noticed that we use "fun" in all sorts of other contexts, too.

For example, we often use "fun" to describe any activity that we
perceive as being unrelated to work—these are the things we say we
do "*for* fun." But this use of "fun" categorizes activities more by
what they are *not* (work) than by the specific characteristics that they
share or the emotional experience they produce. What's more, the
activities we say we do "for fun" include both active pursuits, such as
spending time with friends, and passive things like watching
television—even though the levels of energy that these activities
generate can be radically different.

We also use the word "fun" to describe experiences that we have
deemed to be enjoyable (or that at least were *supposed* to have been
enjoyable). In these situations, we use "fun" in the verb phrase "to

have fun," as in "I had fun at that picnic," or as an adjective—e.g., "That was a fun time last weekend." But more often than not, we don't consider whether we actually mean what we're saying. I've personally heard myself announce, "That was fun," in response to everything from an outrageously fun night out with friends to a *meh* dinner party that did not, in fact, feel fun at all.

Given the wide range of experiences and emotional intensities that we describe as "fun," the idea that fun is a life-changing force may sound hyperbolic. But that's not fun's fault; it's because we've cheapened the word through careless (even if unintentional) over-use. I realized that if we really want to grasp—and harness—the full power of fun, we need to become much more precise about how and when we use the word.

But nailing down a definition of fun is surprisingly difficult to do. The *Oxford English Dictionary* defines fun as "enjoyment, amusement, or light-hearted pleasure"*—but the word "fun" also can refer to things not meant to be taken seriously (e.g., "it was all in good fun") or even to mocking or teasing, as in "make fun." (Indeed, the word itself comes from a Middle English word, "fon," which means "make a fool of, be a fool"—which brings up the important point that making a fool of someone else is definitely *not* included in our definition of fun; we are only talking about experiences that feel fun for *everyone* involved.)[†] And of course, there's also "funny," which refers to anything that amuses us or that strikes us as unexpected or odd.

Do an internet search for "how to have fun" and you'll quickly encounter more evidence of how broadly and sloppily we use the

---

* The OED also offers some fantastic (if not entirely accurate or helpful) synonyms for fun, including "living it up," "whoopee," "jollification" (apparently a real word!), and the enigmatic expression "beer and skittles." Antonyms for fun include "boredom" and "misery."

† "Fon" is also the root of the word "fond" (as in "to be fond of someone").

word. "Roast a turkey," suggests a list of ideas from CNN, which also includes encouragements to get more sleep, to "put together an altar to honor loved ones who have passed," and to watch a documentary about climate change. A similar list from *Real Simple* magazine proposes that if you want to have more fun, you should "make snickerdoodles," "get everyone some fun back-to-school notebooks and supplies," and—I swear I am not making this up—"adorn your table with gourds."*

You might think that the frequency with which we use "fun"— and the many contexts in which we employ it—would make it like catnip to academics, who love debating the definitions of abstract, nebulous concepts such as happiness or joy. But (perhaps because the ambiguity of its meaning makes fun seem frivolous) they have largely ignored the subject. The most prominent scholarly works related to fun aren't about fun at all; they're about play. And even the scholars who study play punt on the definition of fun.

Take Johan Huizinga, a Dutch historian who wrote a seminal book about play, first published in 1938, called *Homo Ludens*—Latin for "The Playing Man." (The version I have is a 1950 English translation based on the Dutch and German editions and is just about as fun to read as its title suggests.) According to Huizinga, fun is an "absolutely primary category of life, familiar to everybody at a glance right down to the animal level." We all know what fun feels like, in other words, and we seem to have a biological drive to seek it out. And yet, he writes, it "resists all analysis, all logical interpretation. As a concept, it cannot be reduced to any other mental category. No other modern language known to me has the exact equivalent of the English word *fun*."

* The suggestions from *Real Simple* are examples of how we sometimes use the word "fun" to describe activities or possessions that seem *playful*—e.g., making a cookie called a "snickerdoodle" or acquiring a whimsical notebook. The suggestions from CNN, on the other hand, are just bad.

Bruce C. Daniels, a historian and author of the book *Puritans at Play*,* sums up the situation well. The definition of fun, he writes, is "maddeningly elusive."

The lack of a solid definition—coupled with the assumption that fun isn't serious enough to deserve attention to begin with—likely explains why so few people have tried to study fun's psychological or physical effects directly.

In a 2017 paper about the general concept of fun—one of the few I was able to find—the authors write that "relatively little research has investigated the consequences of fun" and point out that "the word *fun* does not appear as an index term in any emotion or social-psychology textbook or handbook of which we are aware." Another paper makes the same point. "The psychological literature on fun is very limited," the authors write, adding that "occasionally psychologists have noted that certain concepts never seem to appear within psychological studies"—including fun.

As for physical effects, there's so little specific, relevant research that when I did a search for "fun" on PubMed—the search engine for biomedical literature run by the National Library of Medicine—one of the top results was a paper titled "Putting the *Fun* in Fungi: Toenail Onychomycosis."

Needless to say, this is not the type of fun that I encourage you to seek.

In the absence of scholarly guideposts, I developed my own terminology, starting with the concept of True Fun—which I chose because I wanted to distinguish the euphoria triggered by my experience in my guitar class from our more pedestrian uses of "fun" (not to mention toenail fungus). I also wanted to clarify that

---

* Proposed subtitle: *They Had More Fun Than You'd Think.*

True Fun doesn't rely on the *doing* of any particular activity. Having more of it does not require you to attend more trivia nights or, I dunno, learn how to play pickleball.

But even once I'd named the feeling I was having "True Fun," I still needed to create a succinct definition; I couldn't subject people to a paragraphs-long description that finished with "You'll know it when you feel it."

I started by analyzing my own experiences through the lens of positive psychology—a field of psychology that is devoted to understanding human well-being—to identify possible elements that might be definitional to the experience of True Fun.

In order to make sure that whatever I came up with was universal and not specific to me, I also recruited what I called the Fun Squad, a global group of more than 1,500 people who volunteered to explore their own definitions of fun and spend roughly a month testing out my ideas and giving me feedback. Members of the Fun Squad ranged in age from teenagers to retirees and spanned every income and educational bracket. Some were single, others were married, and they were roughly equally divided when it came to having kids. They included students, teachers, lawyers, homemakers, graphic designers, software engineers, scientists, healthcare workers, financial analysts, writers, receptionists, consultants, and more. They lived all across the United States, and indeed, all around the globe, from Sweden to South Africa to India to Bahrain.

After collecting demographic information from them (and without proposing a definition), I asked Fun Squad members to describe three experiences that stood out in their memories as examples of True Fun, and to write down how old they were at the time, what they were doing, and who was involved. (It's an exercise that I will be suggesting later that you try as well.) The instructions read: "Don't worry about whether your experiences seem trivial, but please do try to focus on experiences where fun is the dominant descriptor—

the ones that would make you say, if I were to ask you about them, 'That was *so* fun.'"

Next, I asked people to describe a fun event or experience that they would love to organize or be a part of in the future. I again asked what they would be doing, whom (if anyone) they'd be with, where they would be, and why this would qualify as fun.

Then I asked what, if anything, made those four experiences different from other experiences or activities that they found pleasurable, relaxing, enjoyable, satisfying, or rewarding.

The anecdotes people shared were fascinating. Memories of True Fun weren't relegated to childhood or early adulthood; people wrote about experiences that had occurred as recently as the day before they filled out the survey (which I sent out in the summer of 2020, during the SARS-CoV-2 pandemic and its associated restrictions and lockdowns). Most striking was the fact that, even though I hadn't yet proposed a definition, all the participants seemed to have the same visceral understanding of what I was getting at when I added the "*so*" in front of the "fun."

Here are some examples:

Playing drums with my husband playing guitar and 15-year-old son on bass, 9-year-old son on keyboard. I got these drums as a gift for my 49th birthday. Whenever I go down to the basement to practice, they drop what they are doing and plug in their guitars and join in. I have so much fun connecting with my family in this way, playing the drums. There's not a lot of talking, but we communicate on another level. We laugh after each song because we're not very good, but we keep trying. . . . I can't tell you how much joy and playfulness this experience brings. I never thought that when I decided to learn the drums at middle age for *me*, it would end up being something that would bring my family together in such a fun, joyous and creative (flow state) way.

The first thing that came to mind was squishing mud through my toes. Walking in mud is fun (and gross). I'm not sure the most recent time I've done this, but I suspect my sense memory is from sometime in high school, along a particular path and probably with my friend Margaret. Squishing toes in wet sand is enjoyable, but not nearly as fun as doing it in mud, possibly because mud is so much messier.

I went to this laughter workshop where I didn't know anyone. We had to do silly things like pretend we were monkeys and greet each other. I was 60. It was so much fun!

At age 75, I took a two-week virtual drawing marathon on my sister's balcony while she and her husband were at their country home. I was alone with my art supplies and computer, with the sun beating down and the only sounds the wind and traffic from the West Side Highway. . . . it was such fun to be totally consumed with a task that seemed almost impossible.

Dance class. I am often overwhelmed by the fun I have on a Friday morning, in a church hall with a bunch of old ladies. I've been doing this class since I was 41, and I'm 46 now. I'm usually the youngest in the room. We do things like dance our imaginary tails (swishy peacock feathers, or fluffy bunny tail?), swish imaginary bathwater, tickle clouds, squawk like birds, claw the air, move as though our feet are in marshmallow. Yeah, it's fun.

Playing fetch with an exuberant, silly dog. This was last weekend. I'm 32.

I was in middle school. My mom and I had just revamped my bedroom into a pink, Parisian oasis. On my first night in this new room, my mom and I had a sleepover complete with our fanciest pajamas, cookies, and long conversations where we could only speak in British accents. It was so silly that we were laughing all night.

I traveled to remote northern Siberia (when it was still the USSR) when I was 20, to formerly closed towns that had never seen westerners. It was a one-month environmental volunteer exchange during the white night summer season, with a dozen other university students from around the world. One weekend, we visited a children's camp, spending a day singing, playing, and splashing in a small lake. I couldn't speak their language, and aside from translators, they couldn't speak mine. . . . The most unadulterated joy of my life occurred that summer day—the deep, essential-to-survival creativity of a hundred children, inviting us into their world with such pure wholeheartedness, silliness, song, and unadulterated wonder, that I could not help but abandon the notion of who I was, and instead, just celebrate being. It feels like short-changing to talk about it (I almost never do), because words are so hard to come by. But it's imprinted on my DNA. It was so, for lack of a better word, *fun*. And it's that combination of feeling—laughing and creating and celebrating a simple and long summer day, with no accoutrements except food and music, with awakened innocence in my soul—that epitomizes fun.

I know, right?

The details of the anecdotes people shared were different—some occurred in the context of nature, others in music, or physical activity, or creativity, or novelty, or silliness. Sometimes they involved friends; in other cases, strangers. But their energy was all the same. There was something joyful but also quite moving about them. There was a lightheartedness, an exuberance, an excitement that feels so electric and freeing and contagious that it jumps off the page. Our moments of True Fun are the moments that we remember. They're the experiences that make life worth living. The emotional power of the memories it creates is proof that True Fun isn't frivolous; it's profound.

Once people had written down their experiences (and again, before I proposed a definition), I asked them how they would define fun to someone who had never encountered the term. I was amazed by how many of their answers touched upon similar themes.

"Fun is unbridled enthusiasm," wrote one person.

"Pure joy, happiness and love!" wrote another.

"It's a visceral feeling of lightness, where your chest expands and you feel like you could lift off the ground," read one of my favorite responses. "It's laughter and joy and feeling like you wouldn't want to be anywhere else in the world. It's doing something you love with other people, where you don't care about what other people think. It's a feeling of freedom. It's being a bit reckless and giving your inner child a chance to come out and play."

When I asked my then-five-year-old daughter what color fun would be, she thought for a second, and then said, "Sunshine."

How could the same effervescent energy be produced by experiences as diverse as doing a painting marathon, singing with Siberian children, walking barefoot through mud with a friend, and playing fetch with a dog? What makes us feel like sunshine?

The more of these experiences I read, the more convinced I became that, while True Fun can occur in an endless variety of contexts, there is, in fact, a universal definition that holds true across people and experiences.

True Fun **is the confluence of playfulness, connection, and flow.** Whenever these three states occur at the same time, we experience True Fun.

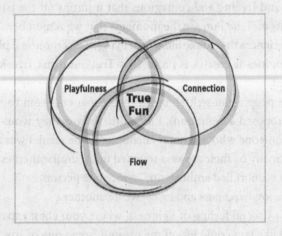

It's simple enough in theory. But to understand it fully, we've got to dissect each of those elements on their own.

PLAYFULNESS

True Fun can only occur when people are being playful.

By playfulness I mean a spirit of lightheartedness and freedom—of doing an activity just for the sake of doing the activity and not caring too much about the outcome. As the examples shared by the Fun Squad made clear, True Fun carries with it no sense of obligation—when we're being playful, we don't mind if there's no tangible reward. Playfulness creates a sense of being outside of your normal reality; you're relieved of your everyday responsibilities and feel carefree; you smile frequently and laugh easily. When people are being playful, they sparkle.

CONNECTION

True Fun always involves a sense of connection—the feeling of having a special, shared experience with someone (or something) else.

It can occur when you feel unusually connected to your physical environment (e.g., nature), the activity in which you're participating, a pet, or even your own body. However, in the vast majority of instances, this connection is with another *person;* when people describe True Fun, they report feeling like they're joining together with someone while at the same time feeling totally themselves. Surprisingly, this applies to introverts as well as extroverts. Based on the Fun Squad's anecdotes, introverts are more likely to experience True Fun in a small group of friends than in a big crowd of strangers, but just like extroverts, their most fun moments do not occur when they're alone.

FLOW

Flow is a term used in psychology to describe when you are fully engrossed and engaged in your present experience to the point that you lose track of the passage of time. (You know the adage "time flies when you're having fun"? That's flow.) Self-consciousness and judgment—whether from yourself or other people—are anathema to flow, as is any form of distraction. Think of an athlete in the midst of a game, or a musician enraptured by the melody she is producing, or the feeling of getting lost in a project or a conversation and looking up to realize that an hour has passed. Its ability to ground us in the present moment makes flow an intrinsic part of True Fun; without it, True Fun cannot occur. Every experience shared by the Fun Squad took place in the context of flow.

Playfulness, connection, and flow are each independently capable of leading to a host of positive emotions, such as achievement, joy, satisfaction, happiness, and awe—I have yet to see anyone come out of an experience that made them feel playful or connected or that put them into flow and say, "Well, *that* was a waste of time."*

You can also experience two out of these three states together. Connected flow can happen in an intense conversation or during a religious service, for example. Playful flow can occur when you're engaged in a solitary hobby you love, such as doing the crossword or making a craft. Playful connection can appear in discrete bursts, like when you give someone a knowing look or share an inside joke with a friend. All of these combinations are also worth seeking.

But when playfulness, connection, and flow happen at once, something magical results. You experience *True Fun*.

Once I'd settled on this definition of True Fun—and had confirmed with Fun Squad members that it described their experiences—a lot of things clicked into place. Playfulness, connection, and flow all make us feel engaged and focused, which helps explain why True Fun is such a life-giving force. They generate energy, which accounts for the electric feeling that's so often associated with True Fun. And the fact that this energy can vary in intensity and duration clarifies how some episodes of True Fun light us up for a flash but don't linger in our memories while others last longer and stay with us for the rest of our lives.

Playfulness, connection, and flow only exist in the moment when we feel them, which explains the fascinating fact that True Fun occurs exclusively in the present tense. Also, unlike positive *states* such as happiness or satisfaction, True Fun is an *experience*. This means that we can't have True Fun continuously, alas, because each instance of it has a beginning and an end. But on the flip side, this makes fun more accessible; it's easier to imagine specific circumstances in which you might *have* fun than it is to imagine how you could become someone who *is* happy or satisfied.

---

* This makes it particularly unfortunate that in our productivity-obsessed, materialistic culture we tend not to use them as metrics or goals.

Fun is also easier to evaluate. If you asked me "Are you happy?" I'd likely be thrown into an internal philosophical discussion with myself (*What does it mean to be happy? What is happiness?* Et cetera) and end up saying, "How the heck do I know?" Ask me if I had True Fun last weekend, on the other hand, and I'd have no problem telling you yes or no.

Playfulness, connection, and flow all encourage us to shed our in-hibitions and formal façades, which is likely why people report feeling in touch with their authentic selves when they have True Fun. And the fact that these states are not dependent on any specific activity explains how the same person, doing the same thing, can have a completely different experience, depending on variables such as their mood, their attitude, and the people they're with at the time. Defining True Fun as playful, connected flow also demystifies one of its most enigmatic elements: how we can all know what it is and yet experience it so differently. True Fun is simultaneously universal and unique.

Defining what True Fun *is* also helped me clarify what it is not. Simply put, if *none* of the three ingredients for fun are present, then we're unlikely to enjoy ourselves at all. And if there's anything that *prevents* us from experiencing one of them, whether it be playfulness, connection, or flow, then we cannot—and will not—have True Fun.

Distraction is probably the greatest offender, since it gets in the way of all three. If we are at all distracted—if our attention is split—we cannot experience True Fun, because fun requires flow, and flow requires that we be fully present. Since the definition of being distracted is that you are *not* present (the word "distracted" is derived from a Latin verb that means "to drag away"), this means that anything that distracts us is going to block True Fun. If we want to experience more True Fun, we need to minimize the amount of time we spend trying to pay attention to multiple things at once.

In addition, distraction gets in the way of playfulness, which requires active engagement. (You can't maintain witty banter, for example, if you're not paying attention to the conversation.) And it destroys connection, too: we've all experienced the frustration and loneliness that comes from being around someone who is physically present but mentally someplace else. True Fun and distraction are like oil and water: they do not mix.

Judgment is also a fun killer. In order to judge something, we have to step out of an experience so that we can evaluate it, and (as we just noted) when we are out of our present experience, we are obviously not in flow. Even everyday forms of evaluation, such as "liking" things on social media or editing the selfie we just took, count as judgment and encourage self-consciousness—another fun killer—and therefore will destroy that moment's capacity to be fun. Comparing ourselves to other people is also a form of judgment and is toxic to fun—as the saying goes, "Comparison is the thief of joy."

The more I thought about the definition of True Fun, the more nuances presented themselves.

For example, there are certain experiences that make a person feel alive but that no one would classify as True Fun. Like, say, childbirth.

What's more, there are many objectively positive states, such as satisfaction or wonder or awe, that don't necessarily fit the definition of True Fun. Sure, having fun can often *lead* to a sense of satisfaction, wonder, or awe, but those states are not "fun" per se. For example, I'm often awed by a beautiful sunset, but I wouldn't say that the sense of awe itself was fun. And on the flip side, you can have True Fun doing things (e.g., car karaoke) that are not awe-inspiring or deep.

While particular activities, settings, and people can contribute to the likelihood that True Fun will occur—and each of us has a collection of activities, settings, and people that are more likely to generate True Fun for us than others (I call these "fun magnets")—no activity, setting, or person is intrinsically fun. You may love cooking and enjoy throwing dinner parties at your home, for instance. But we all know that some dinner parties end up being way more fun than others, even if the same guests are invited, you're in the same spot, and the same food is served.

There are also things that we're drawn to, sometimes compulsively, but that are straight-up not fun. Like, for example, busyness. (This misperception is particularly common on vacations, when we overschedule ourselves in an attempt to maximize our fun.) True Fun is more likely to happen when it has space to unfurl.

Also not fun? Material possessions. Many of us work very hard at our jobs to afford things that are marketed to us as fun. But while possessions can *facilitate* fun (for example, if said possessions are water skis), objects themselves are not fun.

Neither is self-medication. If you take a step back and observe adults "having fun," you may notice that many of the things we pass off as fun could also be described as numbing ourselves from our current reality. For example: getting drunk or high. Binging on movies or TV. Spending hours mindlessly scrolling.

Self-medication can be soothing or enjoyable up to a point, and in moderation, substances can sometimes help us shed our insecurities and inhibitions in a way that actually *is* conducive to True Fun. But this shedding of inhibitions can have some notable costs: you may have a hard time remembering all of the fun you had; you may end up so uninhibited that you do something out of line with your values; and substances come with the risk of addiction and dependence, which are decidedly not fun. Ideally, we want to learn how to loosen up *without* external help (which is something that devoting ourselves to the pursuit of True Fun will help us do).

The fact that playfulness, connection, and flow are all *active* states also means that anything that could be described as passive consumption cannot, by definition, generate True Fun on its own. This is a really important distinction, given that so many of the things that we do "for fun" are passive activities such as watching television or checking our social media feeds, and given how much money and effort goes into convincing us that they're worth our time.

If you find yourself pushing back on this idea, it's likely because passive consumption *can* be relaxing and pleasant, even educational and satisfying. Indeed, there are many situations in which consumption is genuinely enjoyable or rewarding—all of which make it easily confused with True Fun. For example, concerts, live theater, and dance performance can be thrilling, delightful, and even transformative, and I am not suggesting that activities such as going to the movies, reading books, or watching your favorite show are wastes of time, or that you should cut passive consumption out of your life entirely. But if we're being precise about it, these things are not truly *fun*—unless, that is, something about the experience provides a sense of playfulness, connection, and flow (for instance, if a performer is particularly good at connecting with the audience, or if you attend a concert with friends).* And in *that* case, the experience no longer really qualifies as passive consumption to begin with.

As I see it, the main problem with passive consumption is that when it's made too easy and accessible—as it is on our televisions and devices—it runs the risk of becoming a form of drug itself, something we use to seek pleasure and avoid pain (both for ourselves and for our kids). Not only does this habit hold the potential to cause dependence, it can transform passive consumption from an occasional choice into our default, until eventually we forget that other options even *exist*. And every time we use it to numb ourselves, it saps time and energy that we could be putting toward the pursuit of True Fun.

This level of analysis may make it seem like we're getting into the weeds, but it's important: the better we understand what True Fun

---

* In other words, the source of entertainment went from being a form of passive consumption to being fodder for *interaction*, which in turn can facilitate fun. For example, I have a friend who routinely has fun when she and her husband watch cheesy Hallmark movies together and try to predict the dialogue. In this case, the movie itself isn't the fun *per se*; the fun comes from the game that they're playing together (for which the movie provides material).

is and is not, the better decisions we'll be able to make about how to spend our time. Indeed, the beauty of evaluating your life through the filters of playfulness, connection, and flow is that it can help you crystalize the difference between things that hold the potential to catalyze True Fun (i.e., your fun magnets), things that are pleasant (and that thus may be worthwhile, even if not True-Fun-generating), and things that are straight-up time sucks.

The challenge, however, is that you may have to come to terms with the fact that many of the things you ostensibly do "for fun" do not, in fact, generate True Fun. They may not even bring you pleasure.

In some cases, this may be a simple problem to fix. Anything we do for leisure is voluntary, otherwise it wouldn't count as leisure—and leisure is supposed to be enjoyable. So, if you're not enjoying a leisure activity, you should just stop doing it and make room for something else. For example, if you find board games boring, you could suggest something different. No one ever died from refusing to play Monopoly.

Sure, you may find it hard to abandon certain activities because of a sense of obligation—say, if you realize you don't derive much pleasure from your book club but don't want to let down your friends (or if you don't look forward to discussing the book, but you do like the chance to socialize). You may also decide to hang on to other pursuits because you enjoy them occasionally. But once you've put in the work to identify the pastimes that fall into these categories for you, at least you won't keep finding yourself participating in them without knowing how you got there. They're not the type of things that are so mesmerizing that you can't seem to look away, and they're not so easy to engage in that you find yourself drifting toward them on autopilot. If and when you spend time on them, you'll be doing so by choice.

In other cases, however, you may keep finding yourself entranced by things that you have realized are *not* ultimately enjoyable and that will never lead to True Fun—like, for example, descending into social media spirals, or doomscrolling the news, or swiping mindlessly through dating profiles, or spending a beautiful day glued to your couch, or buying things you don't need or can't afford. You may know intellectually that these are not rewarding uses of your time—and be fully aware that they're likely to leave you feeling bad and unsatisfied—and yet keep getting sucked into them anyway. And once you're in their thrall, you may find it very hard to break away.

When this happens, chances are that you have been seduced by what I call "Fake Fun." As I alluded to earlier, Fake Fun is my term for activities and pursuits that are deliberately designed to fool us into thinking that they'll produce True Fun but that don't actually result in playful, connected flow.

Fake Fun can be hard to identify at first, because it's so well camouflaged—it's engineered to trigger the release of some of the same chemicals that are present in our bodies and brains when we're truly having fun. But in reality, it's a mirage of fun that's been created by people and businesses whose incentives, values, and goals are very different from our own. Much like junk food, Fake Fun gives us a quick fix of pleasure but ultimately doesn't make us feel good—and, over time, it can actually harm our mental and physical health.

It also pulls our internal compasses off course. When we succumb to the siren song of Fake Fun, our guiding stars—our actual passions and priorities—become obscured by clouds; Fake Fun takes us in directions we don't actually want to go and leaves us feeling vacant, anxious, unfulfilled, and numb. In short, the more we allow Fake Fun to hijack our compasses, the more dead inside we feel.

So, why is it so hard to keep our compasses pointed straight?

CHAPTER 2

WHY YOU FEEL
DEAD INSIDE

"When Facebook was getting going, I had these people
who would come up to me and they would say, 'I'm not
on social media . . . I value my real-life interactions.
I value the moment. I value presence and I value intimacy.'
And I would say, . . . 'We'll get you eventually.'"
—Sean Parker, founding president of Facebook

BEFORE WE GET INTO WHY WE'RE SO SUSCEPTIBLE TO
Fake Fun and why it makes us feel dead inside, let's pause for a second to discuss why this matters.

It's quite simple, really: we are going to die.

I'm sorry to be so blunt, but I can't think of any more succinct way to explain what's at stake. The reason it's essential for us to address our metaphorical deadness is that it won't be long—decades at the most—before we are all *literally* dead. This is the uncomfortable and very unfun truth about life that no one wants to acknowledge (and that Fake Fun helps us avoid having to think about): it's temporary.*

---

* A friend recently told me about an app that sends you a notification each day reminding you that you are going to die, as a way to inspire you to seize the moment and not waste time on stupid things. When she asked me if I'd ever install it, my answer initially was a hard no—I *already* spend way too much time on existential rumination. But then again, if I could outsource my obsession with mortality to an app—and only be reminded of it once a day, at a predictable and convenient time—that would be *fantastic*.

The Roman poet Catullus* summed up the situation in a love poem to his girlfriend† that has haunted me ever since I read it in high school: "Suns may set and rise again," he wrote. "But for us, when the brief light has set, there is a never-ending night to be slept."‡

What's more, the fact that we're all going to die means that many of the things that keep us up at night don't ultimately matter. Our careers don't matter, our accomplishments and failures don't matter, our net worth does not matter, and our social media followings *certainly* do not matter. At the end of the day, much of what we spend our time obsessing over and stressing out about will be meaningless.

Ha! I bet you weren't expecting *that* when you picked up a book about fun! I promise we'll get back to more lighthearted subjects soon. But I'm getting dark here to make a point.

We can't control the fact that we will die.

But we *can* control whether we actually live.

We *can* control whether we merely endure our days or experience and enjoy them. We *can* control whether we arrive on our deathbeds feeling like we've wasted our time or end up satisfied with how we've spent our brief moment in the sun. While disconcerting, the idea that most things don't matter is also freeing. We can create our *own* meaning and purpose and joy. We can chart our own paths. And True Fun can guide the way.

---

* Now dead.
† Also dead.
‡ "Soles occidere et redire possunt:
  Nobis cum semel occidit brevis lux,
  Nox est perpetua una dormienda." *Sigh.*

OUR LIVES ARE WHAT
WE PAY ATTENTION TO

The first thing we need to acknowledge is that our lives are what we pay attention to. Indeed, our attention is the most valuable resource that we have.

Think about it. We only experience what we pay attention to. We only remember what we pay attention to. Your choice of what to pay attention to in any given minute might not seem like a big deal, but taken together, these decisions are deeply consequential. As Annie Dillard has written, "How we spend our days is how we spend our lives."

This is why philosopher Simone Weil called attention "the rarest and purest form of generosity." If you reflect on your most cherished memories from when you were a child, often they will involve an adult who chose, out of all the things in the world, out of all the other demands on their time, to pay attention to *you*. When I read through the Fun Squad's descriptions of truly fun experiences, this theme often popped up. People described a special weekend with their grandparents, or a time when their mother or father ditched work to spend the day with them. As Weil wrote, "Attention, taken to its highest degree, is the same thing as prayer. It presupposes faith and love."

Our choice of where to direct our attention also affects our emotions and moods. If you habitually direct your attention toward things that upset you—alarmist news headlines, for example, or social media screeds—then you will experience the world as alarming and upsetting. If you choose instead to pay attention to things that uplift you, or that offer opportunities for playfulness, connection, and flow, you will experience the world in a completely different, more positive light.

The words we use to talk about attention and time—we *pay* attention; we *spend* time—are the same verbs we use to discuss money, which implies that we understand their value, at least subconsciously. (It also suggests that we should be wary of anything we do to "kill" or "waste" or even "pass" time.) But what we don't seem to appreciate is that when it comes to experiencing meaning and joy (and, for that matter, fun), attention is actually the *most* valuable of these three currencies. "Spending time" with someone is meaningless if our attention is elsewhere, and while money is certainly a life necessity, if we waste it on something, it is theoretically possible to earn it back. Our attention, on the other hand, is irreplaceable; once we spend it on something, it's gone for good.

Adding to the challenge is the fact that our brains can only pay full attention to one cognitively demanding thing at a time. (This is why you can fold your laundry while listening to the news, but you can't listen to the news while reading a book.) In other words, our brains can't multitask, and if you don't believe me, try this exercise from a Buddhist monk named Haemin Sunim, described in his book *The Things You Can See Only When You Slow Down:* "The mind cannot have two thoughts at once," he writes. "See if you can think two thoughts at exactly the same time. Well? Is it possible?"*

The fact that we can't split our attention means that whenever we make a decision about what to focus on in any given moment, we are also implicitly making a decision about what we're *not* going to focus on. Our attention, in other words, is zero-sum, similar to a narrow spotlight that can only illuminate one small circle, leaving

---

* The answer is "Of course not." And if you are pushing back on this, I encourage you to look into the research about multitasking, which has found that the more you multitask, the worse you're likely to perform on simple memory tasks, and the less efficient and productive you will be. This is likely due to the fact that what we call "multitasking" is actually what psychologists call "task switching"—i.e., rapidly switching between tasks. Just as a car must slow down in order to make a sharp turn, our brains have to slow down every time we force them to change direction. And if you insist that this does not describe you, consider the fact that the people who claim that they are the best at multitasking typically perform the worst; for more information, check out the work of late Stanford professor Clifford Nass.

everything else in the dark. In any given moment—including right now—you're missing nearly all that is going on around you. This is *necessary;* otherwise, we'd be completely overwhelmed. But it further demonstrates how important it is to be intentional about where we direct our light.

Small kids are natural experts at training their spotlights on opportunities for True Fun. If you watch a group of five-year-olds in action, you'll see that they're in flow and are constantly generating opportunities for playfulness; as for connection, if a suitable playmate is not immediately available, they'll seek one out (or make one up).

Unfortunately, these talents atrophy and are stamped out of us as we get older, and by the time we become parents, we often spend much more time and money trying to manufacture engaging experiences for our children than we do for ourselves. As they dance, or sing, or compete, we sit "with the dust bunnies on the power-waxed tile floor, on some windowless lower level of a school, huddled near an electrical outlet to keep [our] devices alive," as Tom Vanderbilt puts it in his book *Beginners: The Joy and Transformative Power of Lifelong Learning.* We work so that they can play.

Don't get too jealous of our kids, however—we're raising them to follow in our footsteps. Much has been written about the mental health problems caused by the pressures and demands that are being put on kids at younger and younger ages, as they're forced to compete for admission at a tiny handful of schools that their parents hope will offer them a golden ticket to "success" (whatever that means).* Far less acknowledged but no less concerning is the fact

---

* It seems to usually mean a career in law, finance, medicine, or business—though judging from the levels of burnout and unhappiness in those fields and the amount of student debt often accrued to gain entry to them, "golden handcuffs" might be the more appropriate term.

that by treating childhood as a résumé-building opportunity, by leaving no space in our kids' schedules for (supposedly) purposeless play, we're also preventing our children from having True Fun.

What's more, we're creating a value system that will reduce their ability to experience it *for their entire lives.* How can you build a life full of playfulness, connection, and flow when you've never been taught that they're important (or, even more concerningly, if you haven't experienced them to begin with)? How are you supposed to appreciate True Fun—and lose yourself in its joy—if you've been raised to view life as a competition in which resources and opportunities are scarce, and you are constantly being ranked and judged?

In short, modern life—at least for Americans—is not set up for *anyone* to attract True Fun. The consequence is that many of us, adults and kids alike, are having so little True Fun that we have forgotten what it feels like, to the point that we don't even realize what we're missing (that is, if we ever consciously knew how to recognize it at all). It's as if we've become trapped in some Dickensian orphanage where the only available food is gruel: we're so used to life being tasteless (and stressful and competitive) that it wouldn't even occur to us to demand other more nourishing and flavorful foods.

I witness this when I give talks about *How to Break Up With Your Phone.* As part of my presentation, I often ask people to call to mind a recent experience that made them feel alive (it's a variation on the question I asked you at the start of this book—i.e., when's the last time you had fun?), and then I ask if anyone is willing to share a memory with the group.

I've asked this of executives, teachers, students, healthcare workers, parents, editors, internet security professionals, spa guests, you name it, and the initial reaction is always the same: silence. When people do volunteer, they tend to speak softly and tentatively, with an up-talking intonation that makes their answers sound more like questions: *"Playing with my nieces?" "Walking my dog?"* The only response I remember that did not include an implied question mark occurred during a talk in Arizona. After a painful pause, a man shot his hand into the air and announced, triumphantly, "This morning, I saw a bobcat!"

Some of this reticence might be due to shyness, of course. But it's happened often enough that I'm confident something else is going on—namely, that we're out of practice, both in terms of seeking and prioritizing True Fun *and* in terms of paying attention to experiences of playfulness, connection, and flow when they occur.

Granted, this might prompt questions about when, historically, human beings have *ever* been in the practice of paying attention to these things, and about which humans have had the freedom and privilege to contemplate them at all. Unfortunately, there are no solid answers to these questions since, as noted, no one has specifically studied our definition of True Fun.

What *is* clear, however, is that humans require social connections in order to flourish (more on that in a bit), that our greatest achievements occur when we are in flow, and that our need for play is intrinsic, biologically driven, and consistent across cultures and throughout time. (Indeed, even most animals are instinctively playful.)* The *ability* to be playful varies based on life circumstances, but opportunities for flow have been relatively abundant for most people throughout history. Geographic constraints and the nonexistence of the internet meant that people couldn't have as many "connections" as we do now, but the connections they did have—through religious and civic organizations and their families—were likely far stronger than whatever you have going on with your followers on Twitter.

We can't know how often people experienced these three states together, or how they felt about the confluence when it occurred. It would also be unwise to make sweeping generalizations about the

---

* One play scholar, Gordon M. Burghardt, presents evidence of playfulness in unexpected groups of animals including marsupials, birds, and lizards; his book *The Genesis of Play* includes intriguing chapter titles such as "Does the Platypus Play?" and "Fish That Leap, Juggle, and Tease."

amount of leisure time available to people in any given historical moment, considering how much it can vary depending on factors such as class, culture, freedom, and wealth.

What is undebatable (at least in the western world) and very relevant to fun, however, is that the past 250 or so years have seen a huge change in how we evaluate time, and therefore in how we use it, including how much of it we make—or more often, *don't* make—available for playfulness, connection, or flow. The Industrial Revolution was indeed revolutionary; the advent of the internet was another important turning point. And the years since 2007 or so have seen an especially dramatic shift in how we spend—and fragment—our time, thanks to the smartphones we all now keep in our pockets.

THE TIME-VALUE PARADOX

The more I thought about time and attention, the more fascinated I became by what I think of as the time-value paradox: we've been conditioned to believe that our time is too valuable to waste, and yet we often end up spending our leisure hours on things that make us feel like we've wasted our time. I figured that if I could understand *why* we do this, I'd be better equipped to avoid falling into this trap myself.

The evolution of how we've thought about time is covered in fascinating detail in Celeste Headlee's 2020 book, *Do Nothing: How to Break Away from Overworking, Overdoing, and Underliving*. In it, she writes that for most of human history, work productivity was measured (and, for paid laborers, earnings determined) by the things people accomplished or created rather than the amount of time they spent on them. "Prior to the Industrial Age, most people worked to complete specific tasks: bring in the harvest, put up the barn, stitch a quilt," writes Headlee. When these tasks were complete, so was the day's work. As a result, prior to around 1800, many people "actually had time to sit around a fire and listen to all 3,182 lines of an epic poem like *Beowulf.*" ("Back then," she says, "that was considered a fun night with the family.")

But the Industrial Revolution and advent of factory jobs caused a huge shift in the way paid laborers were compensated—which is to say, earnings began to be determined not by their accomplishments but by the time they spent "at work." It was the difference, in other words, between a cobbler being paid to repair a shoe (a project that has a defined endpoint and a clear way to measure success) and a factory worker being compensated by the hour for performing tasks that theoretically could be repeated indefinitely. The latter creates financial incentives for people to keep working for as long as they can bear it, in order to earn more money.

The shift to factory work also caused a new issue that has influenced the way we think about leisure time and fun. When you change people's focus from accomplishing tasks to making stuff, you end up, perhaps unsurprisingly, with a lot of stuff. In order to make a profit, you have to convince people to buy the stuff you're producing; in other words, you need to create demand. One way to do this is to build entire industries—i.e., advertising and marketing—to convince people that they want and need more stuff. What's one really effective way to do *that*? You tell people that buying your stuff will make them happy and help them have fun. (This works even better if you can get them to compete with each other to see who can acquire *more* stuff.) But of course, people need money in order to buy your stuff—and pay off the ensuing credit card debt—and making money requires them to work more, often at jobs at which they help produce even more stuff, which then needs to be sold in order to make a profit. And on and on and on. (You have just witnessed my attempt to distill the history of American materialism and consumer culture into a paragraph.)

When it comes to our ability to attract True Fun, this has created a number of connected problems. Our conflation of having lots of money and material possessions with having fun incentivizes us to spend more of our time working so that we can earn more money to buy more things. This has the perverse effect of encouraging us to allow work to invade our leisure time, which both makes us feel like we're never really taking a break and leaves us with less time to participate in experiences that might *actually* produce True Fun. The resulting fun deficit contributes to our sense of emptiness and discontent. But since we haven't recognized the value of playfulness, connection, and flow, we try to fill our emotional voids by working even harder, often during nights and weekends . . . so that we can earn more money and buy more things.

What this all boils down to is that we have internalized the idea that time is a commodity that can be traded, and that the most important thing we can trade it for is money; therefore, any use of time that does not result in financial compensation is not a valuable use of time.

"The transformation this idea caused in the world at large cannot be overstated," writes Headlee. "When time is money, idle hours are a waste of money. This is the philosophical underpinning of all our modern stress: that time is too valuable to waste."

Today, the idea that time is money has been ingrained even in those of us who do not have factory jobs. Indeed, many salaried careers combine the worst of both worlds: the amount of money you can earn is capped by your salary, but there's always more work that you *could* do (and that you may feel pressured to do, in order to prove that you are "committed" and to keep up with your peers). Dangle the carrot of a possible promotion or bonus and we will work even harder.

Some of what we do at work is genuinely productive and fulfilling, of course, but much of it (think email) is not; we spend a lot of time just churning and trying to stay afloat. As Headlee describes it, "Many of us are exhausting ourselves . . . working very hard at things that accomplish very little of substance but feel necessary." Unfortunately, "the *feeling* of being productive is not the same as actually producing something."

Our emphasis on outcomes and efficiency rather than satisfaction and enjoyment may partially explain some of the high rates of depression and anxiety in teenagers, especially those attending schools that serve as feeders for elite colleges. It certainly hints at why it's so hard for many *adults* to prioritize True Fun and to enjoy it when it occurs: we've been indoctrinated to believe that there should be a purpose to everything we do, or else it's a waste of time; as a result, experiences that bring us pure pleasure don't seem worthy of being treated as priorities, and sometimes even come with a side of guilt.

For example, even though I enjoy biking, I very rarely go for bike rides outside, in the fresh air, let alone use the strength and fitness that I work so hard to maintain on physical activities that I actually like.

Instead, I have a habit of sitting in front of my computer for hours at a stretch and then feeling so physically gross that I decide I must counteract my sedentary work life with intense exercise. This urge, combined with my compulsive need to be "productive," means that I often use my free time to attend indoor cycling classes in which I join other people in a dark room (which usually has no windows and is sometimes literally in a basement) on stationary bikes equipped with sensors measuring our energy output, which is ranked on a screen at the front of the room. With an instructor shouting encouragements for us to climb imaginary hills, and pop music blasting so loudly that I often wear earplugs, we then silently compete with each other to see who can bike the fastest to nowhere. Yes, I'm doing good things for my cardiovascular health. But it is more than a bit dystopic, and I would hardly say that I have fun.

In addition to making us less playful, our emphasis on work and productivity reduces our opportunities for connection. Not only do many of us live far from our family and closest friends (often because we've followed a job opportunity) but participation in community organizations has steeply declined since its peak (in America) between 1940 and 1965. In many cases, we've lost or abandoned the social structures and scaffolding that facilitated the casual ties and spontaneous interactions that fostered feelings of connection and community to begin with.

Today, if you're like many people, your moments of in-person connection with friends are often planned far in advance—who has time for spontaneity?—via extended text or email chains. You also probably spend a lot of time "connecting" through text messages and social media. (After all, they're so much more efficient than phone calls!) These can be good ways to stay in touch and can even be enjoyable up to a point, but communicating asynchronously via speech bubbles and emojis hardly feels the same as spending time together in person. And unfortunately, we're not doing much of that, either.

Indeed, we're living in the midst of what many experts call an epidemic of loneliness. A 2018 survey by the AARP Foundation found that more than a third of American adults aged forty-five and older consider themselves lonely (compared to 20 percent in a similar group less than two decades earlier). That same year, a survey of more than twenty thousand American adults by the global health-service company Cigna found that nearly half of the respondents reported "sometimes or always feeling alone"; barely half said that they had meaningful social interactions "such as having an extended conversation with a friend, or spending quality time with family" on a daily basis.

The problem is not just an American one. In January 2018, Theresa May, the prime minister of the United Kingdom, actually established and appointed—I am not kidding; this is a real thing—*a minister of loneliness* to try to assess and reduce the countries' loneliness. (Perhaps one day there will be a minister of fun.)* In response to its crea-

---

* Again, not kidding: given the benefits of fun, I really think we should have one. (Also, can you imagine *being* the minister of loneliness? Just picture the business cards.)

tion, a British filmmaker named Alice Aedy made a minidocumentary called *Disconnected* that featured voicemail messages left for the minister of loneliness by anonymous citizens. They're heartbreaking to listen to, in part because they're so relatable. In the words of one caller: "I sit in my flat and watch people walk by and think, 'How am I so alone in a place with so many people?'"

In an unfortunate irony, our interactions with our phones—i.e., our *communication devices*—often make the problem worse. In a 2017 cover story in *The Atlantic* titled "Have Smartphones Destroyed a Generation?" psychology professor Jean Twenge made this point when she wrote that "it's not an exaggeration to describe [the generation that has grown up with smartphones] as being on the brink of the worst mental-health crisis in decades. Much of this deterioration can be traced to their phones."

The article featured a chart that stood out to me. It showed the percentage of eighth-, tenth-, and twelfth-graders who agree or "mostly agree" with the statements "I often feel left out of things" and "A lot of times I feel lonely." The percentage begins to rise starting around 2008, the year the first smartphones were available. Then, after 2010, it takes off exponentially.

Correlation isn't causation, but it doesn't seem coincidental to me that 2010 is the year Instagram was created. Phones are unlikely to make us lonelier if we are using them *as phones* (i.e., to *call* people)—but passively scrolling through people's feeds is associated with symptoms of depression and lower self-esteem and self-worth. It can make people feel bad about their physical appearance and their social status, not to mention less accepted and more left out. And feeling socially excluded—or even seeing someone *else* be socially excluded—has been shown to activate a network of areas in the brain that are associated with the experience of *physical* pain.

"The greater the proportion of face-to-face interactions, the less lonely you are," loneliness expert John Cacioppo told a reporter from *The Atlantic* back in 2012 (when social media was nowhere near as pervasive as it is today). "The greater the proportion of online interactions, the lonelier you are."

As the reporter concluded, "Within this world of instant and absolute communication, unbounded by limits of time or space, we suffer from unprecedented alienation. We have never been more detached from one another, or lonelier."

Unfortunately, as bad as things may seem for playfulness and connection, the situation for flow is worse. The gig economy and our lack of safety nets (from health and retirement benefits to paid parental leave) make it hard to be present in the moment, let alone enjoy ourselves, because everything feels so precarious. Instead, we live in a constant state of anxiety.

Making flow even more elusive is the fact that, no matter what we're in the middle of doing, we're only seconds away from an interruption, whether it's from a child, an email, a news alert, or a text message or other notification. Indeed, when it comes to our ability to experience True Fun, these perpetual distractions may be the biggest obstacle of them all. Simply put, it is impossible to be in flow—and therefore to have True Fun—if your attention is divided. And, thanks in large part to the devices we carry in our pockets, our attention is divided *all the time*.*

Our output-driven approach to time—and the lack of value we assign to fun—also has the unfortunate result of making us seek quantifiable outcomes for our social lives, too. Without money as a metric, we end up relying on external validation to prove our self-

---

* This is true both because the content on our devices is distracting and (more disturbingly, and as we'll discuss in a bit) because the constant stimulation that they provide is actually changing our brains in ways that make us more distractible.

worth, obsessively documenting our experiences so that we can offer evidence on social media that we are Fun and Interesting People (never mind the fact that you can't be *that* interesting if you're spending all your time on social media, and you can't be having *that* much fun if you're constantly interrupting your experiences to post photographs of them).

The more external validation we receive, the more of it we crave, and the more dependent on it we become. Before long, we end up treating our lives as brands that need to be managed and our children as products that reflect our work as parents (did you *really* humblebrag on Facebook about your kindergartener's reading level out of a desire for connection?); we make decisions based on the public images that we have cultivated rather than on what we actually *want*. Not only does this dissonance make us behave in ways that don't reflect our authentic selves—and, in extreme cases, that prevent us (and our kids) from even knowing our authentic selves to begin with—but it's also exhausting. We're left with no energy to pursue playfulness, connection, or flow, which is an unfortunate irony, given that playfulness, connection, and flow each generate far more energy and satisfaction than any hard-earned "like" on social media ever could.

As if this all weren't bad enough, our prospects for True Fun were further dampened by the global SARS-CoV-2 pandemic and the contemporaneous increase in social, political, and economic unrest. Fear and anxiety kept us distracted and blocked our ability to experience playfulness and flow. Social distancing requirements and lockdowns prevented in-person connection; the preexisting epidemic of isolation and loneliness became even more severe. We weren't great at managing our time or maintaining work-life balance (or, as I like to call it, screen-life balance) before the pandemic; working from home eroded whatever boundaries we had left.

Unsurprisingly, many of us coped with the pandemic by relying even more heavily on our screens, trying to re-create virtually what was no longer available in reality—from school to work meetings to get-togethers with friends. Technology became a lifeline; I don't even want to think about how I would have coped without cell service and a Wi-Fi connection. But it also entrenched our preexisting habits of dealing with reality by losing ourselves in our devices. (And, in the case of children, it created *new* habits that are likely to be long-lasting.) By this point, we're all so dependent on the internet that the idea of disconnecting—even for an evening, let alone a weekend—can seem inconceivable.

I'm not trying to blame all of our problems on technology or suggest that the solution is to quit our jobs, become cobblers, and move to remote cabins in the woods with no cell or internet service. There are lots of forces working against us when it comes to our ability to experience True Fun, and there are obviously circumstances in which we *need* (and want!) technology, especially when it comes to communication, entertainment, and our jobs. Also, in many cases our devices are simply amplifying issues that we already had, such as not having good boundaries between our work and home lives, relying on external validation as a proxy for self-worth, overemphasizing money as a metric for the value of our time, and buying into the idea that the best way to achieve health, success, and happiness is to maximize every single thing we do.

But while there are many aspects of modern life (and side effects of the human condition!) that make it harder for us to experience playfulness, connection, and flow—and thus harder to *achieve* those goals—our dysfunctional relationships with our devices are one of the top obstacles standing in our way.

THE CASE FOR
SCREEN-LIFE BALANCE

When I say that we have relationships with our devices, I mean it. We don't just use them; we *interact* with them, and these interactions are a two-way street.* We check our smartphones in response to a notification just as often as we pick them up with a specific purpose in mind, if not more so. When we do reach for them for a reason, we're frequently sidetracked by a different time-stealing temptation—leading to the experience we've all had where we look up, twenty minutes into a digital black hole, and realize we can't remember what app we were looking for in the first place. Perhaps worse, many of our phone checks are the result of subconscious cravings and habits that have become so automatic that we don't even realize they exist. How many times have you found your phone in your hand with no idea how—or why—it got there?

In addition, we carry our phones with us everywhere: around the house, to the office, on the street, to the bathroom, even into our beds (and in the morning, we often turn to them before we greet whoever else might be in the bed with us). This combination—namely, that they are able (and indeed *engineered*) to interrupt us, that they are manipulating our subconscious (more on that soon!), and that we carry them with us constantly—makes smartphones and other wireless mobile devices different from all other technologies that preceded them, such as radio, television, traditional telephones, and movies.† It also differentiates them from the other

---

* In this book, I'm focusing on smartphones because they are currently the most common (and problematic) form of wireless mobile devices, and thus the biggest impediments to screen-life balance. But everything I'm saying about smartphones could also apply to other WMDs, too, including tablets and smartwatches and things that haven't even been invented yet.

† Their closest ancestor is arguably Blackberries, the handheld devices (with very basic functions, and primarily owned by businesspeople) that many people mockingly referred to as "Crackberries," due to the way they made their owners act like addicts.

technologies in our lives; I may have written a book called *How to Break Up With Your Phone,* but it's unlikely I'd write a follow-up called *How to Dump Your Toaster Oven.*

I still have a smartphone, and obviously am not writing this book with a quill; I'm grateful for technology and wouldn't want to live without it. But at this point, much of our screen time isn't the result of a conscious choice; our devices are controlling us rather than the other way around. We're in a relationship, and it's not a healthy one.

If you want to keep the needle on a compass pointed north, you need to make sure that you're protecting it from other magnets. The same principle applies to life: if we want to live meaningful, joyful, fully engaged lives, we need to protect our attention from anything that distracts us and pulls us toward Fake Fun—starting with the temptations on our screens.

At its most basic level, the challenge we face is time—not just how we think about its value but how much of it is being consumed by our devices. There are only twenty-four hours in a day, and we sleep for at least a quarter of them. Before the SARS-CoV-2 pandemic, the average adult was spending upward of four hours a day on their phone, and for many of us, the number is now even higher.

Four hours a day adds up to nearly sixty full days a year. It's *nine months'* worth of forty-hour work weeks. It's a quarter of our waking lives.

And that's just our phones. Add in our tablets and televisions, our computers and videogame consoles, and I think it's safe to say that many people are now spending *most* of their waking lives staring at screens. Yes, obviously some of this is necessary for work. But think about it: How much time each day, if you're being honest with yourself, do you actually spend on your hobbies or with your partner, family, or friends, in person? Even if you add them all up, does it come anywhere close to four hours—let alone the *total* time you spend on all screens?

It's not even just the sheer *amount* of time that's affecting us. The way we interact with our devices—or, more specifically, the way they fragment our attention as we flit back and forth between real life and our screens (or the apps or posts that they contain)—is resulting in what some experts call "polluted time," or "time confetti," a term that journalist Brigid Schulte coined that refers to all the seconds and minutes lost to unproductive and unsatisfying multitasking. (The default settings on our phones and computers often make this worse by dinging us on all of our devices every time we get a new text or email.) This likely accounts for the discrepancy between the amount of leisure time that experts *say* that we have—they claim that most people have more time for leisure than they had in the 1950s!*—and the amount that we *feel* is available.

"People end up enjoying their free time less and, when asked to reflect on it, estimate that they had less free time than they actually did," writes time management expert Ashley Whillans in her book *Time Smart*, describing an experiment in which people were asked to shift their attention from their present experience to a stress-inducing activity. "That's how invasive the technology time trap is: time confetti makes us feel even more time impoverished than we actually are."

Whereas flow rejuvenates us, time confetti makes us *exhausted*. Trying to hold too many things in our heads at one time taxes our working memories and leaves us drained. (As defined by *Psychology Today*, working memory is "a form of memory that allows a person to hold a limited amount of information at the ready for immediate mental use." It's what enables you to do a math problem in your head or temporarily recall the names of the people you just met at a

---

* I know. I don't believe it, either.

party.) When we do this for an entire workday, we end up so fried that, even though we know that we'd feel much better if we met up with a friend, or went to the gym, or took the dog for a walk—and even though we just spent the entire day staring at a screen—we don't have the energy to do anything but sink into the couch and reach for the remote control or the phone.

As a result, we end up spending a lot of our *leisure* time on screens, too, doing things "for fun" that (while possibly relaxing, enjoyable, educational, soothing, or numbing) actually do not create playful, connected flow, let alone make us feel more alive, and that thus will never generate *True* Fun.

Instead, many of the leisure activities that we do on our screens fall into the category of Fake Fun, usually in the form of self-medication, entertainment, consumerism,* or distraction that—while sometimes satisfying in small doses—ultimately only leaves us feeling more anxious and alone.

HOW OUR BRAINS HAVE BEEN HACKED

That night when I had my out-of-body experience with my daughter—the one where she was looking up at me as I looked at antique doorknob listings on my phone—was a real-life version of the scene in *A Christmas Carol* where Scrooge is visited by the Ghost of Christmas Yet to Come, sees what his future will be if he stays on his current path, and resolves to change his ways. In that moment, the scales fell from my eyes, and I was able to see clearly both what

---

* One of the ironies caused by our lack of work- and screen-life balance is that we are starved for fun but too tired to *do* anything that might produce it. So instead we just buy more stuff. It's much easier, for example, to order a new flat-screen television than it is to organize a party. (Unfortunately, you may have to then work even longer hours to pay off the credit card debt you accrued when you bought the television, which may leave you so tired that you spend your leisure time watching said television instead of doing other more fun-generating things.)

was happening in the present and what would happen in the future if I didn't fix my habits—namely, I'd end up wasting my life on things that didn't actually matter (and would risk encouraging my daughter to do the same). I freaked out, I decided I wanted to change, and I embarked on a journey that has led to me writing these words today.

I'm deeply grateful to have had that realization, but I can't help but wonder: Why did it not happen sooner? My screen-life balance was obviously out of whack, and I had been exhibiting symptoms of a compulsion, if not an outright behavioral addiction, for years. Why did it take a brief hallucinatory moment likely brought on by sleep deprivation for me to see the situation clearly?

It reminded me of when I was diagnosed with type 1 diabetes when I was twenty-two years old. In retrospect, I had *all* of the symptoms of undiagnosed type 1. I was ravenously hungry. I was so thirsty that I had dreams about seltzer and woke up in the middle of the night to drink water from our dorm bathroom's faucet. Despite eating constantly, I dropped twenty pounds. And yet it took prodding from my roommate to get me to go to the doctor, where I was promptly diagnosed. Looking back, it all seems obvious. But in the moment, I wasn't aware of what was happening—both because type 1 diabetes wasn't on my radar to begin with and because, thanks to the effects that high blood sugars can have on cognitive function, my brain literally wasn't working right.

Something similar is now happening with technology. In theory, it might seem like it should be easy for us to recognize the degree to which our devices are deadening us and keeping us from experiencing True Fun (while simultaneously amplifying our anxiety). If we could rationally analyze our relationships with our phones, we would acknowledge that while, sure, we often do need them for work, many of the things we do "for fun" on them actually are not fun at all in the true sense of the word, let alone meaningful or satisfying—and then we would reject them.

For example, we would realize that choosing our activities based on how many "likes" we think we'll get is a pretty unsatisfying way to live. We'd see that, while we'd originally signed up for a dating app out of hope that we'd find love (and, indeed, many people *do* find love through dating apps), we're thwarting our chances by swiping through people's profile pictures on autopilot, almost as if it's a game, without even thinking about the actual human beings that the pictures represent (and ignoring the actual real-life humans that might be nearby; I once had a fascinating and depressing conversation with a bartender about how he often witnesses a row of single strangers sitting at the bar, swiping through dating apps instead of talking to the person next to them). We'd notice that looking at other people's idealized photos on social media, or doomscrolling the news, or compulsively refreshing our email, or playing games for hours, or binge-watching TV, or shopping online for things we don't need, doesn't make us feel good. We'd know that checking our phone in the middle of a conversation is rude and makes the other person feel bad. So we'd stop.

But we don't. Why?

Because our brains have been hacked.

They've been hacked by sophisticated companies using sophisticated algorithms that are specifically designed to keep us glued to our screens. These companies have figured out how to use our own brains against us, triggering changes in our neurochemistry that make us *think* we're having fun when in fact we're not—and making us behave in ways that benefit the app makers, rather than us.

In other words, please don't blame yourself if you have an unhealthy relationship with your smartphone and other wireless mobile devices. It's not your fault. I meet a lot of people who flagellate themselves for their supposed lack of self-control when it comes to their screen time. But in reality, blaming ourselves for being hooked would be the equivalent of a smoker blaming themselves for the fact that cigarettes are addictive. If we find it difficult to change our habits, it doesn't mean that there's something wrong with us or that we have no willpower. It's because *apps have been designed to hook us.*

They're designed this way because nearly all of our most problematic, time-sucking apps are part of what's known as the "attention economy" (or, more menacingly, but no less accurately, "surveillance capitalism"): an economy in which our attention, rather than goods and services, is the commodity that is being bought and sold.

A lot of attention (ha) has been paid recently to the attention economy, thanks to films such as *The Social Dilemma* and former tech insiders who are raising the alarm, such as Tristan Harris, founder of the Center for Humane Technology. But it's having such devastating effects on our ability to experience True Fun that it's worth taking a moment to clarify how it works.

In the attention economy, we are not the customers or the vendors; we are the *users* (an ominous term!), and our attention is the product that is being sold. *Advertisers* are the customers, and they are paying another company—for example, a social media app—for the chance to capture our attention.* The more attention we devote to an app, the more opportunities there will be for the app to present us with personally targeted ads and content, and to gather data about us that can be used to show us even more targeted ads and content in the future—and the more money it will make.

All apps and sites that are part of the attention economy therefore have the same ultimate goal. No matter what their taglines say, it's not to "connect" us, or delight us, or inspire us, or educate us, or make us feel good about ourselves, and it's certainly not to help us

---

* Note that they are not paying *us*. Tech expert Jaron Lanier estimates that if companies had to compensate us for our data and attention, a four-person family could be entitled to roughly twenty thousand dollars a year. Regardless of whether Lanier's plan could ever actually become reality, it is worth asking how we have allowed the executives at companies such as Facebook, which owns Instagram and WhatsApp, to become among the world's wealthiest people (and, in the case of Facebook, to have had the company's value at one point exceed one *trillion* dollars) by selling a commodity that they have stolen from us. When it comes to the way they profit off our attention, they are essentially the robber barons of modern times.

have fun. It's to interrupt our real-life experiences as frequently as possible and keep us glued to our screens for as long as they can.

"Our attention can be mined," Justin Rosenstein, a former Facebook engineer who helped to develop the Like button on Facebook, said in *The Social Dilemma*. "We are more profitable to a corporation if we're spending time staring at a screen, staring at an ad, than if we're spending that time living our life in a rich way."

And it's not *just* our attention that they're after. Jaron Lanier, a tech expert and virtual reality pioneer, points out that advertisers—and the other people and companies behind paid content—aren't paying money to companies like Facebook just to have us glance at their ads and move on. They're paying money in hopes of producing gradual, slight changes in our perceptions, emotions, and behavior that will serve their interests, and/or benefit their bottom line. In other words, their goal is to get us to *do* something. "What might once have been called advertising," writes Lanier, "must now be understood as continuous behavior modification on a titanic scale." As he summarizes it, "Your specific behavior change has been turned into a product."

Companies modify our behavior with the help of what are called "adaptive algorithms"—basically, computer programs that allow the apps to learn from our interactions with them and show us ever more personalized ads and content.*

These adaptive algorithms are what's behind the unnerving experience when you talk with a friend about something—let's say, their new shoes—and the next day an ad for those exact shoes shows up in one of your feeds, despite the fact that you never searched for them yourself.

---

* The world's best AI algorithms are *extremely* valuable to the companies that created them, a fact that is demonstrated by how carefully they are guarded. As Lanier writes, "algorithms behind companies like Facebook and Google are stored in some of the few files in the world that can't be hacked; they're kept *that* secret. The deepest secrets of the NSA and CIA have been leaked, repeatedly, but you can't find a copy of Google's search algorithm or Facebook's feed algorithm on the dark web."

If this has happened to you, you may have concluded that your phone's microphone is eavesdropping on your conversations. But according to Roger McNamee, an early investor in Facebook, now a critic who wrote a book called *Zucked: Waking Up to the Facebook Catastrophe*, that's "not practical today." Instead, "a more likely explanation is that the behavioral-prediction engine"—i.e., the site's algorithm—"has made a good forecast."

In other words, the algorithm has a hunch, based on data it's collected from you and other people like you, that you might be interested in buying shoes—even if you aren't yet aware that you're interested in shoes at all. It may know, based on location data and your chat history, among other sources of information (known collectively as metadata), that you recently spent time with this particular friend, and that your friend recently bought a pair of shoes from a brand that pays for advertising on the site or app. So the algorithm shows you one of its ads.

This, generally speaking, is how algorithms decide what to show us: they compare data about us and our past behaviors to the profiles and past behaviors of thousands if not millions of other users who resemble us in some way, whether in terms of demographics or behaviors. This information can be gathered, writes Lanier, from sources including our communications, interests, movements, contacts with others, emotional reactions to circumstances, facial expressions, purchases, and even vital signs—what he describes as an "ever-growing, boundless variety of data." Then the algorithms use what they've determined about those other people's *subsequent* behaviors to predict what we are primed to do next.

I say "primed to do next" rather than "*will* do next" deliberately. The phrase "will do next" suggests that we are in control of our own decisions, and that the algorithms are merely acting as crystal balls.

But in reality, the best algorithms are more like sorcerers, able to manipulate which options are presented to us in a way that nudges us toward the desired outcomes of *their creators*. Algorithms' predictions are not always accurate. But when they are—and they become more so with every passing day—algorithms can steer us toward taking whatever path is most beneficial to the people or company that designed them.

"It is deeply creepy," writes McNamee. "It will get creepier as the technology improves."

At first glance, the cost of these algorithm-driven behavior changes might seem negligible (even if they're creepy). So what if you spend a minute of your time standing in line for lunch looking at a news story or post on social media that an app's algorithm chose for you? It's just a minute. And so what if you make a choice based on an algorithm's recommendation? It's possible that the algorithm nudged you in a direction you actually wanted to go—for example, by showing you an ad for something you're interested in. And besides, it's just one out of countless decisions in your day.

But it's not just what these algorithms get us to do that's the problem; it's all the other things we *aren't* doing as a result, especially given the fact that the incentives of the people designing apps and algorithms (most of whom are not nefarious; just profit-minded) usually don't align with how we actually want to live our lives. Instead of being consumed by the fear of what we might miss if we were to put down our phones, we should think about all the things we *definitely* miss when we pick them up. In short, every moment spent following algorithmically generated links is a moment we're not doing something *for ourselves,* whether it's reading a book, or practicing an instrument, or talking to a friend, or even just gazing at the sky. The more we allow our time to be shredded into confetti, the more we treat *ourselves* as products with public images that need to be cultivated and maintained—in other words, *the more complicit we become*—the less we're able to slip into flow, be our authentic selves, and experience True Fun.

Algorithms are also shaping our *emotions* by exposing us to content that has deliberately been chosen to manipulate how we feel—and, therefore, influence how we behave.* For example, a news site's algorithm will know that sensational headlines get the most clicks—so those are the headlines that will be prioritized and sent to us as alerts (as the old journalist adage goes, "If it bleeds, it leads"). Who cares if it adds stress to our day? Even some algorithmically chosen content that doesn't have an obvious financial incentive behind it can color our moods in ways that we would not necessarily have chosen for ourselves (and that are usually not fun). Consider, for example, the feature on Apple's photo app that auto-generates slide shows drawn from our personal photo libraries, sets them to sentimental music, and presents them to us with a notification that chirpily announces "You have a new memory." These little nostalgia bombs, as I call them, are unwelcome reminders of the passage of time that have the power to derail my day.

Also, we're not exposed to content that algorithms have chosen for us just once or twice a day; we're exposed to it every single time we open an app. And we open apps every time we look at our phones. And we look at our phones dozens if not hundreds of times a day. Taken in isolation, each of these moments might not be a big deal, but in the aggregate, their effects raise questions about free will.

"Look around you and ask what drives your product, media, and people choices," writes Kartik Hosanagar in his book about algorithms, *A Human's Guide to Machine Intelligence*. "Unless you are a tech Luddite, algorithms are silently rearranging your life. The conventional narrative is that algorithms will make faster and better decisions for all of us, leaving us with more time for family and leisure. But the reality isn't so simple. In this brave new world, many of our

---

* Facebook caught a lot of flak for a 2012 study in which it altered the feeds of nearly 700,000 users (without notifying them or obtaining their explicit consent) to see how the emotional tone of the content to which they were exposed might affect their moods.

choices are in fact predestined, and all the seemingly small effects that algorithms have on our decisions add up to a transformative impact on our lives. Because who we are, ultimately, is the sum total of the various decisions we make over a lifetime."

If we find it hard to pull away from our screens, if we see ourselves behaving in ways that don't align with our actual values or priorities or the definition of True Fun, it doesn't mean that we are failures; it's a reflection of the app makers' ingenuity and the effort they put into controlling us.

"Imagine bookshelves, seminars, workshops and trainings that teach aspiring tech entrepreneurs techniques [to get people to spend their time and attention on apps]," writes Tristan Harris, who was a "product philosopher" at Google before he became disillusioned and cofounded the Center for Humane Technology. "Imagine rooms of engineers whose job every day is to invent new ways to keep you hooked."

These engineers—or, as I prefer to think of them, attention thieves—use techniques that they themselves call "brain hacking" to keep us glued to our screens, thus creating more opportunities to nudge our behaviors in directions that serve their interests. As Sean Parker, Facebook's founding president (who has since become something of a conscientious objector to social media), remarked at a 2017 Axios event in Philadelphia, "The thought process that went into building these applications, Facebook being the first of them . . . was all about 'How do we consume as much of your time and conscious attention as possible?' "

The answer that the attention thieves came up with was to copy tactics from a different device—and another source of Fake Fun: the slot machine. In fact, there are so many similarities between our phones and slot machines that experts such as Harris refer to phones as slot machines that we keep in our pockets. This is a big deal, because slot machines are considered to be some of the most addictive machines ever to have been invented.*

"When we pull our phone out of our pocket, we're playing a slot machine to see what notifications we have received," writes Harris. "When we swipe down our finger to scroll the Instagram feed, we're playing a slot machine to see what photo comes next. When we 'Pull to Refresh' our email, we're playing a slot machine to see what email we got. When we swipe faces on dating apps like Tinder, we're playing a slot machine to see if we got a match."

The more I've learned about these techniques (which are known, quite euphemistically, as "persuasive design"), the more terrified I've become—both for us adults and for our kids. Many of us are behaving in ways that Larry Rosen, a psychologist and co-author of *The Distracted Mind*, describes as being similar to those displayed in psychiatric conditions such as obsessive-compulsive disorder (OCD) and attention-deficit/hyperactivity disorder (ADHD). My friend Miriam Stewart captured the degree of our dysfunction in an essay called "My Not-So-Silent Retreat," about feeling drawn to her smartphone during a meditation retreat. "No sane person would have utilized any other means of communication as often as I was checking my phone," she wrote. "You would never turn the TV on and off or open and close the newspaper twelve times in 20 minutes, or call someone several times in an hour to say one sentence and then hang up."

Indeed, in many cases our habits have become so extreme that they look a lot like a behavioral addiction.† This isn't entirely surprising: according to Robert Lustig, MD, emeritus professor in pediatric

---

* As Natasha Dow Schüll, author of *Addiction by Design: Machine Learning in Las Vegas*, explained to CBS, "The gambling industry is designing machines that can addict people"; according to CBS news, Americans spend more on slot machines than they do on theme parks, baseball, and movies combined.

† The basic definition of an addiction, according to the American Psychiatric Association, is "uncontrolled use of a substance despite harmful consequences." In other words, you know something is bad for you, but you feel powerless to stop. Addictions

endocrinology at the University of California San Francisco and author of *The Hacking of the American Mind*, their ability to light up our dopamine systems (more on this in a second) means that "phones affect our brains in the same way as drugs." And we certainly *use* our phones like drugs: to give us jolts of pleasure and help us avoid emotional pain. But yet we're reluctant (or perhaps unable) to acknowledge the depth of the problem because it is so widespread.

As a way to gain perspective, I encourage you to spend a few days paying attention to the way the people around you are interacting with their phones. The next time you're out in public, for example, notice the people "watching" their children's soccer games while tending to their work email. Notice the people crossing busy intersections while texting. Notice the people typing on their phones *while driving*. Notice the scene at restaurants, where nearly every diner has their phone next to them on the table, as if it's part of the place setting, and entire families sit "together" with each person lost

---

are marked by powerful cravings, even obsession, and a tendency to use the addictive substance as a way to seek pleasure and avoid emotional pain.

As people's addictions worsen, their relationships may start to suffer. They may stop engaging in hobbies and social activities that they used to enjoy. They may structure their lives around making sure that they always have access to whatever they're addicted to and become agitated, even angry, when their supply is cut off. (Have you ever become irrationally upset when your hotel's internet connection doesn't work while you are on vacation?) And when confronted, addicts are likely to deny that a problem exists.

Usually, the term "addiction" refers to *substance* addictions, such as tobacco or alcohol. But in the most recent edition of the *Diagnostic and Statistical Manual of Mental Disorders* (more commonly known as the *DSM*), the American Psychiatric Association included gambling disorder as the first-ever "behavioral addiction," opening the door to classifying other behaviors as addictions as well. The most recent version of the *DSM* (the *DSM-5*) also included "internet gaming disorder" as a condition worthy of further research—the first internet-related activity to be classified in this way.

As I write, the APA has not recognized smartphone or internet addiction as an official disorder—a point I want to emphasize for all the addiction psychologists in the audience who are concerned about my use of the term. I'm not doing so lightly; I believe that it is only a matter of time before some form of it is recognized as such. It's worth noting that the *DSM-5* was published in 2013, when some of today's most time-sucking apps were brand new or didn't even exist. (Instagram was launched in 2010; Snapchat in 2011; Tinder in 2012; and TikTok in 2016.) When it comes to technology, 2013 was light-years ago.

in their own device. Notice your friends' behavior. Notice your family's. Notice *your own*. Then imagine that instead of phones, we were holding cigarettes or syringes.

David Greenfield, founder of the Center for Internet and Technology Addiction, created an evaluation tool called the Smartphone Compulsion Test to help illustrate how dysfunctional our relationships with technology have become. The fifteen-question quiz asks you to answer yes or no to questions such as "Do you seem to lose track of time when on your cell or smartphone?" and "Do you find yourself viewing and answering texts, tweets, and emails at all hours of the day and night—even if it means interrupting other things you are doing?"*

Saying yes to more than five of the statements suggests that "it is likely that you may have a problematic or compulsive smartphone use pattern." If your score is higher than eight, "you might consider seeing a psychologist, psychiatrist, or psychotherapist who specializes in behavioral addictions for a consultation."

Spoiler alert: if you own a smartphone, you are going to fail this quiz. Even Greenfield himself says that he would score poorly. That doesn't mean that there is a problem with the test. It means that the problem is more serious and pervasive than we'd like to admit. A report from Google, of all places, noted "addictive patterns of engagement" in the ways people interact with their phones, such as repeatedly refreshing apps in hope that new content will appear. In short, we're all hooked.

If we want to have any chance of taking back control and having True Fun, we have to know how we're being manipulated.

So, here's what's happening.

* You can take the test for yourself on the Center for Internet and Technology Addiction's website.

Apps and slot machines hook us by hijacking our brain chemistry. More specifically, they're designed to trigger the release of dopamine— a chemical that is released in response to both true *and* Fake Fun. (We're about to simultaneously get a little dorky *and* oversimplify some biochemistry; bear with me.)

At a basic level, dopamine is a salience indicator. You can think of it as a tool that our brains use to record when something is worth doing again and to motivate us to repeat the behavior in the future.

Dopamine is like a biochemical guiding star: we're pulled toward activities that our dopamine systems have tagged as important, in the same way that a compass needle is pulled toward magnetic north.

The most important role of the dopamine system is to help us identify and remember—and motivate us to repeat—activities that are essential for the survival of our species; for example, dopamine is released in response to food and sex. It's also released in response to activities that are helpful for our survival, even if not absolutely essential, such as social bonding or, for that matter, *fun*.

Regardless of the trigger, dopamine heightens our senses and focuses our attention, creating a state of increased awareness and engagement that helps us remember the details of the experience so that we can re-create it in the future. When you reflect back on the moments in which you felt the most alive (and the moments in which you had the most True Fun), dopamine was undoubtedly involved. Its role in motivation and memory also explains why dopamine helps us learn.*

So, here's the problem: our dopamine systems are nondiscriminatory. Just as a compass can't tell the difference between the pull of

---

* Dopamine is particularly helpful when we're trying to acquire skills that require rote memorization—say, learning new vocabulary words, studying a foreign language, memorizing basic math facts, or learning how to read music. Indeed, if you look at some of the most popular—and effective—learning apps, there are multiple dopamine triggers embedded in their designs (for example, the vibrations and dings that you receive when you get something right). In my opinion, this is a *good* use of artificial dopamine triggers because it helps us achieve a desired goal.

the earth's magnetic force and the pull of a refrigerator magnet, our brains can't tell the difference between dopamine triggers that are *good* for us and dopamine triggers that are not. Nor can they differentiate between fun that's real and fun that's fake.

Instead, their responses are entirely automatic. When our brains encounter a dopamine trigger, they release dopamine, full stop. We will be compelled to seek that trigger again, regardless of whether it is *actually* worth repeating. (Indeed, dopamine plays an important role in addictions.) This is the reason that Fake Fun is so powerfully seductive: it's designed to trigger the release of dopamine in a way that fools us into thinking that it's real—often providing a hit of instant gratification before ultimately leaving us feeling empty inside.

The nondiscriminatory nature of our dopamine systems means that throwing off our internal compasses is quite simple: you just bake dopamine triggers into your product's design.

This is exactly what app makers do.

"We give you a little dopamine hit every once in a while because someone liked or commented on a photo or a post or whatever," explained former Facebook president Sean Parker, describing the techniques platforms like Facebook use to capture our time and attention. "And that's going to get you to contribute more content, and that's going to get you . . . more likes and comments. It's a social validation feedback loop . . . it's exactly the kind of thing that a hacker like myself would come up with, because you're exploiting a vulnerability in human psychology."*

There are dopamine triggers all over our phones, from the blood-red color of notification bubbles to the slight vibration that results when we put something into our shopping carts. The three that are

---

* "The inventors, creators [of Facebook and Instagram and other similar apps] . . . understood this consciously," he continued. "And *we did it anyway.*" (Ominous emphasis his.)

most relevant, when it comes to deceiving us into wasting our time on the pursuit of Fake Fun, are novelty, rewards, and unpredictability. Each is powerful on its own, and when we experience them together—as we often do when we look at our phones—they are nearly impossible to resist. But the better we understand them, the greater our chances to resist become.

NOVELTY

Any time we experience something new, we're going to get a little spritz of dopamine. It's easy to see why we evolved this way: the pursuit of novelty often leads to progress.

The evolutionary advantage of seeking out new things may also explain why novelty is so often associated with fun. Indeed, many of our most fun memories involve activities that felt new to us at the time. Think of a first kiss, or driving your first car, or the first time you traveled someplace new. (It might also suggest a fascinating flip side: that the feeling that we call "fun" might serve an evolutionary purpose, as a way to use enjoyment and delight to motivate us to try new things.)

Of course novelty, by definition, can't last forever; in your offline life, it eventually wears off, and you move on to something—or someone—else. But we never tire of checking our phones, because they offer us something new every time we pick them up. If you don't have new email you can always check social media. Social media isn't satisfying? Try the news.

Just as it's possible to build up tolerance to a drug, the more accustomed your brain gets to receiving these regular hits from your devices, the more dopamine it will take to satisfy your cravings, and the more dependent on your devices you'll become. Formerly enjoyable activities like listening to music or hanging out with a friend feel less stimulating and satisfying than the rapid-fire jolts of Fake Fun that you get from checking social media again.

"This is one of the worst parts of tech addiction," David Greenfield explained to me. "It dulls reality."

If we really thought about it, we'd probably agree that most sources of novelty offered by our phones are unimportant and not actually fun. But they're new, so they trigger dopamine, and the dopamine motivates us to seek out those sources again. Eventually we become like lab rats, conditioned to repeatedly press a lever to get a new reward.

REWARD

Speaking of which, rewards are also a huge dopamine trigger. In the case of a slot machine, the reward is obviously money. In the case of True Fun, the reward is joy in the moment, and a memory to look back on and treasure. Our phones, on the other hand, offer us ephemeral and less meaningful rewards, often in the form of "likes" or comments on social media.

On some level, we all know that most online affirmation is meaningless, that being "connected" on social media isn't the same as feeling connected in real life, and that online "communities" too often turn into polarized tribes. But it doesn't matter. Humans are a social species, and even the most introverted among us still evolved to exist in groups. We care what other people think.

We also care about our rank. Indeed, our need to demonstrate our social status is so strong that we are willing to turn our lives into exhibitions just to prove ourselves to our peers.

Jaron Lanier sums up the situation in his book *Ten Arguments for Deleting Your Social Media Accounts Right Now.* "Suddenly you and other people are being put into a lot of stupid competitions no one asked for," he writes. "Why aren't you sent as many cool pictures as your friend? Why aren't you followed as much? This constant dosing of social anxiety only gets people more glued in. Deep mechanisms in the social parts of our brains monitor our social standing, making us terrified to be left behind, like a runt sacrificed to predators on the savannah."

What's particularly crazy about our obsession with external validation is that many of the people we seek affirmation from online aren't actually *real*. There are millions of fake accounts on social media platforms—it's a constant struggle for social media companies to identify and purge these accounts—so it's quite possible that some of the "likes" and follows that you're interrupting your life to earn are actually coming from bots, not people.*

But we contort our lives around them anyway. Chamath Palihapitiya, former vice president of user growth at Facebook, described this in stark terms at an event at the Stanford Graduate School of Business in 2017.† "We curate our lives around this perceived sense of perfection because we get rewarded in these short-term signals: hearts, likes, thumbs up," he said. "And we conflate that with value, and we conflate it with truth. And instead, what it really is is fake, brittle popularity that's short-term and leaves you more—admit it!—vacant and empty than before you did it."

Part of the reason that treating our lives like performances leaves us feeling so vacant and empty is that it encourages us to behave in ways that are downright toxic to fun. Perfectionism doesn't leave space for playfulness (and, as we'll talk about in a bit, it can be devas-

---

* It's also likely that some of the "influencers" you look up to because of their enormous followings have paid to increase their followings, specifically to manipulate you into thinking that they are worth paying attention to. In a 2018 report, *The New York Times* found that it was possible to buy twenty-five thousand Twitter followers, using a company called Devumi, for $225—roughly a penny apiece. (Devumi, according to the article, at that point had "more than 200,000 customers, including reality television stars, professional athletes, comedians, TED speakers, pastors and models.") Some of these accounts are obviously fake if you look at them closely, but others actually use profile photos and bios that have been scraped from those of real people (it's a form of identity theft), so that they appear to be real.

† "User growth" is Silicon Valley speak for getting more people hooked on the platform.

tating to our mental health). Staging the perfect selfie removes you from your experience and destroys flow.* And instead of connecting us, passively scrolling through pictures of other people's supposedly perfect lives leaves us feeling insecure and jealous. We compensate by posting idealized photographs of our own lives to make ourselves feel better (which is another way of saying that we post them to make *other* people feel insecure and jealous), creating a performative competition that destroys any chance of experiencing *real* connection—or True Fun.

But dopamine throws our rationality out the window. And the fact that we never know for sure how or when people will respond to us only makes it harder to stop.

UNPREDICTABILITY

That brings us to the third main dopamine trigger tech companies use to manipulate us into conflating fun that's real with fun that's fake—and that we need to understand and watch out for if we want to wrest back control: unpredictability.

You might think that we'd be more compelled to do something if we knew it was going to have a positive outcome. But that gets boring. To our brains, an uncertain outcome is far more seductive than something that's guaranteed. Think about movies: they're usually more enjoyable the first time you see them. Even the most routine-oriented among us have brains that like suspense.

When unpredictability is combined with rewards—in other words, when rewards are delivered on an unpredictable schedule, as is the case with slot machines and our most time-sucking apps (and, for that matter, in many psychology lab experiments involving

---

* It also can literally kill you. Stories abound of people taking selfies in national parks next to scenic waterfalls or cliffs, only to tumble to their deaths.

rats)—the effects are even more potent. Psychologists refer to this as "intermittent reinforcement," and it's such a powerful dopamine trigger that it's considered to be one of the *most* effective techniques to manipulate people's behavior. (It's also a very common pattern in emotionally abusive relationships.)

Much of the power of intermittent reinforcement has to do with anticipation—namely, the fact that our brains release more dopamine in anticipation of a possible reward than they do when the reward is guaranteed. That's why, once you hear the sound or feel the vibration of a notification, it's so difficult to resist the urge to check, even if you are in the midst of an important task or conversation: your brain is essentially drooling in anticipation of what might be waiting for it.* Our attraction to uncertainty, coupled with the biochemistry of anticipation, also likely explains why people get so wrapped up in arguments on social media: we engage someone in a fight, which triggers the release of a whole host of other survival-related chemicals in our bodies—and this biochemical combination causes us to become consumed by the anticipation of our opponent's response and obsessed with convincing them that we are right. The fact that we don't know if or when they'll respond makes it even worse.

App developers use the uncertainty and anticipation of intermittent reinforcement to keep us tethered to our phones. If we knew that email or followers or likes or news stories would only be delivered at 4 P.M. on weekdays, we wouldn't keep checking our phones

---

* Worse, we receive notifications so incessantly that we've begun to drool at the anticipation of notifications themselves, to the point where our brains release dopamine (which in turn makes us experience cravings) any time our phones are nearby—even when they're *off*. This constant state of anticipation can actually make you hallucinate: many people report experiencing what researchers call "phantom vibrations," in which they feel their phone vibrating in their pocket when their phone isn't even there. This is one of the reasons that minimizing your notifications is an important step in taking back control of your phone.

during other times. But our phones do not deliver new information on any semblance of a schedule. We never know when something new will arrive, or what it will be. So we keep our phones with us, and part of our attention trained on them, at all times. Regardless of how meaningless the eventual rewards are, the unpredictability and anticipation causes our brains to release dopamine, which in turn makes us want to keep checking. As David Greenfield once put it to me, "Our brains love maybe."

It's important to note that there's nothing inherently wrong with our brains' attraction to novelty, rewards, and unpredictability. In fact, there's an evolutionary advantage to it, because it makes us curious—and if we weren't curious, we would become complacent and never try new things. It also makes life more enjoyable by opening us to new experiences and leading us into situations that are unexpectedly delightful.

But the dose makes the poison. Our smartphones contain so many dopamine triggers that the result is often not curiosity, but hypnosis; every one of us has had the experience of looking up from a device and wondering where the last hour of our life has gone. Time flies when we're *truly* having fun, but it also flies when we are in a dopamine-induced, Fake Fun–fueled trance.

And as always is the case with dopamine, we need to be careful about what sorts of behaviors we're being conditioned to repeat, and at what frequency. After all, there are consequences to our actions. When we interrupt conversations every time we receive a notification, we weaken our connection to the person we're with. When we repeatedly check the news just in case something has happened, we raise our own anxiety levels and keep ourselves in a state of high alert. When we refresh our email just in case we've received a new message, we distract ourselves from the task at hand. When we do this over and over again, day after day, the effects add up. And every time we succumb to our urges, it pulls us out of flow and lessens the chance that we will experience True Fun.

THE CONSEQUENCES

When Steve Jobs announced the first iPhone in 2007, no one thought to set up a randomized, controlled trial to measure the effects of these "revolutionary devices," as Jobs accurately described them. Instead, we just all got smartphones. As a result, we're now living in the midst of a giant, uncontrolled experiment.

We have a sense of what we've gained—mostly convenience, easy communication, and access to limitless entertainment and information. We have a much *less* solid sense of what we've lost—or, in the case of people who have grown up with smartphones and nonstop internet access, what we never had at all.

By this point, however, one thing's certain: our interactions with our devices are powerfully affecting us. This has been confirmed, disturbingly, by the very people who created them.*

"You have one brain," Chamath Palihapitiya told his Stanford audience. "So, you're training your brain here whether you think it or not, whether you know it or not, whether you acknowledge it or not. . . . These things, where you're spending hours a day, are rewiring your psychology and physiology."

Palihapitiya summed up his approach, and the gravity of what's at stake, in stark terms. "I can control my decisions, which is 'I don't use this sh*t,'" he said to his audience, in reference to social media.

* Steve Jobs himself didn't give his kids iPads. ("They haven't used it," Jobs told *New York Times* reporter Nick Bilton in 2014. "We limit how much technology our kids use at home." According to Jobs's biographer, Walter Isaacson, "Every evening Steve made a point of having dinner at the big long table in their kitchen, discussing books and history and a variety of things. . . . No one ever pulled out an iPad or computer. The kids did not seem addicted at all to devices.") Bill and Melinda Gates had a similar no-tech-at-the-table policy and didn't get their kids smartphones until they were 14.

"I can control my kids' decisions, which is 'They're not allowed to use this sh*t.' . . . But everybody else has to soul-search a little bit more about what you're willing to do, because . . . you don't realize it, but you're being programmed. It was unintentional, but now you've gotta decide how much [of your intellectual independence] you're willing to give up."*

PERPETUAL DISTRACTION

When it comes to the ways in which our phones are rewiring our psychology and physiology—and affecting the way we experience our own lives—their ability to distract us is at the top of the list. The constant distractions served up by our devices are causing us to exist in what tech expert Linda Stone calls a state of "continuous partial attention," which is exactly what it sounds like: paying partial attention, continuously.

As we touched on earlier, existing in a state of continuous partial attention—i.e., being perpetually distracted and distractible—is a guaranteed way to block your ability to have True Fun, because when you're distracted, you're not in flow, and if you're not in flow, you can't have True Fun.

It also blocks connection. Being truly connected with someone requires you to be fully present, which you can't be if part of your attention is trained on your phone; indeed, studies show that the mere presence of a phone on a table can reduce the perceived quality and intimacy of a conversation.

Our inability to stay focused also interferes with our ability to create memories. We obviously can't form memories of things we didn't pay attention to in the first place, which means that every real-

---

* Speaking of social media, here's what Facebook founding president, Sean Parker, had to say at the aforementioned 2017 Axios event in Philadelphia. "It literally changes your relationship with society, with each other. . . . It probably interferes with productivity in weird ways. God only knows what it's doing to our children's brains."

life moment that we miss as a result of burying our heads in our phones represents an experience that we won't have, and a memory that will never be created. What most of us don't realize, however, is that our phones are preventing us from remembering the things we *do* experience, too. The process of transferring short-term memories into long-term storage requires physical changes in our brain (more specifically, the creation of new proteins), and this process is disrupted by distraction.

If we don't have long-term memories, we can't have insights (which I define as the ability to draw connections between seemingly unconnected things), because we don't have information or experiences to connect—it'd be like trying to make a meal from an empty pantry. This, in turn, suggests to me that the constant distractions served up by our devices may be impacting our ability to think deeply and have interesting thoughts.*

The sheer amount of information available on (and shoved into our brains by) our phones is also likely harming our creativity. In their book, *The Distracted Mind,* neuroscientist Adam Gazzaley and psychologist Larry Rosen make the point that human beings forage for new information in the same way that other animals forage for food. This is another one of those evolutionary quirks that served us well in the past: seeking information was helpful when information

---

* I had an unusual chance to fact-check the idea that the distraction from phones could be affecting our ability to store long-term memories (and thus our ability to have insights) when I was on a train from Washington, D.C., back to Philadelphia and randomly sat down across from Eric Kandel, a scientist who won the 2000 Nobel Prize in Physiology or Medicine for his discovery that the storage of long-term memories requires the creation of new proteins in the brain and that this process is interrupted by distractions. Upon realizing who he was, I let out an expletive, leapt across the aisle, and knelt next to his seat.

I then proceeded to ask him point-blank: Could the distractions from our smartphones be impeding the formation of the proteins that we need for long-term memories, and thus having negative effects on our ability to think creative and independent thoughts?

He thought about it for a second. "Yes," he said. "I think that would make sense."

was limited, just as our drive for food helped us when calories were scarce. But now, the abundance of cheap, sugar-filled food has led to an epidemic of obesity and type 2 diabetes, and our easy access to endless, often low-quality information is overwhelming our brains. Just as too much sunlight makes it impossible to see, too much information makes it impossible for us to think.

There's a reason, after all, that many of our most creative ideas and insights occur when we're in the shower: it's one of the very few contexts in which we allow our brains to relax, to wander, and in a sense, to play. (This used to also be true for walking, but now so many of us text or listen to podcasts on our walks that they no longer really qualify as downtime.) When we spend all of our time scrolling and surfing, listening and watching—in other words, when we spend all our time *consuming*—we're spraying our brains with an unrelenting fire hose of information and giving them no chance to come up with new insights, ideas, or thoughts.

As Greg McKeown writes in his book *Essentialism,* "By abolishing any chance of being bored we have also lost the time we used to have to think and process." If we want to be creators rather than consumers, if we want to be interesting people instead of automatons, we need to take a break from our devices and give our brains some room to breathe.

FOMO AND CORTISOL

The ultimate solution to many of these issues would be to create distance from our devices and reconnect with our lives (that is, if we still have them!). But it's very difficult to even consider giving ourselves this breathing room, let alone to create long-term healthy relationships with technology, because we're trapped in a self-perpetuating cycle. Not only does dopamine pull us back to our devices, but—thanks to dopamine—we've been so conditioned to think of checking our devices as something worth doing again and again that when we can't check, we feel consumed by what's colloquially known as FOMO: fear of missing out.

Whereas True Fun focuses our attention—when we're having it, there's nowhere else we'd rather be—FOMO makes it impossible for us to ever be fully present. It scatters our attention and makes us anxious, often to the point at which our bodies release a stress hormone called cortisol.

"Your cortisol levels are elevated when your phone is in sight or nearby, or when you hear it or even *think* you hear it," David Greenfield told me. "It's a stress response, and it feels unpleasant, and the body's natural response is to want to check the phone to make the stress go away."

So, what do we do? We reach for our phone. And what do we encounter? A dopamine trigger, which reinforces the idea that using our phone to soothe our anxiety is worth doing again . . . and the cycle continues.

Cortisol is meant to help us respond to and survive *physical* threats, such as being chased by something. Unfortunately, just as the dopamine system can't distinguish habits that are good for us from habits that are bad, the cortisol system can't differentiate between threats that are physical and threats that are emotional (or, for that matter, threats that are consequential and those that are trivial). It responds the same way regardless.

And here's where things get truly concerning. When it's released in short bursts in response to acute physical threats, cortisol helps us survive by doing things such as speeding up our hearts, increasing our blood pressure, hyper-focusing our attention, and flooding our muscles with energy so that we can run away.

But when we're not facing acute physical threats and are instead trying to deal with *emotional* stresses—including those common in daily life—chronically elevated cortisol levels can be harmful, rather than helpful. Among other things, they can weaken our attention span, willpower, and self-restraint; hurt our processing speeds, eye-hand coordination, and ability to plan and execute tasks; and negatively affect our emotional regulation, learning and retention, and visual and verbal memory.

A lot of these effects have to do with the fact that when we're stressed-out and our cortisol levels are high, the prefrontal cortex—the area of our brain responsible for decision-making and rational thought——goes offline.* At the same time, having elevated levels of cortisol "makes dopamine go hog wild," Rob Lustig said to me. It also decreases the brain's sensitivity to serotonin, a chemical that's believed to play a role in contentment.

Under normal circumstances, the prefrontal cortex and the dopamine system work hand in hand to keep our internal compasses pointed in the right direction: the dopamine system highlights anything that *might* be worth repeating, and the prefrontal cortex steps in to make the judgment call. For example, your dopamine system encourages you to have another beer; your prefrontal cortex takes the glass out of your hand and reminds you that you are about to drive home.

"The prefrontal cortex is the brain's Jiminy Cricket," said Lustig. "It keeps us from doing stupid things."

But when the prefrontal cortex is offline, we're left with less self-control and a powerful desire to make our anxiety go away—the faster, the better. This combination leads us to do things that provide a quick hit of dopamine but that are unsatisfying in the long run, bad for us, or downright dangerous, such as abusing alcohol or drugs, or

---

* For a vivid example of this, do an internet search for "Name a Woman (Billy on the Street)." You'll find a short video in which a man, presumably named Billy, aggressively confronts a young woman by shoving a microphone in her face and demanding that she "name a woman." Caught off-guard and visibly flustered—and with her prefrontal cortex presumably suffering the cognitive effects of a sudden burst of stress hormones—she is unable to do so.

texting while we drive. (Think of how you coped during the last time you were really stressed-out. Was a lot of ice cream involved? That's what I'm talking about.)

Depending on your temperament and life circumstances, your cortisol levels might be chronically high regardless of whether or not you have a smartphone—and indeed, there's nothing inherently stressful about a smartphone itself. But for many of us, our phones function as communication and delivery devices for some of the main sources of anxiety in our lives—for example, the news, or our job, or particular relationships. This suggests to me that we should be doing a lot more to protect ourselves from the potential emotional landmines lurking in our devices, and helps explain something David Greenfield once said to me: "The smartphone shuts down our ability to use judgment."

The emotional and cognitive effects of elevated cortisol are concerning enough. But the physical consequences are even scarier. When cortisol levels remain high over the long term—which they do when we exist in a heightened state of anxiety for extended periods of time—it affects our physical health in ways that could actually shorten our lives. Indeed, it's well established that chronically elevated cortisol levels increase the risk for a wide range of health problems including depression, obesity, type 2 diabetes, high blood pressure, heart attack, stroke, fertility issues, digestive problems, Alzheimer's disease, and even cancer.[*]

It might seem nuts to think that your relationship with your phone could be doing something as serious as raising your risk for a

---

[*] Our habit of staying up later than we mean to because we're binge-watching shows or scrolling through our phones is also causing problems. Our bodies' cortisol levels follow a regular twenty-four-hour cycle, and not getting enough sleep—as in, anything less than seven or eight hours—can throw this natural day-night rhythm out of whack. When our cortisol rhythms are disrupted, it makes our bodies less adaptable to stress and increases our risks for all of the health conditions mentioned above.

heart attack, and I'm certainly not suggesting that it's as toxic as, say, smoking. But when I wrote an article for *The New York Times* about the possibility that our always-on relationships with our phones could be raising our stress levels and affecting our hormones in ways that could harm our long-term health, I explicitly asked the researchers whom I interviewed, "Is this a crazy idea?" and all of them said no.*

"Every chronic disease we know of is exacerbated by stress," Rob Lustig told me. "And our phones are absolutely contributing to this."

Put this all together, and here's my conclusion, drawn from more than half a decade of studying and thinking about this subject: our lack of screen-life balance is hurting our relationships, productivity, creativity, self-esteem, memory, focus, sleep, authenticity, and mental and physical health. (And any effects in adults are probably even more dramatic in children and teenagers, whose brains are still developing.) It's sapping our happiness and leading us to languish. It's inhibiting our ability to set priorities and make good decisions. It's exhausting and depleting us. It's encouraging consumption and eroding the barriers between work and home life. It's steering us away from what really matters to us, making us feel dead inside, and damaging our ability to have True Fun.

And that last part is much more important than you might think, because not only does True Fun *feel* better than nonstop work and screen time, it can actually prevent and even reverse many of their negative effects. True Fun isn't a distraction from our problems, in other words. It's a solution.

---

* I'm serious: I literally asked them that.

CHAPTER 3

WHY FUN—TRUE
FUN—IS THE ANSWER

"I'm going to keep having fun every day I have left, because there's no other way to play it."
—Randy Pausch, *The Last Lecture*

BEFORE WE LAUNCH INTO A DISCUSSION OF THE MANY
ways in which True Fun is good for us—as in life-changingly, astoundingly good—I want to emphasize that the *most* important benefit of orienting our lives toward True Fun is the fun itself. We should
seek out more playfulness, connection, and flow because those states
all feel great—*really* great, much-better-than-anything-you-could-do-
on-your-smartphone great—in the very moment when we experience them. True Fun is *fun*, in other words, and that should be reason
enough to pursue it.

With that said, it's astonishing to consider just how powerfully
positive True Fun can be for us mentally, physically, and emotionally,
and how little attention has been paid to its potential as a health intervention. While a lack of screen-life balance creates a whirlpool of
negative effects that sucks us down, pursuing True Fun helps us tap
into a rising current of air that lifts us up.

Let's start by taking a look at True Fun's ingredients.

Things That Are Unquestionably Bad for Our Health	Things That Are Unquestionably Good for Us*
(And That Are Often Amplified by Things We Do on Our Devices)	*(And That Are Facilitated by Fun)*
• Feeling chronically anxious and stressed	• Not being chronically anxious and stressed
• Not feeling confident	• Feeling confident
• Not being able to find humor in life	• Being able to find humor in life
• Not laughing	• Laughing
• Being socially isolated	• Having strong social ties
• Feeling lonely	• Being part of a community
• Not spending time in nature	• Spending time in nature
• Being physically inactive	• Being physically active
• Being perpetually distracted	• Feeling focused, engaged, and present
• Feeling purposeless	• Feeling purposeful
• Feeling like we don't have control	• Feeling a sense of control

* By "good for us," I don't mean that the items on the second list just make us feel nice in the moment (though that's important); I mean that they have been scientifically proven to lower our risk for disease and lengthen our lives.

PLAYFULNESS

According to the founder of the National Institute for Play (and one of the world's foremost experts on the subject), Stuart Brown, "The times we feel most alive, those that make up our best memories, are moments of play." And yet many adults reflexively resist the idea of becoming more playful, to the point that Brown writes that he is sometimes "taken aback . . . by the outright hostility to play." In his book *Play: How It Shapes the Brain, Opens the Imagination, and Invigorates the Soul*, Brown describes one experience in which someone responded so angrily to his suggestion that we prioritize play that Brown worried the man might punch him.

That particular person's issues aside, I think that our discomfort is caused by a misunderstanding of what playfulness and play actually mean. When adults hear the word "play," their minds often jump to the situations in which we use "to play" as a transitive verb—i.e., "to play [something]"—and then they freak out and tell you they don't like it. We play games. We play sports. We play make-believe with kids. If you don't find any of those activities appealing—and indeed, many people do not!—then you might assume that you don't like to play. Similarly, people assume that the adjective "playful" only applies to children, or that it means that you have to be a jokester, someone who clowns around (or, heaven forbid, someone who likes clowns)—in other words, that being playful requires you to be a goofball.

But while sports, board games, dress-up, goofballing, and make-believe are all forms of play (and kids are definitely play experts), they are far from the only ways that humans play. According to Brown, "play" describes any activity that is "absorbing [and] apparently purposeless" and that "provides enjoyment and a suspension of self-consciousness and sense of time. It is also self-motivating and makes you want to do it again." In other words, play depends less on the activity itself than it does on the attitude we bring to it. *Any* activity can count as play if we approach it with a playful state of mind.

Speaking of playfulness—it, too, doesn't require you to pretend to be something (or someone) you're not. Instead, playfulness refers to the ability to let down your guard, shed formality, not care too much about outcomes, and open yourself to—indeed, proactively seek out—opportunities for humor and lighthearted connection. (For example, consider the difference between "having a conversation" and "bantering": you're doing the same thing—talking—but the latter involves a playfulness that makes it more fun.) Indeed, *all* of us are capable of recognizing playfulness and being playful ourselves—even people who consider themselves to be "serious." Just think about the last time you interacted with a puppy. (Or, if you're more of a cat person, a kitten.)

It's important to clear up these misconceptions, because to hear Stuart Brown describe it, a life without play would hardly be worth living. "It's not just an absence of games or sports," he writes. "Life without play is a life without books, without movies, art, music, jokes, dramatic stories. Imagine a world with no flirting, no day-dreaming, no comedy, no irony. It would be a pretty grim place to live. In a broad sense, play is what lifts people out of the mundane. I sometimes compare play to oxygen—it's all around us, yet it goes mostly unnoticed or unappreciated until it is missing."

"When we stop playing," writes Brown, "we start dying."

In *Homo Ludens,* his seminal book on play, Johan Huizinga makes a similarly strong statement: he argues that play is "an integral part of life," one that "has its place in a sphere superior to the strictly bio-logical processes of nutrition, reproduction and self-preservation." As a result, writes Huizinga, "Play cannot be denied." (As evidence that there is a biological "play drive," Brown points out—as I alluded to earlier—that most animals play, including all mammals and even many reptiles.)

What's more, play and playfulness can help us get back in touch with (or figure out for the first time) who we actually *are*. In the words of British psychoanalyst D. W. Winnicott in his classic 1971 book, *Playing and Reality,* "It is in playing and only in playing that the individual child or adult is able to be creative and to use the whole personality." Brown elaborates on this idea, writing that "the self that emerges through play is the core, *authentic* self."

It may be a smarter and healthier self, too: play has been found to increase the brain's production of a protein called brain-derived neurotrophic factor (BDNF), which stimulates nerve growth in areas of the brain associated with emotional processing and decision-making, and Brown cites research that has found that people who continue to play games, and to explore and learn (both of which are forms of play) throughout life, "are not only much less prone to dementia and neurological problems, but are also less likely to get heart disease and other afflictions that seem like they have nothing to do with the brain." Scientists have also found that the periods in life when animals play the most often overlap with periods of the greatest development of the cerebellum, a part of the brain that is involved in the coordination of body and eye movements, balance, learning motor skills such as riding a bicycle or playing a musical instrument, and possibly more cognitive tasks such as processing language and regulating our moods.

Allowing your playfulness to come out—or cultivating playfulness, if it's not your normal *modus operandi*—can have a remarkable ripple effect on your happiness and satisfaction in other areas of life as well. According to Caroline Adams Miller, life coach and author of *Creating Your Best Life*, "Once our clients begin to incorporate more play into their lives . . . they experience more well-being and feel better in other ways, including improved health, stronger friendships, more creativity and greater zest for life."

As Miller's quote alludes to, playfulness also strengthens our relationships—which totally makes sense. Playfulness is often a proxy for confidence and closeness; if you're comfortable with someone, you're more likely to allow yourself to be playful. But playfulness itself also brings people closer, makes them feel comfortable, and creates special, shared experiences. You can see this in your own life: if you call to mind your oldest, most treasured friendships and some of your favorite moments that you have shared with those people, there will likely be an element of playfulness running through them.

Playfulness is also a great way to attract new people to you—whether as romantic partners, colleagues, or friends—because people who are playful are simply more fun to be around. Think about the people you enjoy spending time with the most, the ones who bring you joy and consistently make you smile. And then think about some of the adjectives you'd use to describe them. Chances are playfulness will be toward the top of the list.

When we are actively playing with people, the emotional result can be what Johan Huizinga described as "an absorption, a devotion that passes into rapture and, temporarily at least, completely abolishes that troublesome 'only' feeling."* What's more, when you're playful with the same people over time, it can create bonds between groups of people that persist even when you're not actively playing, making play what play scholar Miguel Sicart has called "a string with which we tie our memories and our friendships together." This is why we can reunite with certain friends we haven't seen in decades and instantly feel connected (and also explains the specific pleasure that comes from sharing inside jokes). As Huizinga puts it, "The feeling of being 'apart together' . . . of mutually withdrawing from the rest of the world and rejecting the usual norms, retains its magic beyond the duration of the individual game."

This is exactly what happened in my guitar class. As I've described, it offered me the chance to spend an hour and a half every week playing with other adults, both literally and metaphorically. At first, I only spent time with my classmates during class. But before long, my "play community" expanded beyond Wednesday nights. The owner of the music studio began hosting monthly open mics. I organized a few large weekend jam sessions for anyone who wanted to come, and several of my classmates and I started retreating to the

---

* As someone who frequently suffers from "that troublesome 'only' feeling," I am particularly appreciative of this effect.

studio's basement after class to sneak in an extra hour or so of music. (Initially we'd been going out to a nearby bar, but eventually we realized that what we *really* wanted to do wasn't to drink; it was to keep playing.)

One weekend, some separate friends of mine invited me and a classmate to come over to play at their house, and after an unexpectedly rapturous afternoon, we decided we were a band (albeit a band whose performances are limited to occasional open mics, and whose primary audience consists of our spouses and children). We began getting together regularly to play music; when the SARS-CoV-2 pandemic made in-person gatherings impossible, we did regular video calls (these sometimes lasted for hours, despite the fact that latency issues made it impossible to actually play *together*). We maintained a running conversation over text messages, made music videos for one another's birthdays, and dropped off care packages at one another's homes. Being a part of the group made me happy—and kept me sane.

In all these cases, what started as shared interests blossomed into bona fide communities. We had become connected through play.

CONNECTION

As it turns out, this is enormously important. Humans are social creatures; we have evolved to live in groups. This is why social exclusion hurts so much, and why we're so vulnerable to FOMO. When it comes to environmental factors that are important for our physical and mental health, strong relationships are at the top of the list—not just for our well-being but for our physical survival (and not just for extroverts but for introverts, too).

Indeed, according to a 2010 meta-analysis of interventions designed to reduce loneliness, "loneliness influences virtually every aspect of life in our social species"—to the point that loneliness expert John Cacioppo wrote that he and his colleagues had found that "loneliness somehow penetrated the deepest recesses of the cell to alter the way genes were being expressed."

That is a big deal. Roughly speaking, "gene expression" refers to whether particular genes are turned on or off (and thus are active or not) at any given point in time. For example, I was born with genes that made me predisposed to developing type 1 diabetes, but I only developed the disease when something caused those genes to be expressed. (If you'd like a more cheerful example, think of what happens when a caterpillar transforms into a butterfly. That's the result of certain genes being expressed at a particular moment in its lifespan.) It's well known that external factors in our environments, such as exposure to particular chemicals (e.g., those in cigarette smoke), can influence how and when certain genes are expressed, but most of us have never considered how emotional triggers such as loneliness might affect the process.

We should consider it—and indeed I did during a particularly unpleasant stretch of the book-writing process, when I spent four cold winter days alone at home in the midst of the SARS-CoV-2 pandemic, while my husband and child decamped to my parents' house so that I could make progress on the manuscript. (Imagine, if you will, me slouched in front of my laptop with about fifteen browser windows open, each containing a different research paper about the horrible health effects of loneliness and isolation, as I sat on the couch, isolated and alone.)

Among the disturbing things that I discovered: when it comes to dying early, being socially isolated is thought to be an even bigger risk factor than physical inactivity and health problems associated with obesity. Some experts believe that the health risks of loneliness and social isolation are comparable to those caused by smoking *fifteen cigarettes a day*.

There are so many health problems associated with loneliness that Steve Cole, PhD, director of the Social Genomics Core Laboratory at UCLA, refers to loneliness as being a "fertilizer for other diseases." Social isolation and loneliness are associated with higher risks for everything from high blood pressure, heart disease, stroke, and obesity to depression, Alzheimer's disease, and cognitive decline. And, for the last two, the risk is particularly noteworthy: social isolation and loneliness have been associated with about a 50 percent increase in the risk of developing dementia.

Loneliness is a risk factor for inflammation and weakened immunity. It increases the levels of stress hormones in our blood and impairs our sleep—which is particularly worrisome given that inadequate sleep is itself an independent risk factor for all of the conditions listed above. What's more, loneliness encourages FOMO by making us hypervigilant for potential social threats, such as any sign that we're being rejected or excluded—and hypervigilance itself is both a manifestation and a source of stress.

Like depression, loneliness also affects our brains in ways that impair our ability to think clearly and pull ourselves out of our ruts. When we're lonely, we pay more attention to negative feedback than positive. The lonelier we feel, the more we gravitate toward things that will make our loneliness worse—a category that includes many of the most popular apps on our phones.

Unlike passive scrolling, the pursuit of True Fun reduces loneliness and increases our sense of connection by encouraging active engagement with other people in real life. And when it comes to our health, that is very important.

"High-quality social relationships are vital for health and well-being," says a 2020 report from the National Academies of Sciences, Engineering, and Medicine about social isolation and loneliness. In his book *Spiritual Evolution*, psychiatrist George Vaillant sums up their importance even more succinctly: "Joy is connection."

Vaillant knows what he's talking about. He's a former director of the Grant Study, which is one of the world's longest running studies about human health and well-being. And as he and his fellow researchers have discovered, feeling connected to other people doesn't just bring us joy. It also has a huge impact on how long—and how well—we live.

The Grant Study, which Vaillant led from 1972 till 2004, began in 1938 with 268 sophomores at Harvard University and continued to track the men throughout their lives. (The current version of the study has been expanded to include women.) The goal was to try to identify what factors and life experiences best predicted healthy aging.

When the study began, the researchers assumed that the biggest factors were likely to be things like personality traits, intellectual ability, and physical characteristics such as the size of their skulls. But those weren't the most important factors. Nor were money or fame. (The initial group of sophomores happened to include several men who rose to prominence, including President John F. Kennedy.) Instead, the biggest factor that separated men who aged well and lived the longest from those who did not was the quality of their relationships.

"When we gathered together everything we knew about them at age fifty, it wasn't their middle-age cholesterol levels that predicted how they were going to grow old," said Robert Waldinger, the current director of the study, in a 2015 TEDx talk called "What Makes a Good Life? Lessons from the Longest Study on Happiness."

"It was how satisfied they were in their relationships," he continued. "The people who were the most satisfied in their relationships at age fifty were the healthiest at age eighty."

The study has found that the people with the strongest relationships lived longer, reported higher levels of happiness and satisfaction, and suffered less cognitive decline. In Waldinger's words, "Good relationships don't just protect our bodies; they protect our brains."

Indeed, strong close relationships had a bigger impact on longevity and happiness than money, fame, social class, IQ, or genes.* As George Vaillant summarized it, "When the study began, nobody cared about empathy or attachment. But the key to healthy aging is relationships, relationships, relationships."

The idea that the quality of our connections to other people is crucial to our well-being resonated with me, in part because I'm an only child, born of an only child, with an only child of my own. My father grew up estranged from his siblings, whom I never met and who are now dead; I therefore have no aunts or uncles, and if I have living cousins, I don't know them. Creating a "chosen family" and a sense of community has always been important to me, and Vaillant's comment confirmed that it's worth the effort. But it's *hard,* especially now that my friends are married, with children of their own. I've found fun to be a useful tool to coax people together, with the ulterior (benevolent) motive of creating an extended "family" of people who all know each other (and whose kids know each other), and whose company I enjoy.

I've also found that fun can expand the number of people with whom we can connect to begin with, because of its ability to bring us closer with people who have different opinions or backgrounds from our own—you may deeply disagree with someone's political views and yet have a great time dancing with them at a wedding, for example. True Fun brings out our shared humanity, which, as we'll see in a bit, is extremely good for our emotional well-being (not to mention the future of humankind).

Interestingly, you don't need to *know* a person particularly well in

---

* Human connection also helps our productivity. You'd think that staying at your desk with your nose to the proverbial grindstone would be the best way to maximize your productivity, but in reality, people who take breaks to socialize get more done than people who spend their day working alone.

order to experience the positive effects of playful in-person human connection. Exchanging genuine smiles with someone, even if they're a stranger, boosts our mood and lowers our levels of stress hormones. Even engaging in what's known as a "fleeting relationship"—say, a conversation with a ride-share driver or a fellow passenger on a plane, or bantering while ordering coffee—has been proven to have a positive effect on mood. (And again, this is true for introverts, too.)

What's more, the connections we experience when we are having fun aren't just limited to other *people*. True Fun frequently occurs alongside physical activity—which is a form of connection with our bodies—and physical activity is good for our health and for our moods. Fun also often occurs when we escape our normal man-made environments and engage with the natural world. Interactions with nature (provided they don't involve being caught in a storm or encountering something that might eat us) have themselves been proven to reduce stress; that's why "forest bathing" has become a thing. In fact, being in nature has so many positive psychological benefits that some researchers quasi-jokingly use the word "outdoorphins" to describe the types of endorphins that are triggered by being outside.

With that said, when we *do* experience an unexpected sense of connection with other people, the resulting energy can be rapturous. There's even a term for it: "collective effervescence," which was coined in 1912 by sociologist Émile Durkheim to describe the feeling of connection, meaning, and joy that occasionally arises from collective events.

"Collective effervescence happens when joie de vivre spreads through a group," wrote Adam Grant in a *New York Times* column about the phenomenon. "It is the synchrony you feel when you slide into rhythm with strangers on a dance floor, colleagues in a brainstorming session, cousins at a religious service or teammates on a soccer field."

To me, the concept of collective effervescence helps nail down why, exactly, True Fun is more likely to occur around other people: when it involves a playful spirit, collective effervescence is itself a form of fun.

FLOW

If you're feeling connected (or, for that matter, playful), chances are that you're also experiencing the third component of True Fun, flow—that is, a state of total engagement, in which you are so engrossed in the activity at hand that you lose track of time; in fact, flow is so absorbing that people often don't even realize that they're in it until after it's over.

Not only does connection often produce a state of flow but flow itself can create connection. (Flow can even be contagious: if you spend time around people who are in flow, you may well find yourself in flow, too.) It can also contribute to collective effervescence: during a period of flow, writes Mihaly Csikszentmihalyi, the psychologist who coined the term, "we might even feel that we have stepped out of the boundaries of the ego and have become part, at least temporarily, of a larger entity."

What's more, flow is also marked by a total lack of self-consciousness, leaving us with what Csikszentmihalyi describes as a "stronger self-concept"—which is to say, confidence in our authentic selves—and is often accompanied by a sense of mastery and control. When we are in flow, we don't fear failure.

I experience this myself when I play music. I do *not* like playing or performing alone; my worry that I'll screw up makes it impossible for me to slip into flow (which, ironically, makes it *more* likely for me to mess up). But if I'm in a group, I get so absorbed by the pleasure and challenge of playing with other people that I forget to judge myself. Afterward, when I listen to recordings of what we've played, I'm frequently amazed by what we were able to create.

Flow isn't necessarily rapturous or long-lasting—you can experience it a few minutes (or moments) at a time, in low-intensity bursts—but it *can* be, which explains why it is so often present in what psychologists refer to as the "peak" experiences of our lives. As Csikszentmihalyi describes it, when we're in this kind of peak flow, "we feel a sense of exhilaration, a deep sense of enjoyment that is long cherished and that becomes a landmark in memory for what life should be like." Learning to get flow from as many of our experiences as possible might just be, says Csikszentmihalyi, "the secret to a happy life."

The study of a Japanese concept called *ikigai* backs this up—and gives a great example of how our life trajectories can change when we're guided by fun. *Ikigai*, roughly speaking, is what the French call *raison d'être*—our reason for being. (The characters that make up the Japanese word translate to "worthwhile life.") It's what makes us excited to get out of bed in the morning, and is described in detail by authors Héctor García and Francesc Miralles in their appropriately titled book, *Ikigai: The Japanese Secret to a Long and Healthy Life.*

Interested in the science of longevity and the question of what makes a long and happy life, García and Miralles traveled to Okinawa, a Japanese island known for its higher-than-average number of people over the age of a hundred. There they noticed "an uncommon joy flow[ing] from its inhabitants and guid[ing] them through the long and pleasurable journey of their lives." It was, they concluded, their *ikigai*, which they described as "the happiness of always being busy."

But not busy in our western, always on, working 24/7 sense of the word. Busyness, in *ikigai*, refers to the happiness of always being engaged and present in something—or with someone—you care about. It refers, in other words, to a particular kind of flow. The more you're in flow, say García and Miralles, "the closer you will be to your *ikigai*."

The type of flow that people experience when manifesting their *ikigai* is the same type of flow we experience when we're having fun. "We didn't see a single old grandpa sitting on a bench doing nothing," wrote García and Miralles, describing the residents of Ogimi, the particular town they were visiting. (Ogimi is known as "the village of longevity" because of the number of seriously ancient people who live there.) "They're always coming and going—to sing karaoke, visit with neighbors, or play a game."

At the time of the researchers' visit, Ogimi had no bars and only a few restaurants but more than a dozen community centers. The residents were constantly getting together to socialize—and bringing García and Miralles along with them. During their time in the village, García and Miralles went to a joint birthday party for a ninety-nine-year-old, a ninety-four-year-old, and a "young" man who was turning eighty-nine. They danced. They went to festivals. They had leisurely chats while drinking tea. They sang a *lot* of karaoke.*

One of the elderly residents they interviewed summed up the community's values: "Spending time together and having fun is the only thing that matters."

The flow of *ikigai*—and, for that matter, of True Fun—stands in stark contrast to the eyes-glazed-over state we often slip into while staring at screens. This is what Csikszentmihalyi calls "junk" flow: a state that can be pleasant but is also mind-numbing (or, in some cases, *stressful* and mind-numbing, such as the one I get into when staring at my list of unanswered emails).

Junk flow encourages consumption without actually engaging us. Think, for example, of binge-watching a television show, or

---

* It sounds very similar to my experience in college and makes part of me wish I were an Okinawan retiree.

mindlessly scrolling through memes on your phone. Like junk *food*, it satisfies a craving—but in excess, it can leave you with the gross feeling you get when you pass out on the couch and wake up to find an empty ice-cream container beside you and potato chip crumbs all over your sweater. Unlike fun, junk flow doesn't nourish our souls.

LAUGHTER

The fact that playfulness, connection, and flow are all so good for us on their own suggests that when they're experienced together, their impact should be even greater. But this is tricky to tease out, given the lack of research that's been done on our specific definition of True Fun.

Thankfully, there is a telltale sign of True Fun that *has* been relatively well studied: laughter.

True, sometimes we laugh when we're not having fun. But when we're truly having fun, we nearly always laugh—to the point that I've begun to use laughter as a way to differentiate True Fun from enjoyment. (For example, you can genuinely enjoy a Friday night you spent reading or baking a cake alone, but if you didn't laugh, then you likely weren't having True Fun.)* When I asked Fun Squad members to describe what they felt or experienced during their moments of True Fun, nearly 90 percent said that there had been laughter—in fact, of the entire list of options that I offered, it was the most popular response.† Most of the positive effects of laughing therefore also likely apply to True Fun.

Let's start with physical health. Laughter reduces levels of corti-

---

* Also interesting to ask yourself: how often do you fully, deeply laugh in response to something on your phone? (And if you *do* find yourself deeply laughing, notice how often it is immediately followed by a desire to share the source of your laughter with someone else.)

† Respondents were allowed to check as many boxes as they wanted. Other popular responses included "being fully absorbed and present" and "losing track of time."

sol and an accompanying stress hormone, adrenaline, which—with the caveat that correlation and causation are not the same—may help explain why people who laugh more often have been found to have lower risks for cardiovascular disease and early death from all causes. Good-humored, genuine laughter also triggers a cascade of reactions that can reduce inflammation in blood vessels, reduce clotting, decrease blood pressure, and improve vascular health. (It probably also doesn't hurt that when we're really laughing, we breathe more deeply.)

When we laugh easily and frequently, it indicates an ability to find humor in life, which both increases our chances of having fun and is a very adaptive coping mechanism that boosts resilience in the face of everything from mundane, mild stresses to the most unfathomably horrible of circumstances; in his 1946 book, *Man's Search for Meaning*, psychiatrist and Holocaust survivor Viktor Frankl (who writes that he and his fellow prisoners used a "grim sense of humor" to help them survive) describes humor as one of "the soul's weapons in the fight for self-preservation."

In addition to lifting our moods in the moment, humor also reduces our risk of stress- and anxiety-related diseases such as heart attacks and strokes in the long run. What's more, appreciating humor has been found to improve the short-term memory of older adults, an effect that is likely also due to laughter's ability to reduce cortisol. (As we touched on in the last chapter, high cortisol levels impair our memories and make it harder to process information and learn new things.) Laughter also releases endorphins that have been found to increase people's tolerance for physical pain.*

---

* How, you might wonder, does one measure pain tolerance ethically? Here is what the researchers have to say: "Pain tolerance was assayed using a frozen vacuum wine cooler sleeve (frozen to −16°C for the start of each trial; maximum duration 180 seconds) in experiments 1 and 2, and a mercurial sphygmomanometer"—i.e., a blood pressure cuff, which was then inflated. "In each case, subjects were asked to indicate when they could no longer stand the pain." (We can add this to my list of research experiments for which I will never volunteer.)

The Continuum of Pleasant Experiences

Enjoyment   True Fun

Laughter

*Laughter often indicates the moment at which
an experience has crossed the line from enjoyable to fun.*

Researchers also believe that the particular types of endorphins triggered by laughter play an important role in social bonding and help buffer us against the physical effects of stress. This is likely why humor and playfulness have been found to bring people closer together and increase a sense of warmth and connection. In fact, even the act of reminiscing about shared laughter has been shown to increase people's satisfaction with their relationships, and *anticipating* what researchers call "mirthful laughter" (i.e., the friendly, fun kind) increases levels of health-protecting, immunity-boosting, and depression-lifting hormones and reduces levels of those associated with stress.*

The more we laugh together, in other words, the more connected (and less lonely) we feel; as comedian John Cleese has observed, "It's almost impossible to maintain any kind of distance or any sense of social hierarchy when you're just howling with laughter." And the more connected we are, the more we laugh; in fact, laughter is thirty times more likely to occur in social contexts than when we're alone.

---

* Also, "When we laugh, our brains release a cocktail of hormones that make us feel happier (dopamine), more trusting (oxytocin), less stressed (lowered cortisol) and even slightly euphoric (endorphins)," Stanford University professors Jennifer Aaker and Naomi Bagdonas write in their book, *Humor, Seriously.* "By working humor into our professional interactions, we can serve our colleagues this powerful hormone cocktail, and in so doing we can literally change their—and our—brain chemistry on the spot."

(This may help explain why most of our experiences of True Fun happen when we're with other people.)

The lead author of one study about laughter summed it up simply: "By seeking out positive experiences that make us laugh, we can do a lot with our physiology to stay well." Given how often True Fun leads to laughter, this also suggests that if we care about our health, we should prioritize True Fun.

HOW FUN MAKES US HAPPY

Many people, especially Americans, are obsessed with the pursuit of happiness. (It's right there in the Declaration of Independence!) We read books and listen to podcasts about happiness; we lament to friends and therapists about our *lack* of happiness, and we buy anything that marketers promise will give us more.

And I get it: I want to be happy, too. But announcing that we'd like to "be happy" is about as practical as announcing that we'd like to be taller. Great, but in the absence of artificial growth hormones or a medieval torture device, how exactly are we supposed to *do* that?

That's yet another power of fun: it produces happiness. More specifically, the pursuit of fun provides a blueprint for happiness by shifting our focus from an amorphous emotional state (I want to *be* happy) to an active experience (I want to *have* more fun). Given that we are invariably happy while having fun, the more fun we have, the happier we're likely to be; the ingredients for fun are in many ways the ingredients for happiness, but with better instructions. Fun also helps us sneak up on happiness without scaring it away. In fact, one of the reasons that orienting our lives around fun may make us happier is that happiness *isn't* the direct goal.

The pursuit of fun results in a self-perpetuating positive cycle: having fun makes us happy, and when we're happy we're more likely to have fun, which in turn makes us happy, which makes it easier for us to have fun—and on and on and on. As Barbara Fredrickson, director of the Positive Emotions and Psychophysiology Laboratory (aka the PEP lab) at UNC-Chapel Hill, has written, each experience of positive emotion "increases the likelihood that people will feel good in the future."

It's also worth noting that researchers who study happiness believe that, while a certain amount of our happiness is determined by our genes and circumstances, 50 to 80 percent of it may be under our control. In fact, they've actually created an equation for it:

S(et point) + C(ircumstances) + V(oluntary behaviors) = H(appiness)

Your happiness "set point" depends on your genes, which obviously can't be changed. Your circumstances include both controllable things like where you live, and uncontrollable things like the family dynamic you were born into. Voluntary behaviors are exactly what they sound like: they're the things you *choose* to do—including how you spend your leisure time and how much energy you devote to creating more opportunities for True Fun.

To me, the beauty of True Fun (and more specifically, the beauty of defining it as the confluence of playfulness, connection, and flow) is that it can help us generate concrete ideas for what these happiness-inducing voluntary activities could *be*. In other words, it helps transform something abstract and elusive into something that is attainable and under our control.

HOW FUN HELPS US FLOURISH

Flourishing is a term psychologists use to refer to a state of optimal human functioning in which we feel engaged, open, purposeful, self-accepting, resilient, robust, motivated, and satisfied. It's the opposite of languishing—which is to say, the all-too-familiar sensations of hollowness, emptiness, or being stuck in a rut. Many psychologists believe that, when it comes to feeling good about ourselves and our lives, flourishing—even more so than happiness—should be our goal.

According to Martin Seligman, director of the University of Pennsylvania Positive Psychology Center and author of the book *Flourish: A Visionary New Understanding of Happiness and Well-Being* (and a flourishing convert himself), there are five fundamental elements of flourishing: positive emotions, engagement, positive relationships, meaning, and positive accomplishment. The more you experience them, the more you will flourish.

When I thought about it, I realized that each of these five elements is often present in—and often directly generated by—fun. When I'm in playful, connected flow, I am engaged, I experience positive emotions, and I'm usually with people whose company I enjoy. While an experience doesn't have to result in a sense of meaning or accomplishment to be fun, I've noticed that many of my fun experiences leave me with one of these feelings, if not both.

Fun's ability to help us flourish is visually captured in Maslow's Hierarchy of Needs: a list created in 1943 by a psychologist named Abraham Maslow, usually illustrated as a pyramid, that attempts to summarize the elements that intrinsically motivate human beings, in the rough order in which they must be achieved. The bottom two layers of the pyramid contain the basic needs that must be satisfied before we can focus on flourishing, or prioritize (or even think about) True Fun—namely, having adequate food, water, warmth, rest, security, and safety. The top three layers—having friends and intimate relationships, possessing a strong sense of self-esteem, and achieving our full potential—are factors that take us beyond mere survival and into a state of flourishing. They also just happen to be some of the side effects of fun.

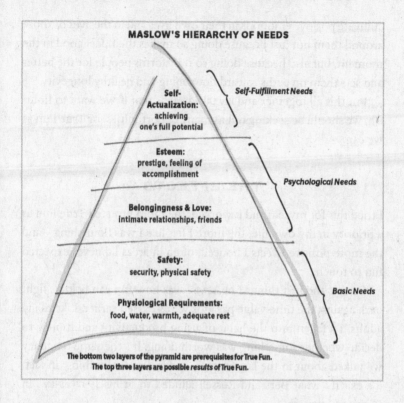

MASLOW'S HIERARCHY OF NEEDS

Self-Actualization: achieving one's full potential — *Self-Fulfillment Needs*

Esteem: prestige, feeling of accomplishment

Belongingness & Love: intimate relationships, friends — *Psychological Needs*

Safety: security, physical safety

Physiological Requirements: food, water, warmth, adequate rest — *Basic Needs*

The bottom two layers of the pyramid are prerequisites for True Fun. The top three layers are possible *results* of True Fun.

The idea that fun helps us flourish also aligns with the broaden-and-build theory of positive emotions, created by Barbara Fredrickson. It asserts that positive emotional states, even if fleeting, aren't just *signs* of resilience, well-being, and health; they actually *build* resilience and health, and help people weather *future* periods of stress. According to this theory, positive emotions can lead to new ideas, activities, and social bonds that in turn build our physical, intellectual, social, and psychological resources—resources that can "function as reserves that can be drawn on later to improve the odds of successful coping and survival."

The takeaway, according to Fredrickson, is that "people should cultivate positive emotions in their own lives and in the lives of those around them not just because doing so makes them feel good in the moment, but also because doing so transforms people for the better and sets them on paths toward flourishing and healthy longevity."

Put this all together and *my* takeaway is that if we want to flourish, we should be seeking out as many opportunities for True Fun as we can.

THE EFFECTS

I tried this for myself, and it worked: the more I treated True Fun as a priority in my own life, the more I felt like I was flourishing—and the more positive effects I noticed, often in areas I'd never expected fun to touch.

One of the first things I observed was how fun can help us fight back against the time-value paradox we discussed earlier. Like many adults, I'd fallen into the habit of using productivity and money to decide whether something was worth doing. It's the same tendency we talked about in the last chapter, and it isn't a new thing; in fact, it's exactly what Bertrand Russell alluded to in his 1932 essay "In Praise of Idleness."

"There was formerly a capacity for lightheartedness and play which has been to some extent inhibited by the cult of efficiency," he wrote. "The modern man thinks that everything ought to be done for the sake of something else, and never for its own sake."

Minus the "man" part, it was as if he had looked into the future and written an essay about *me*. Like many people, if I got paid money to do something, I assumed it must have been worth my time. If I worked for ten hours without a break, I concluded that I must have had a good day—even if it left me exhausted and depleted.

My research on fun has taught me that this approach is misguided. Instead, I now try to keep in mind a paraphrased version of an observation from Henry Thoreau: "The price of anything is the amount of life you exchange for it."

Yes, we all obviously have to get work done and earn money; as we've discussed, we require a base level of economic security before we can devote attention to our emotional well-being. But if our basic needs are met and our ultimate goal is a meaningful, joyful life, then we're not actually gaining much psychologically by stacking up accolades and excess wealth—and money and productivity are not the primary metrics we should rely on when we evaluate our use of time. Instead, I propose that we use True Fun.

The pleasure produced by True Fun makes it intrinsically motivating, meaning that when we're having it, we would gladly continue doing whatever we're doing without any need for an external reward. It kicks us out of response mode and inspires us to live proactively, keeping our own priorities top of mind.

True Fun also helps us tap into a sense of shared humanity, a form of connection that researchers believe is essential for our well-being and ability to flourish (and, for that matter, to experience collective effervescence). Indeed, according to Adam Grant, "Psychologists find that in cultures where people pursue happiness individually" (as we in the United States tend to do), "they may actually become lonelier. But in cultures where they pursue happiness socially—through connecting, caring and contributing—people appear more likely to gain well-being."

Unfortunately, shared humanity is not something we tend to put much thought into, let alone to prioritize. As Celeste Headlee writes in her book *Do Nothing*, "Few of our daily activities are focused on helping us become more naturally playful or thoughtful or, god forbid, social."

"We've cut out expressions of our basic humanity because they're 'inefficient': boredom, long phone conversations, hobbies, neighborhood barbecues, membership in social clubs," she writes. "We smile indulgently at the naiveties of the past, when people had time for things like pickup basketball and showing slides of Hawaiian vacations to their friends. How quaint, we think, that our grandparents had time for things like sewing circles and lawn bowling."

At first, I felt inclined to agree. (Sewing circles? Lawn bowling?) But once I'd experienced what playful, connected flow felt like in my mind and body, I realized that, far from being quaint or a waste of time, seeking fun through social activities with other human beings is one of the *best* uses of our time—regardless of what the activity might be. Today, having a relaxed lunch with a friend or taking a break in the middle of the day to call someone no longer seems like an unnecessary luxury, and organizing a weekend away with friends no longer seems like too much work. Instead, I now recognize them as valuable investments in my well-being. (And also, I once had a truly fun time lawn bowling with some friends. So maybe don't knock it till you've tried it.)

Fun can also help us flourish by changing the way we approach decisions. These days, when I encounter a nonmandatory request—even if it's potentially positive, such as a new opportunity—I ask myself: Does this feel fun? Will it generate playfulness, connection, or flow? If so, I consider saying yes. If not—or if saying yes will reduce the time I have available for *more* meaningful, enjoyable, or rewarding activities—I do my best to say no.

I also try to pay attention to my body—it doesn't lie. If I feel any sort of tightness or clenching, or if my breath becomes shallow or short, it's a sign that I shouldn't agree. On the flip side, if I notice lightness or excitement, I consider saying yes, even if the idea of doing so makes my stomach flutter. That's often a sign of nervous excitement, which probably means I'm stepping out of my comfort zone in a good way.

Using fun to guide our decisions can also make us more productive. Many of us in white-collar jobs get sucked into doing things that give us the impression we're being "productive"—say, checking email constantly, or ticking small things off our to-do lists, or getting sucked into office politics and gossip—when in reality we're just filling time to make ourselves *feel* like we're getting stuff done. (Take a hard look at your workday, in other words: How much of your time are you spending on things that are meaningful or essential to your job—or you—versus on being reactive?)

Whereas spending leisure time on my phone and computer tends to scatter my attention and make me less efficient, creating space for fun (and always having opportunities for fun on the horizon to look forward to) can keep me motivated and on task.

This is especially true if I'm able to incorporate a sense of playfulness into my work, an idea that is backed up by research done by Adele Diamond, a professor of developmental psychology at the University of British Columbia. She has demonstrated that if you ask four-year-olds to stand still for as long as possible, they typically can last about a minute. But if you tell the children to pretend that they are guards at a factory—in other words, if you invite them to treat the task as *play*—they can stay still for an average of *four.* Just imagine how much more *we* could accomplish with a four-fold increase in our ability to stay on task.

Paying more attention to our need for fun can also help us flourish by giving us more resilience with which to cope with life when it's *not* fun—if I've had a frustrating day of work, for example, I've noticed that an evening dose of fun can erase my bad mood. (And microdoses of fun *definitely* helped me maintain my sanity during the SARS-CoV-2 pandemic.) This has led me to believe that fun may play a role in the "undo" hypothesis, put forth by Barbara Fredrickson, the aforementioned director of the PEP lab. According to this theory, positive emotions, such as those produced by fun, can actually "correct" or "undo" the effects of negative emotions.

For example, Fredrickson found that when people were shown

videos that elicited what she called "mild positive emotions" right after she asked them to perform an anxiety-producing task (giving a one-minute speech about why they are a good friend), their bodies recovered more quickly from the stress: their heart rates, blood pressure, and perceived anxiety all went back to normal faster than those of the control group.

Fun can also help us avoid burnout. For example, in moments of writer's block, I used to do one of two things: I'd either stare at the problematic paragraph till my eyes glazed over, hoping for divine inspiration, or I would "take a break" by toggling over to my internet browser and staring at news headlines and the list of unanswered messages in my email inbox until I needed a break from *that,* at which point I'd go back to staring at the problematic paragraph. (And then I'd wonder why I kept finishing my days feeling like I never wanted to write again.)

The problem was that I wasn't actually taking a break. In most cases, the reason I felt burned out to begin with was that my working memory was overtaxed, and my ability to process new information and come up with new ideas had been depleted. (As a reminder, your "working" memory refers to all the things you're holding in your consciousness at any given moment in time.) The last thing I needed was to add *more* information to my working memory by scanning news headlines and my inbox. This just contributed to my mental exhaustion.

Then I read Alex Soojung-Kim Pang's book *Rest: Why You Get More Done When You Work Less.* In it, he writes that many of the world's greatest writers, scientists, and artists "balance busy lives with deep play, forms of rest that are psychologically restorative, physically active, and personally meaningful."

This is a strong argument for vacations, or even for taking a weekend away from your computer and devices to spend on your passions and priorities. But I realized that I could do something similar in my everyday work life, too, by setting aside a few minutes throughout the day to do something that held the potential for playfulness, connection, or flow (or, ideally, all three). In other words, I could take breaks by microdosing on fun.*

Given that I work alone with limited opportunities for socialization during the day, my best idea so far has been to take breaks by playing the drums. (That's another side effect of my interest in fun: I've started to take drum lessons.) When I feel my attention slipping, I turn away from my computer and practice for a few minutes instead. Shifting my focus to something rhythmic and physical brings me back into my body and activates a different part of my brain. (It also sometimes makes me feel like my head is going to explode, but in an oddly pleasant way.) This, in turn, replenishes my attention span, and I come back to the computer feeling refreshed—and often with a new idea. I experience what Soojung-Kim Pang is describing when he writes that "when we stop and rest properly, we're not paying a tax on creativity. We're investing in it."

Speaking of which, the pursuit of True Fun can also make us more creative; the more regularly we experience it, the more new ideas we are likely to have. This may be due in part to the fact that playfulness, connection, and flow all reduce stress, and stress dampens creativity. It could also be the result of the surge of energy that we experience when we have fun, which enables us to put our ideas into action.

In all these cases, the boost in creativity likely has to do with fun's effects on our body's chemistry. True Fun often involves new experiences, and as we've discussed, all forms of novelty cause the release of dopamine, which is our brain's way of recording when an experience is worth remembering and motivating us to repeat it. (Laughter is also a dopamine trigger, which further helps explain why we pay more attention when we find things humorous or fun, and are more likely to remember them afterward.)

---

* We'll be talking about fun "microdoses" in detail later in the book.

Whereas the dopamine triggers on our smartphones often reinforce habits that are useless or downright bad for us, the dopamine that's released in response to True Fun is *helpful*. Not only does it motivate us to seek even more new and potentially fun-generating experiences in the future that might contribute to our sense of flourishing, but it primes our brains to better remember the details of these experiences afterward.

This is important because, as we discussed in the last chapter, memories are the raw material for insights. The greater the diversity of our experiences and the more details we remember from them, the more ideas and connections we can generate—and the more creative and insightful (and, for that matter, *interesting*) we become.

What's more, the lack of self-consciousness we experience when we're having True Fun puts us in a safe, open psychological state that is itself conducive to creativity. As an example, consider what happens during musical improvisation, a form of flow in which musicians meld with their instruments and the other people with whom they're playing, and are open to new ideas without judgment. (The lack of self-judgment part may explain why I've personally always found improvising so difficult!)

In 2008, researchers did a fascinating study in which they scanned the brains of jazz musicians as they improvised on a special iron-free piano that had been designed to fit inside an MRI scanner. When the musicians were improvising as opposed to playing scales or a piece of memorized music, their brain activity was "fundamentally different," according to Charles Limb, a surgeon, musician, and neuroscientist at UCSF who was one of the study's lead researchers.

As an article in *National Geographic* described the findings, "The internal network, associated with self-expression, showed increased activity, while the outer network, linked to focused attention and also self-censoring, quieted down." (In Limb's words, "It's almost as if the brain turned off its own ability to criticize itself"—and, in so doing, gave itself permission to play.) These effects aren't limited to musical improvisation: Limb has subsequently done similar experiments with freestyle rappers and theatrical improvisers and found similar results.

If you think about it, fun itself is an improvisational state, with no predetermined outcome. When we're having fun, we're entirely in the moment, responding spontaneously to whatever comes our way. Our usual judgmental tendencies—whether they're directed toward ourselves or others—are temporarily silenced and replaced by a spirit of openness and playfulness. When we're freed from self-consciousness, we have more courage to try new things. We have more ideas. We are insulated from our usual insecurities and fear of rejection. Our potential for creativity goes through the roof.

Put this all together and it's not surprising that in the scientific research on creative thinkers, writes David Epstein in his book *Range: Why Generalists Triumph in a Specialized World,* "an enthusiastic, even childish, playful streak is a recurring theme."

When I reflected on the many ways in which prioritizing fun can help us flourish, it became clear to me *why* fun is such a powerful tool for building a meaningful life—and why not treating it as a priority can leave us so vulnerable to technology's thrall. Simply put, the pursuit of fun requires us to decide how we want to fill our days. It demands that we identify what makes us feel the most alive.

If we don't know what True Fun looks or feels like, and don't have a sense of which activities and contexts are the most likely to produce playfulness, connection, and flow, then we will be left with empty space and no idea how we want to fill it. The companies behind our most time-sucking apps have an economic incentive to take advantage of this vacuum and suck up our energy and attention, leaving us too exhausted to do anything else.

But when we *do* understand the value of True Fun and orient our lives around its pursuit, not only are we happier in the moment, but we're motivated to continue to seek out energizing activities in the future. Fun creates a self-reinforcing cycle that helps us prioritize the things that bring us joy.

So, where does this leave us?

While the dinging of notifications distracts us and makes us feel anxious, True Fun focuses us and reduces stress. While being on call to our devices depletes us, fun leaves us rejuvenated and refreshed. While social media encourages us to treat life as a performance, fun demands that we live life directly, authentically, without worrying about what a possible audience might think. While our apps encourage FOMO, True Fun is so intrinsically satisfying that when we experience it, there's nowhere else we'd rather be. While online "connections" often leave us feeling hollow, vacant, and competitive, the sense of connection we experience when having fun breaks down walls, encourages vulnerability, and brings us closer to other people by helping us tap into our shared humanity.

If we put in the effort to understand the factors that contribute to our personal experience of True Fun and shape our lives around the pursuit of playfulness, connection, and flow, the cumulative effect can be life changing—even if, as is often the case, we don't experience all three elements at once. With fun as our compass, not only will we be inoculated against the siren song of screens but we will cure ourselves of many of their negative effects.

True Fun makes us healthier and happier. It enables us to flourish. It helps us feel—and, for that matter, *stay*—alive.

It is also, as we noted at the outset, *fun*.

So, let's talk about how to have more of it.

PART II

How to Have Fun

CHAPTER 4

THE FUN AUDIT

> "If you don't prioritize your life, someone else will."
> —Greg McKeown, *Essentialism*

HOPEFULLY, YOU'RE CONVINCED THAT FUN CAN CHANGE
your life, and now you are chomping at the bit to discover what fun
means to you and to try to have more of it. That's so great! Here's
the first thing I want you to do:

DON'T TRY TO HAVE MORE FUN

Yes, I know, that might seem like an ironic thing for me to say. But
hear me out. It's not that I don't *want* you to have more fun. I do! I
desperately want fun to become your personal compass and guiding
star.

The problem with trying to have more fun is that the phrase
"have fun" isn't specific enough; it doesn't tell you what you're actually supposed to *do*. (I know how to "have a croissant." But how does
one "have fun"?) It's almost as useless as telling someone to just "be
happy."

Also, if we try to force True Fun, we will risk becoming like a
man I once was partnered with in a swing-dancing class who spent

our entire song together avoiding eye contact and muttering, "We're having fun. We're having fun. We're having fun," to himself over and over again. This poor man was not having fun, and neither was anyone he danced with.

In other words, True Fun is like romance: we can set the mood for it, but if we try too hard, our attempts will likely backfire.

So, here's the plan.

The first step of our fun audit* will be to zero in on what playful, connected flow feels like in our minds and our bodies—the logic being that you can't have more True Fun if you don't know how to recognize it when it occurs. This is also an attempt to balance things out: a lot of us already have put plenty of work and therapy dollars into learning to identify what stress and anxiety feel like, which is a useful skill. But how many of us have put the same effort into learning how to identify the effects (especially the physical ones) of *positive* feelings?

Next, we'll get a baseline sense of how much True Fun you're currently having (or not having). We'll take a *fun history* to identify some of your past experiences of True Fun and start a fun times journal to track playfulness, connection, and flow in the moments when they happen. (Chances are high that you're already encountering them in more contexts than you realize.) We'll also analyze the things you do "for fun" to suss out whether they *actually* hold the potential to attract True Fun, or if they're really Fake Fun in disguise.

We'll use your memories of True Fun and your recent instances of playfulness, connection, and flow to identify your personal *fun magnets*: specific activities, people, and settings that often attract True Fun for you personally. Then we'll analyze your magnets to figure out your *fun factors*—that is, the *characteristics* that create this magnetism. This is important because the better you understand the

---

* I promise that this will be more enjoyable than the word "audit" makes it sound.

characteristics that have made certain settings, activities, and people generate fun for you in the past, the easier it will be to judge whether something is likely to attract fun for you in the future—and to brainstorm ideas for other potential fun magnets that you may not yet have tried.

We'll also identify your personal *anti-fun factors*—i.e., things that block you from having fun—so that you can make sure to avoid them. (On the flip side, there may be cases where you decide to revisit and experiment with them—you might be surprised to find that something you thought was an anti-fun factor (or that was an anti-fun factor for you in the past) actually *is* conducive to True Fun for you.)

The process of identifying and analyzing your personal fun magnets and fun factors is interesting in and of itself. But this is not meant to be an intellectual exercise; we don't just want to *understand* these things—we want to put them into action. To do that, we'll use an acronym called SPARK—short for "make space, pursue passions, attract fun, rebel, and keep at it"—to orient your internal compass toward your personal fun North Star.

That may sound like a long list of things we need to do, so let me clarify a few things. First, you're right: there *is* a lot we need to do. This makes sense, given how little thought most of us have put into defining, recognizing, and generating fun. Imagine what it would be like if you were ravenously hungry but didn't know that the gnawing in your stomach was hunger, didn't know that the solution to hunger is to eat food, and didn't know how to get food, let alone what types of foods you like. Many of us are similarly naïve about fun. But there's no need to stress out about (or feel overwhelmed by) any part of this process—I'll walk you through it step by step.

Also, please remember: the whole point of this process is to *enjoy yourself.* To that end, you may want to invite someone whom you like or want to spend more time with to join you. (This is part of creating a personal fun squad, which we'll be talking about later on in the process—and it can include more than just one other person if you'd like.) Going through these steps with a friend or loved one will provide fodder for conversation and exploration, bring you closer, and increase the likelihood of you both having more True Fun.

And on that note, please remember that this is meant to be a chance for self-exploration and enjoyment, not a homework assignment. While you do need to engage with the questions and experiments if you actually want to see changes in your life, you do not need to do every single exercise that I describe or take me up on all of my ideas. Follow the plan's basic structure, in other words, but feel free to customize the details. If you ever start feeling like your pursuit of fun is turning into work, back off a bit. Yes, we have a lot to do, but the process should feel like play.

The goal isn't to turn every second of your life into an outrageous explosion of fun. That would be impossible (and, honestly, a bit much—someone has to take out the trash). We also don't want to set the bar too high—*any* moment of playfulness, connection, and flow, no matter how fleeting, is a step in the right direction and will make you feel more engaged and alive. I like to imagine that we're playing darts on a board where the outer ring represents moments of playfulness, connection, *or* flow, the inner rings represent experiences that involve two of these states, and the bullseye is the magical confluence of all three. We're aiming at the center, but hitting any part of the dartboard is worth points.

At first, the effects of this refocusing might be subtle, but it won't take long before you find yourself surprised by how many aspects of your life fun has touched—from the quality of your relationships to your energy level to the way you choose to spend your time. Set True Fun as your compass, commit to sticking with it, and you will find your life transformed.

STEP 1: KNOW THE SIGNS
OF TRUE FUN

We can't appreciate or seek out fun if we don't know how to recognize it when it occurs, which is why our first step is to learn to identify some of its most common physical and emotional effects.

When I asked my then-five-year-old daughter to describe what fun feels like, her response was "happy and excited." She hit the nail on the head: True Fun is a mood boosting *and* energizing state.

Here are some other signs to watch for:

- Laughter
- A sense of release/freedom/letting go
- Feeling like you're having a special, shared experience
- Losing track of time
- Feeling free from self-judgment and self-consciousness
- Feeling like you've temporarily "stepped out" of normal life
- Being fully absorbed and present
- Not caring too much about the outcome
- A feeling of childlike excitement and joy
- A positive boost in energy
- Feeling totally yourself

If any of these are present, you're likely experiencing some combination of playfulness, connection, and flow. If all three apply, chances are that you've identified a moment of True Fun.

Also, note that True Fun can vary in intensity and duration—it can feel mind-blowing or mild, and it can occur in a flash or last for a more extended period of time. (Think of the difference between sharing a moment of laughter with a friend and spending an entire weekend with that friend.) If you're the kind of person who enjoys categorizing things, you can think of this as the difference between everyday fun and peak fun—or, as we'll discuss later, microdoses of fun and booster shots—both of which are worth seeking out.

Indeed, one thing this process has helped me realize personally is that even before my life-changing crisis on my couch, I was having more moments of playfulness, connection, and flow than I realized; I just hadn't explicitly labeled them as True Fun and thus hadn't been fully appreciating them or benefiting from their ability to boost my mood.

I encourage you not to make the same mistake. As we move through this process, don't only focus on major moments of playfulness, connection, and flow. Part of building a more fun-filled life is appreciating the moments of micro fun that pop up nearly every day, whether they be a few seconds of banter with a supermarket clerk, or a chance to give someone a compliment or playful smile. If we want to take full advantage of the life-giving power of fun, we want to train ourselves to notice and value these smaller moments, too.

STEP 2: ESTABLISH A BASELINE

Now that you know what you're looking for, we'll use a tool I developed called the *fun frequency questionnaire* to establish a baseline of how much True Fun you're currently having (or not having) so that you can identify areas that need help—I recommend revisiting it every few months to measure your progress.

The fun frequency questionnaire asks you to indicate on a scale of one to five how much you agree with the following ten statements, with 1 being "strongly disagree" and 5 being "strongly agree":

- Having fun is a priority for me personally.

  1   2   3   4   5

- I know/understand what "fun" means to me.

  1   2   3   4   5

- Friends would describe me as a fun person.

  1   2   3   4   5

- I can identify the characteristics that make certain experiences feel fun to me.

  1   2   3   4   5

- I can easily name five activities or settings in which (or people with whom) I often have True Fun.

  1   2   3   4   5

- I make it a point to incorporate these activities (and put myself in those settings and spend time with those people) on a regular basis.

  1   2   3   4   5

- I make a point of always having something to look forward to.

  1   2   3   4   5

- I go out of my way to try to make things more fun for myself and other people.

  1   2   3   4   5

- I regularly experience delight.

  1   2   3   4   5

- I have enough fun.

  1   2   3   4   5

Then add up your numbers.

Score _____

If you score between forty and fifty, congratulations: you are already embracing the power of fun; keep reading to learn how to manufacture even more of it. If you scored between thirty and forty, you're well on your way; with a few adjustments and some attention, you should be able to amplify the fun in your life. And if you scored below a thirty, don't despair: the fact that you have made it this far in the book means that you are committed to having more fun—which itself is an important sign of progress and an early sign of success. If you follow the suggestions in the following pages, you should see some big changes. Also, regardless of your total score, take note of any questions for which your answer was below three. These are specific areas that likely need more attention.

When I first started my own journey toward designing a more fun-filled life for myself, my score was pretty low. I knew fun was important, I went out of my way to make things more fun for other people, and I felt pretty confident that friends would describe me as a fun person. But I didn't know the characteristics of the sorts of experiences in which I had fun, I couldn't easily name specific activities or settings that attracted it, and I certainly wasn't having enough of it. (Nor, as I noted, was I noticing or labeling smaller moments of fun when they occurred.)

It didn't feel great to realize this, but judging from the responses of the Fun Squad, I was not alone. The good news is that once you've acknowledged your fun deficit, you can start digging yourself out of your hole.

STEP 3: TAKE YOUR FUN HISTORY

The next step in our fun audit is to take a fun history. The goal is to bring to mind several peak experiences of True Fun—as in full-on playful, connected flow—and analyze them so that you can better understand *why* they felt fun and re-create the feeling in the future. (Stuart Brown, the play researcher, often has people take a similar history for play, with the same purpose.)

Start by getting yourself a journal or a notebook—ideally, one that you like and enjoy writing in, since you'll be using it in other steps, too. Set aside sixty or so undistracted minutes for the next few exercises. (Turn off your phone!)

Begin by reflecting back on three experiences in your life that you would describe as True Fun: moments in which you felt completely present, engaged, and alive, in which time seemed to simultaneously stand still and fly by, and that were so joyous and energizing—so *fun*—that they count as some of your most treasured memories.

Note that there are a lot of things in life that are genuinely relaxing, pleasurable, or enjoyable, and that you might previously have described as fun but that probably do not qualify for this exercise—for example, taking a bath, or eating a delicious meal, or watching a favorite television show. There are also "peak experiences" that are true life highlights but that are not necessarily *fun*, such as graduation or the birth of a child. Please try to focus on memories where "fun" is the dominant descriptor—the ones that would make you say, if I were to ask you about them, "That was *so* fun."

Once you have one in mind, close your eyes and try to put yourself back in the moment. Immerse yourself as fully as you can. Imagine the sights, the sounds, the smells, the *feeling* in your mind and body. Then ask yourself: What exactly were you doing? Where were you? Roughly how old were you? What objects, if any, were involved? Who, if anyone, were you with? What in particular made it feel so fun?

Here are some examples from the Fun Squad:

I was 21 and traveling by myself, and I had just arrived in Croatia after getting the overnight ferry from Italy. I met three Canadians in my youth hostel and invited them to go on a day trip the next day with a couple of other people I had met in Italy who had traveled on the ferry to Croatia as well. The whole thing was such a fun experience, full of freedom to do whatever

I wanted as there were no expectations. . . . The following day we had a wonderful day together, spending time at the bar while it was raining, going on a boat trip, swimming, walking around and exploring and just getting to know each other and learn about our different backgrounds. We then ended the day by going on a bar crawl at night, ending up at a club in a castle and spending the whole night dancing.

I was on a roller coaster, one of my first big ones, at the age of ten, give or take. I remember it was a warm night, and I went with my family to the amusement park. . . . My stomach was in my throat and I was one hundred percent certain that the seatbelt was not secure. I was screaming and I wanted out. Then the roller coaster reached the very top, just before the drop. In that moment I saw the whole city, lit up. I could see the ocean. I could suddenly feel the salty breeze. It was so beautiful. I started laughing. With the tears from the fear still wet on my cheeks, I put my hands up and felt free, all the way to the moment when I got off that seat, knees buckling. It was absolutely *thrilling* and so much fun.

Just this last weekend my partner and I took our daughter to see his parents in southern NM. . . . One afternoon, I announced that I was headed to the pool while the others were enjoying an activity indoors. I had half an hour to myself in the beautiful pool and surrounding courtyard. I immediately dove in. My dive was clumsy, being out of practice. I swam across the pool, climbed the steps, ran back around toward the deep end and dove in again. Better. I repeated this several times, often giggling as I ran back toward the deep end. I did some other free form jumps, feeling again like my ten-year-old self in my childhood pool with my little brother. Then I swam several laps across the pool, practicing every stroke I remembered. Then I spread out my towel and lay in the sun, cooled by the water, my heart beating palpably, my breath quick. And I remember thinking, "That was so fun!"

Note that your memories of True Fun do not have to involve trips to Croatia or to theme parks—smaller moments count, too. A few other examples:

Playing on a floatable raft in the lake with my daughter. It was a sunny summer day. I was about 40, she was about 5. We were singing and dancing, bouncing and screaming . . . and inevitably falling into the water together.

Riding a bike on a summer day with my boyfriend. I had my bike tuned up recently and had not ridden it in quite a while. Riding through our local park and on trails, I felt electric energy and could not wipe the grin off my face. The weather was perfect and I, frankly, felt like a kid again.

This past weekend my wife and I got a babysitter for the kids for a few days to celebrate our five-year anniversary. . . . If one moment in particular stands out, it was sharing a beverage while playing guitar and singing together. This is something we did before kids and have lost the time to do.

Once you've written down your three past fun experiences, once you've really marinated in the memory of how they made you feel, look forward in time and describe something that you would love to organize or participate in in the future that you think might hold the potential to spark True Fun. What would you be doing? Who, if anyone, would you be with? Where would you be? Why would this create True Fun for you?

Again, some examples from the Fun Squad:

I would get my neighbor friends together to go roller skating. We would go to the local rink I went to as a kid, which still rents old-school four-wheel roller skates and plays terrific music. That rink "brings out the happy" in people. Everyone there is smiling and enjoying themselves. It would be fun for me because I love the skating, I love the music, and I love seeing my friends and other people have so much fun. Being there transports me out of my regular working-mom mindset. When I'm listening to music and trying to stay on my feet and not fall down, I can't think about my to-do list or worry about my family and friends. Plus, I love watching people who can really skate—and I love watching my friends enjoy this unexpected fun.

I'd go to an open mic. Open mics are fun because you never know what might happen. They bring together earnest creators who want to share their original work (or a creative take on a cover) and who are, by and large, receptive and encouraging to all the other performers. Sometimes two performers will come up with a spontaneous collaboration. Sometimes someone with truly amazing talent shows up and totally wows the room. No two shows are the same—every one is unique and ephemeral. They epitomize that old line about how "you just had to be there."

I would organize a trip with my husband. We would go to a place full of antique shops, try new dishes, meet local people.

We'd talk a lot during our walks. We'd take pictures and find hidden places like small villages or ruins. This would happen in some European country. It'll be pure fun, because we love traveling together. We tend to laugh a lot when we face weird situations abroad, and we know—when that happens—that we're creating more private jokes for the future. It'll be fun because we won't be thinking about work, or paying bills, or life passing by. We'll be living deliberately; we'll be present.

If you're feeling stumped (or even if you're not), these questions might help:

- What were you passionate about when you were a kid?
- When in your life have you laughed the hardest? What were you doing? Who were you with?
- What are some of your favorite memories of holidays, celebrations, or traditions?
- What's a memory of a time when you felt playfully rebellious or harmlessly deviant?
- What are some moments from your life in which you felt the most alive? What were you doing? Who were you with?
- Which people are often present in the moments when you have the most fun?

Try not to judge yourself as you're doing any of this—there are no right answers. And don't worry if you find this exercise hard; many people do. If so, just let the questions percolate in your subconscious and jot things down as ideas arise. (You may want to discuss them with a friend.)

Once you have a description of three past memories of True Fun and an idea for something you'd like to do in the future (or just fantasize about), ask yourself what, if anything, makes those four experiences different from things that you find (or have found) plea-surable, relaxing, enjoyable, satisfying, or rewarding.

STEP 4: KEEP A FUN TIMES JOURNAL

The next step in our fun audit is to start a fun times journal to help you identify the activities, people, and settings in your *everyday* life that energize you and get you into a state of playfulness, connection, and/or flow. While our more intense memories of True Fun are often associated with things that are novel or unusual, you do not need to be in an exotic context to experience its elements—as I al-luded to, they're probably already present in more situations than you realize.

We'll be using this information, combined with your memories of past fun, to home in on your personal fun magnets and fun fac-tors, so that you know what sorts of experiences to focus on finding and creating more of. We'll also use your fun times journal to ana-lyze the things you *say* you do for fun, to see if they really hold the potential to generate playfulness, connection, or flow, or if they're actually sources of Fake Fun that need to be reduced or eliminated. This will help you create more space for things that make you feel alive.

The fun times journal is inspired by the "Good Times Journal" from the book *Designing Your Life,* and the basic idea is simple: you set aside a few minutes each day to record moments in which you felt a sense of connection, playfulness, or flow, as well as anything you did "for fun." (You may be surprised by how much these two categories do *not* overlap—and how often you experience playfulness, connection, or flow in unexpected contexts.) I recommend keeping your journal for at least two weeks so that you capture enough data; you might want to keep it on your bedside table so that you can write in it before you go to sleep, during the time you might other-wise spend scrolling through your phone.

It doesn't matter how small or fleeting your moments of playfulness, connection, and flow are: write them down, label them with a *P*, a *C*, and/or an *F*, and for each instance, note what you were doing, who you were with, where you were, and what, if any, objects or devices were involved. Anything that resulted in one or two of these three states probably left you feeling good and is worth seeking out in the future. And if an experience included playfulness, connection, *and* flow, circle it: you were probably having True Fun!

An example from the Fun Squad:

F: Work (giving written feedback to students on their writing). I noted this yesterday too, which is giving me a new appreciation for my work and the realization I easily enter flow when I am deep into giving feedback.

C: Long telephone conversation with my son who had a birthday today. Felt close to him.

C, P, F: Impromptu dance with my husband in the kitchen to Ella Fitzgerald and Count Basie's "Tea for Two." We choreographed some dance steps and I got out some teacups. It was really fun!

Once a week or so, review your notes from your daily fun times journal and see if any themes emerge. (If you're the type of person who finds such things appealing, you can keep a tally of the instances of playfulness, connection, and flow that you experienced, and see if you can increase their frequency over time.) Then ask yourself: Were there any particular activities, settings, or people that were (or were not!) consistently associated with playfulness, connection, or flow? (If so, what could you do to create similar conditions in the coming week?) Did you find yourself in one or two of these states more or less frequently than the other(s)? And did anything surprise you?*

As you review your journal, also note things you did (or people you spent time with) "for fun" and ask yourself whether they actually produced playfulness, connection, or flow. If so, they can stay in your schedule and are worth seeking out again and spending time on (or with) in the future. But if they left you feeling drained instead of energized, they're likely sources of Fake Fun, and you may want to cut back on them. Here are some examples from the Fun Squad of things people did for fun that, upon reflection, turned out not to be fun at all:

- Looking at my phone
- Eating too much junk food
- Scrolling through Instagram
- Checking Facebook every couple of hours—just a lot of junk. Not fun.
- Duolingo for way too long
- Watching YouTube

If you're a visual person, you may even want to consider plotting "Things I Do For Fun" on a graph to determine what to keep doing and what to skip, based on the quadrant in which they fall.

I'm not kidding! This can be really useful. The x-axis should rate them by enjoyment, and the y-axis by the energy they produce.

Here's one I made for myself.

Anything on the right half of the graph is enjoyable and thus worth your time, though only the items in the top right quadrant hold the potential for True Fun, because they are both enjoyable *and* energizing. The bottom right quadrant is home to activities that you like, but that aren't energizing *per se*—and that therefore are unlikely

---

* I had a recent surprise myself when I realized that a trip to the dentist had, in fact, been fun.

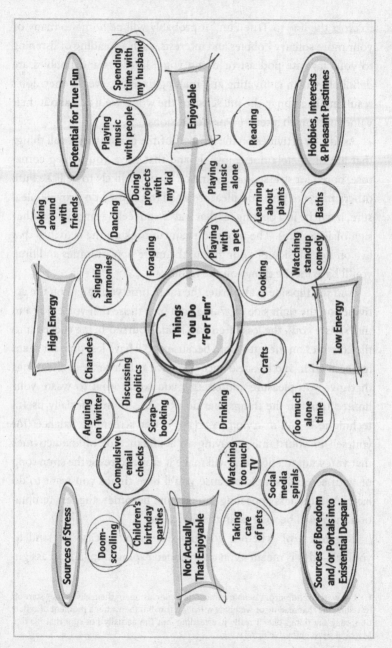

to cross the line to True Fun.* It probably will be home to many of your more solitary hobbies and interests, such as reading or listening to your favorite podcast or doing yoga. Interests and hobbies are definitely worth cultivating and making time for, even if they don't result in True Fun in the full sense of the word; we'll talk about their value more in chapter 7 ("Pursue Passions").

As for the activities on the left half of the graph, they're all things that are ultimately not enjoyable and that leave you feeling comatose, bored, or stressed-out. Some of them are likely to be Fake Fun; others may not give you pleasure at all (or, if they do provide pleasure, it will be in a fleeting hit that leaves you feeling empty—another sign of Fake Fun). The more you can cut back on the activities that live on the left side of your graph, the more opportunities and time you'll have for the things on the right.

And the flip side is also true: the more time you spend on the activities on the right side of your graph (i.e., those that you enjoy and that satisfy you), the less often you'll find yourself being sucked into the activities on the left—both because you'll have less time for them to begin with, and because once you have a clear sense of the things that give you pleasure and energy, you won't *want* to waste your limited time on the things that do not. This is an especially useful technique if you're trying to create better screen-life balance (for yourself *or* your family): having an abundance of offline activities that you want to engage in will make it easier to resist the siren song of your screens, simply because you'll have things you want to do *more*. And the less appealing screen time becomes, the less temptation there will be to resist in the first place.

Regardless of whether you make a graph, please be kind to yourself—this is meant as an open-ended exploration, not an assign-

---

* I've watched numerous people come to this conclusion for themselves: they start off by telling me that reading or watching movies is fun, but then, after a moment of reflection, they say things like "I really like reading, but I'm actually not sure that it's *fun*. Maybe it's just enjoyable or relaxing."

ment that will be graded. On many days, playfulness, connection, and flow won't happen all together; on some days, you may not notice them at all. That's normal, especially in the beginning. Your goal is to get in the habit of tuning in to your everyday life so that you recognize the moments in which they *do* occur, with the ultimate goal of creating more opportunities for them in the future.

From the Fun Squad:

> For the first time in this journaling practice, I had a PCF moment: Talked for almost an hour with my boss on the phone. We were talking about work, but we also laughed, connected. I felt playful. We talked about my sewing, creativity, her mother who saved fabric for over 60 years (she gave me a whole basket of their heirloom fabrics to play with and upcycle in my sewing). This was a very nourishing phone call, I realized after I hung up. Fun!

And be sure to take note of anything *proactive* that you did that sparked fun. Like, for example, this experience someone wrote to me about, which apparently was directly inspired by her participation in the Fun Squad.

> Today I was standing on the diving board of my parents' pool, fully clothed, talking to my mother. I had this urge to jump into the pool with all of my clothes on. But I kept talking, kept nodding along in the conversation. And then I let out a humongous childish laugh and jumped into the pool.

First of all, I want to be friends with that person. And second, I think it's a great metaphor. We are all standing at the edge of a pool of potential fun. We're tempted by it but can't quite bring ourselves to jump. The trick is learning how to shed our inhibitions, say yes to our inner urges, and find the courage to dive in.

CHAPTER 5

FIND YOUR FUN

"Men would not know how to fill their days
if they had only four hours of work out of the twenty-four.
In so far as this is true in the modern world, it is a
condemnation of our civilization."
—Bertrand Russell, "In Praise of Idleness"

ONCE YOU'VE GOTTEN ACCUSTOMED TO RECOGNIZING playfulness, connection, and flow when they occur and have a sense of what True Fun feels like to you, the next step is to understand the preconditions for True Fun and to identify your personal fun magnets and fun factors—that is, the specific activities, situations, and people that typically attract True Fun for you, and the characteristics that are responsible for their magnetic pull.

STEP 1: KNOW THE PRECONDITIONS

While everyone has a different collection of fun magnets and fun factors, there are several *universal* preconditions that are necessary in order for True Fun to emerge. You can think of these as being like the foundation of a house: they're the base that supports everything you build. If these preconditions are not met, playfulness, connection, and flow can't occur, which means that you cannot have True Fun.

We've discussed the first two earlier, but they're so important that they bear repeating.

BEING ENGAGED AND PRESENT

You must be present and undistracted in order to have fun, because flow is a foundational element of fun, and flow requires total absorption. This has implications for devices: you might find that one of your personal preconditions for fun is to put your phone away while you're spending time with people, and you might even want to (politely) request that everyone you're with do the same.*

NOT FEELING JUDGED OR SELF-CONSCIOUS

If you feel judged, either by yourself or by someone else, you will not be able to have fun. Likewise, it's difficult to have fun if you feel like the other people around you aren't also having fun, or if there's a wet blanket or spoilsport present.

GOING ALL-IN

Speaking of which, fun requires everyone's buy-in. You (and your companions) must be fully invested in and connected with the activity or the people you're with (or both). Fun doesn't emerge when people are only *sort of* doing something.

NOT CARING TOO MUCH ABOUT THE OUTCOME

When the stakes are too high, the fun runs away. This doesn't mean that you can't care *at all* about the outcome of whatever it is you're doing—your objective, after all, is to be engaged, and having a goal (or even a competition) can energize you, bring you closer to other people, and keep you focused. It just has to be accompanied by a sense of playfulness, and you need to be okay if you don't win, or if things don't ultimately work out in the way you'd hoped.

* An important note! There are times when devices actually can *facilitate* fun. For example, when I play music with friends, we often use an app to look up the chords of the songs we're trying to play. Thanks to technology, we have instant access to nearly any song ever written, which greatly expands our possible repertoire and definitely *adds* to the fun. The trick is to make sure that people are using technology to help them connect more with the people they're with, as opposed to retreating into their screens.

BEING WITH OTHER PEOPLE

Yes, it *is* possible, in certain circumstances and for certain people, to have fun alone (e.g., the Fun Squad member who found True Fun in her solo swimming session). With that said, it is *remarkable* how consistently members of the Fun Squad mentioned other people when they reminisced about times that were truly fun—even if they were self-described introverts.

I mean this literally: they remarked upon it. When I asked participants if anything surprised them about their memories of fun, quite a few of them said that they were shocked that most, if not all, of their memories of True Fun included other people—even though in general they preferred being alone. As one person put it, "I find it really fascinating and sort of counterintuitive that while I am definitely an introvert and find pleasure in many solitary activities, all of my fun moments involve other people." Said another: "I'm incredibly surprised by how much the things I consider 'fun' have to do with other people, especially since I'm such an introvert and appreciate alone time."*

While it might seem counterintuitive to think that introverts' fun moments tend to involve other people, the phenomenon of collective effervescence that we talked about earlier explains why it actually makes a lot of sense; indeed, many psychological studies have found that interacting with other humans tends to have mood-boosting effects, even for introverts. (One such paper says so right in the title: "Fun is More Fun When Others Are Involved.") The Fun Squad's comments also align with a comment from positive psychol-

---

* "A lot of my examples of fun involve shared experiences with loved ones, even though I am a self-proclaimed introvert," wrote another Fun Squad participant. "So, I can unwind and relax solo, but to truly have fun I need to have other people around me."

Said another, "I'm a little surprised that my concept of fun seems so tied to being with other people. I don't think of myself as a super-extroverted person—I think I'm probably somewhere toward the middle of the spectrum—and I can certainly be happy on my own. But the experiences that immediately stood out to me as *fun* involved other people."

ogy expert Martin Seligman in his book *Flourish*. "When was the last time you laughed uproariously?" he asks. "The last time you felt indescribable joy? . . . Even without knowing the particulars of these high points in your life, I know their form: all of them took place around other people."

I suspect that when it comes to fun, the difference between the experiences of extroverts and those of introverts may be less about the presence of other people and more about the qualities of the relationships, the level of energy, and the size of the group. Introverts seem most likely to have True Fun when they're in the presence of a small group of people whom they know (and who know them) well. Extroverts often enjoy small, close groups, too, but are also able to find fun in more boisterous and less intimate situations. In other words, even if you are a full-on introvert, don't immediately write off other people as a precondition or catalyst for fun. You may just need to find the right ones.

STEP 2: FIND YOUR FUN MAGNETS

The fact that True Fun is an emotional experience means that, while activities can help *generate* fun, *activities themselves are not fun*. This is a very important point! Too often people assume that if they want to have more fun, they have to do more activities, so they start packing their schedules with random stuff and then become frustrated when, rather than having fun, they feel exhausted.

With that said, each of us has certain activities—and, for that matter, people, and settings—that are much more likely than others to trigger or enhance our feelings of playfulness, connection, and flow, and thus more likely to attract True Fun.

I call these "fun magnets," and each of us has a collection that's unique to us. If you want to up your chances of experiencing True Fun, you should seek out and prioritize your fun magnets as often as you can.

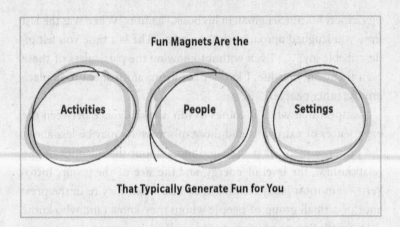

Fun Magnets Are the

Activities   People   Settings

That Typically Generate Fun for You

Chances are high that you know a few of your magnets already, even if you've never classified them as such. Maybe you have a particular friend who always seems to light you up, or an activity that often sparks fun for you, such as skiing or singing or cooking, or a setting, such as a campground or beach or lake, in which many of your fun memories have taken place.

If so, great: make a note of them. But don't worry if none immediately come to mind; thanks to the work you've done in the previous steps, you now have material that you can mine.

Start by looking at the anecdotes you described in your fun history and scanning your fun times journal for any entry in which playfulness, connection, and flow were *all* present, and that thus represent moments of True Fun. (You may already have circled them.) Jot down any specific activities, settings, or people that were involved. You may notice that a few activities, people, or places recur—these are examples of your personal fun magnets.

Also note the activities, settings, and people that were involved when you experienced playfulness, connection, or flow on their own (or in a combination that didn't include all three). These are magnets for pleasure and enjoyment (and possibly relaxation), and are worth keeping track of, too, even if they never cross the line to full-on fun.

Comparing your fun magnets to those of other people in your life is an interesting exercise that may make it easier to understand your differences and create more experiences that lead to True Fun (or playfulness, connection, or flow) for you, either together or on your own. For example, here are some things that attract fun for my husband and repel it for me:

- Taking hikes on which we wander off-trail through the brush (because ticks)
- Going on overnight camping trips that involve carrying all of your food, bedding, and clothing on your back and that require you to avoid physical contact with greenery (because *ticks*)
- Games that involve strategy or aim (e.g., poker, chess, darts)
- Swimming in ponds or streams that are so cold that they have ice in them

Here are some of my fun magnets that he inexplicably does not share:

- Spending long car rides brainstorming new business ideas
- Spending weeks after the car ride executing those ideas*
- Playing long rounds of a game I created in which you pick two unconnected professions and come up with a name or

---

* As just one example, early in our relationship, my then-boyfriend-now-husband casually mentioned the term "boutique law firms." I, not really listening, just heard "boutique," which for some reason made me think of lingerie, which then gave me an idea: Wouldn't it be funny to come up with an online boutique that sold clothing and underwear featuring law-related puns? The result is a business I call Illegal Briefs, which offers products including "Harmless Error" baby bibs and "Request for Admission" thongs. While not yet as successful as I feel it should be, Illegal Briefs caught the attention of a reporter for the main legal newspaper in California, who wrote a story about the venture, accompanied by a photograph of me standing in a library, cradling a law book as I used my other hand to cheekily pull the hip of my (decidedly legal) underpants above my jeans. This photo ran on the front page of the paper, to which my husband's boss was a subscriber.

tagline for a pretend business that specializes in both (e.g., a plastic surgeon's office combined with a tattoo parlor called "Tit for Tat" or a personal trainer-slash-couples therapist with the slogan "Work It Out")

- Playing music with other people for hours on end
- Cardio hip-hop
- The accordion

Here are some of our shared magnets:

- Hosting dinner parties
- Traveling
- Eating good food
- Playing frisbee
- Exploring the world with our daughter
- Spending time with close friends
- Hiking on well-groomed trails
- Swimming in lakes that do not have ice in them
- Making each other laugh

STEP 3: FIND YOUR FUN FACTORS

Once you have used your fun history and fun times journal to identify some of your fun magnets, the next step is to figure out the general *characteristics* that create their magnetic pull. These are your personal "fun factors," and once you've identified yours, you will have given yourself a powerful tool that you can use to find and create new experiences that are likely to generate True Fun.

For example, do you tend to have True Fun when you're engaged in physical activities, like dancing or playing sports? Does True Fun often pop up when you're doing something more intellectual, such as playing a strategy-based board game or bantering with quick-witted friends? Does it occur when you're in nature? Do you have

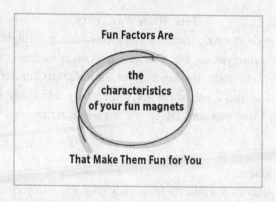

Fun Factors Are

the characteristics of your fun magnets

That Make Them Fun for You

fun when you're creating or organizing something? When you're being silly? When you're mastering a new skill? Does having a sense of community attract fun for you? How about competition? Do you need to be interacting with other people in order to truly have fun? Are you able to do so when you're alone?

It may seem counterintuitive, or even counterproductive, to analyze fun in this level of detail, but it's important: the better you understand your fun magnets and fun factors, the easier it will be to attract more fun.

To find your fun factors, start by reading through the following list of fun factors and their descriptions, and circling the ones that resonate with you the most. Don't think too hard; listen to your gut.

If you'd like, you can also look back at the list of fun magnets and the moments of playfulness, connection, and flow that you've recorded in your fun times journal and put a checkmark next to the fun factors that apply to each experience. For example, let's say I were to analyze why playing music in a group so consistently attracts fun for me. I might put checks next to music, mastery, learning, challenges, silliness, teamwork, community, socialization, intimacy, and small groups. My love of swing dancing incorporates many of the same factors, plus physicality.

THE FUN FACTORS

Note: I've deliberately included fun factors that you might initially think are synonymous, but that have important nuances. Also, I've grouped them under the headings of Playfulness, Connection, and Flow, but as you'll see, there are some that could easily reside in more than one category. (Keep reading for more detailed explanations.)

Playfulness:

Which qualities or contexts frequently contribute to your ability to feel playful?

1. Silliness
2. Creativity
3. Imagination
4. Intellectual stimulation
5. Challenges
6. Games
7. Absurdity
8. Uncertainty
9. Spontaneity
10. Control
11. Loss of control

Connection:

Which styles of connection do you typically prefer?

1. Big groups
2. Small groups
3. Intimacy
4. Strangers
5. Anonymity

6. Being alone
7. Teamwork
8. Community
9. Teaching/sharing knowledge
10. Leading
11. Sexuality

Flow:

Which qualities or contexts are the most likely to put you into flow?

1. Physicality
2. Nature
3. Music
4. Risk
5. Thrill-seeking
6. Performance
7. Being the center of attention
8. Learning
9. Demonstrating mastery
10. Sensuality
11. Competition
12. Novelty

Some of these fun factors are self-explanatory, but some could use a bit of clarification, especially in terms of how they differ from fun factors that at first glance might appear to overlap or be synonymous. So let's run through them.

Physicality refers to activities that involve physical movement and a connection with your body (e.g., dancing, or sports).

Nature involves being outside and engaged with the natural world.

Intellectual stimulation includes any sort of activity that tickles your brain and requires you to think (e.g., debating, bantering, problem-solving, or strategizing).

Silliness is any kind of goofing or joking around (but not necessarily in a slapstick kind of way).

Some people who count **music** as a fun factor love *making* music (e.g., singing or playing an instrument), but others find fun when they listen to music, or use music to facilitate or amplify other experiences.

Creativity encompasses activities that involve an act of creation of any kind, including the creation of physical objects, new ideas, or experiences—so cooking would count, as would brainstorming or organizing a party.

Demonstrating mastery refers to the feeling of being really good at something and having an opportunity to show it. A **challenge** is anything you have to strive for or put effort into accomplishing (challenges can be physical or mental). **Learning** is the process of acquiring new knowledge or skills, and **teaching/sharing knowledge** refers to situations in which you connect with other people by, well, teaching or sharing your knowledge!

Leading is a form of connection in which you are in some way acting as a coach or director or guide—for example, leading while dancing, or directing a play, or being the captain of a team.

Speaking of which, **teamwork** means working together with a group of people to accomplish a particular goal; **community** means feeling connected with people you care about, without necessarily trying to achieve anything specific. Think of the difference between a sports team and a church group.

Sensuality refers to any activity that connects you with your five senses. It can have overlaps with **sexuality** (which is what it sounds like, including flirting), but sensuality can occur without any element of sexual frisson.

Novelty refers to *any* type of exploration or new experience.

While an element of novelty is often intrinsic to True Fun, for some people the pursuit of novelty is *so* likely to generate fun that it counts as an independent fun factor. The same thing is true for **absurdity**, which can be roughly defined as things that are unexpected or out of the ordinary, often in a humorous way.

Imagination refers to any activity that immerses you in some sort of fantasy world, such as role-playing or make-believe, or reading fiction.

Risk and **thrill-seeking** are often grouped together in our minds because they both produce an adrenaline rush. But while risk is nearly always thrilling, thrills don't always require risk—for example, roller coasters are thrilling but not risky. People who have risk as a fun factor derive enjoyment from knowing that there is an element of danger or a chance that they might lose something important. People whose factors include thrill-seeking but *not* risk like the adrenaline, but not the danger. If your fun factors include risk, in other words, they probably *also* include thrill—but the reverse is not necessarily true.

Loss of control is often lumped in with risk and thrill-seeking, but it, too, is a fun factor on its own. In fact, for many risk- and thrill-loving people, the enjoyment comes from going right up to the line of losing control but *not* crossing it. Think of car racing (another activity that is thrilling *and* risky): drivers find fun in pushing themselves right up against the limits of their abilities, but I doubt that many of them would say that they relish the idea of spinning out of control.

People who have loss of control as a fun factor, on the other hand, sometimes gravitate toward activities that help them escape or let loose, such as drinking alcohol. (Note that losing control through substances comes with obvious caveats.) But it can also refer to anything that takes you metaphorically out of the driver's seat and frees you of the burden of being in charge or making decisions. For example, I am usually an obsessive logisticizer, but a few years ago my husband and I went on a vacation where I asked if he would take charge of all the planning. While it's not usually my approach to travel—and loss of control is not typically a fun factor for me*—on that particular trip, it was just what I needed; relinquishing control made it much more fun.

Enjoying **control** is the opposite—though it's worth noting that this does not involve controlling *other people* but rather enjoying feeling in control of yourself, your decisions, or your abilities. (Controlling other people—which is different from leading them—is a pathology, not a fun factor.)

Competition and **games** often coexist, but they're not synonymous. Games provide structures, rules, and goals, but it's possible to play a game without being competitive—think of a game of catch, or a casual round of golf. Competition adds an energy and intensity that is enjoyable to some people but is a total anti-fun factor to others.

Performance and **being the center of attention** might also seem to overlap, but it's possible to enjoy being the center of attention without performing *per se*, and it's also possible to enjoy performing without being the center of attention—for example, if you're a backup musician.

Spontaneity refers to the act of being open to opportunities and ideas as they present themselves, and not being wedded to a particular plan. **Uncertainty**, on the other hand, is deriving enjoyment from not knowing the *outcome*. For example, you could make a plan to go to a night club (i.e., not be spontaneous) but enjoy the uncertainty of not knowing what will happen, or who might be there. Or you could spontaneously decide to go out with a group of people but like having a plan for what you're going to do.

As noted earlier, for some people, fun is most likely to occur

---

* The friends who helped me edit this book would like you to know that this is an understatement.

when they are spending time with people whom they know (and who know them) **intimately**; for others, it may be more likely to happen when they're around **strangers**. Ditto **big** versus **small groups**— think, for example, of the difference between a crowd at a concert and a small group of friends that can fit around your kitchen table. (And, of course, it's possible to like both.) Some people derive particular enjoyment—and/or a sense of freedom—from **anonymity**. And, while most fun experiences occur in the presence of other people, there are indeed some people who primarily find fun **alone**.

Once you have ticked off or circled the fun factors that resonate with you, and that describe your fun magnets and past instances of playfulness, connection, and flow, finding themes should be easy: just notice which fun factors you circled or that have lots of checkmarks next to them. These are your most powerful fun factors and can be used to brainstorm *other* activities or situations that might generate fun. Recognizing that I love physicality, learning, and music, for example, recently inspired me to sign up for a tap dance class for adult beginners—and it was indeed fun.[*]

Also note the fun factors that only have one or two checkmarks next to them. They're not major fun factors for you, but the fact that they *sometimes* are present when you're having fun might give you ideas for future exploration and experimentation.

I also recommend doing a scan of your current life to see whether you have adequate opportunities for the three foundational elements of fun—playfulness, connection, and flow—and determine whether they're in balance. Do you have lots of opportunities for flow but not

---

[*]   Not all of your experiments will be successful. For example, my love for music and physical movement once led me to try a Brazilian martial art called capoeira, which incorporates elements of gymnastics, music, and dance. While I enjoyed it, it ended up not being a fun magnet for me—apparently the "martial" part of martial arts stresses me out. But it was a worthwhile experience nonetheless.

many for playfulness and connection? (As a freelancer, that certainly describes most of my workdays.) Or do you have lots of relationships that make you feel connected but that aren't particularly playful? In other words, do any of these three tanks need to be topped off? If so, you can use your fun magnets and fun factors to help you come up with ideas for how to do so.

STEP 4: RECOGNIZE YOUR ANTI-FUN FACTORS

While you were reading through that list of fun factors, chances are that a few of them jumped out as being totally antithetical to fun, the metaphorical equivalent of the end of the magnet that repels other magnets. I call these anti-fun factors, and they're useful to identify, too—both so that you can avoid situations that involve them and so that you can better understand *why* you don't enjoy certain activities that attract fun for other people.

As part of the survey that I sent to the Fun Squad, I asked people to list activities that other people found fun that they did not, and vice versa. When I looked at their responses, several of the fun factors were clearly much bigger dividing lines than others. Risk was the most obvious one: some people gravitate toward risk while others want nothing to do with it. Knowing your own risk tolerance (and teasing out how you feel about risk versus thrill) is very important when you're trying to figure out what types of new activities might be worth exploring; it's also useful to compare your risk tolerance with that of other people in your life, because it can often be an unacknowledged source of conflict. If you recognize your differences, then it becomes easier for the more risk-averse person to not feel bad saying no, and for the risk seeker to recognize the need to find outlets for that side of their personality.

There is also a stark division between people who enjoy boisterous crowds—for example, at a concert or party or bar—and those who find crowds stressful and unfun. The same thing is true for control—a lot of people explicitly mentioned *not* enjoying the loosening of control that comes from drinking alcohol, while others found it freeing. Imagination also provoked strong feelings: people who do not count imagination as a fun style tend to *really* not like it.*

With all that said, before you automatically write something off as an anti-fun factor, I invite you to challenge your own assumptions. As one friend put it to me, "I think some of us—*ahem, me*—would benefit from doing some things that might feel awkward at first. And some of us probably *really* need to broaden our list of what can be fun. That's the downer of adulthood, right? We've trimmed a lot of things out of our life, even things we used to enjoy (see: concerts) because of some belief that we either don't enjoy them any longer or don't have the space for them in our lives."

As she concluded, there may well be things that you really do not find fun, or things that used to attract fun for you that you no longer enjoy. But other assumptions, upon investigation, may turn out not to be true.

PUTTING IT INTO ACTION: SPARK

By this point (even if you didn't take the time to plot every moment of True Fun you've ever had on a hand-drawn graph), you should have a very good sense of your personal fun magnets and fun factors and some new ideas for ways to incorporate more playfulness, connection, and flow into your life. If you stopped right now and did nothing else, you'd already be succeeding.

But it's one thing to *understand* your definition of fun, and it's

---

* While I didn't ask about it explicitly, there was also one activity that popped up over and over again in people's answers and that represented an (almost literal) line in the sand: the beach! Some people think of the beach as the epitome of fun, a catalyst to an infinite number of enjoyable experiences. Other people hate everything about it. (The sun, the sand, the salt: *everything*.) The fact that I did not mention a beach anywhere in the survey itself makes this even more interesting to me, and amusing.

another thing to put it into practice. If you truly want to turn fun into a guiding star, you need to make long-lasting changes to your routine—and to your mindset—to transform True Fun from an occasional houseguest to a regular companion.

In the next chapters, we're going to use the acronym SPARK—which, as you may remember, is short for "make space, pursue passions, attract fun, rebel, and keep at it"—to explore ways of doing so. As you read them, don't feel obliged to do everything that I suggest; as always, feel free to pick the ideas and exercises that seem the most interesting and relevant to you.

Regardless of what you choose to try, the ultimate goal is to help you structure your life in a way that is more conducive to fun, and to keep fun at the top of your priority list even when the rest of life threatens to get in the way. In other words, we're figuring out how to spark True Fun—and how to feed and nourish the resulting flame.

CHAPTER 6
MAKE SPACE

*"The notion of free time is as distant from
most people's everyday experience as open space."*
—Stanley Aronowitz and William DiFazio,
The Jobless Future

MY PARENTS' HOME WAS BUILT IN THE 1840S WITH A
simple, rectangular footprint, its rooms centered around the fireplace and stairs. Over the years, previous owners constructed various additions—a living room, extra bedrooms, a porch—and the building served many purposes, from the main house of a horse farm to (rumor has it) a mafia hangout and bordello.

The land the house sits on is beautiful, with mature trees, former horse fields, and a small pond. Inside, however, the space feels cramped. Despite the fact that it's surrounded by pleasant views, the house is oriented inward, with most activity gravitating toward the kitchen—the darkest room in the house. Getting from one room to another requires twists and turns. There are hardly any windows that face the prettiest vistas. As a result, while the house is spacious, it feels claustrophobic. The additions were tacked on with no master plan.

This haphazard building scheme reminds me of life. Most of us have built our lives without a blueprint in mind of what, ultimately, we *want* them to look and feel like. Instead, we start off following whatever path has been laid out for us—with our parents picking our schools and teachers telling us what to do, in an educational system that was developed for training workers for the Industrial Revolution, not for inspiring creative and fulfilling lives. We drift into careers, often based more on what is expected of us, or what opportunities are presented to us in critical moments, than on what we ourselves actually *want*.

Then we add friends and colleagues—some of whom nourish us, others who are toxic or drain our energy. At some point many of us find a spouse and start having kids, maybe because we proactively want these things, maybe because we've reached an age or position where it seems like the right thing to do. We take on responsibilities and say yes to "opportunities" because we want to prove our competence or don't want to let other people down. We get phones and tablets and laptops because we need them for work and communication, and then suffer the unintended consequence of being on call to anyone who wants a sliver of our time.

Obsessed with productivity, we end up with no hobbies. Consumed by the pursuit of "connections," we have no time for friends.

Our responsibilities, anxiety, and distractions leave us drained and tired, with little energy for our own interests, or the passions we used to have before life got in the way; our to-do lists feel endless, and yet rarely include anything that would count as play. Instead, we spend our days consuming and reacting, toggling between tabs on our computers before we go home and collapse on the couch, where we self-soothe with substances and screens until it's time for sleep. When our alarms go off, we wake up, already exhausted, reach for our phones (which are on our bedside tables, if not under our pillows), see the lists of emails to be answered and news stories to be read and social media posts to be scrolled through—all other people's priorities—and are thrust back into reaction mode as another day begins.

Our lives, in other words, have become like my parents' house:

functional, and in many ways quite comfortable—most of us probably wouldn't want to pack up and move—but designed by someone else.

If we want to have more True Fun, we need to become the architects of our own lives. And just as you can't construct a new building without clearing the ground first, we can't attract more True Fun until we make space.

Making space means clearing mental and physical clutter. It means reducing resentment, letting go of unnecessary responsibilities, and creating boundaries to protect your time and attention from people and companies trying to steal it from you. It means building stillness and openness into your schedule so that you have room for more moments of playfulness, connection, and flow. The goal is to create space for you to design and build the life you actually *want*.

This can be a challenge, to put it mildly. As we've discussed, you can't experience and prioritize True Fun unless you feel safe and secure, and have your basic needs met. That means that there are obviously situations and life conditions that make it harder (and occasionally impossible) to have True Fun, and even those of us living in relative comfort likely have work to do before we can clear space for more of it. With that said, most of us have the ability to create more space for fun. Here's how to start.

GIVE YOURSELF A PERMISSION SLIP

If you're like many people, you may feel a little weird or irresponsible about prioritizing fun, let alone your *own* fun. You may also feel like you have somehow been tagged as "unfun" (either by yourself or by someone else), or that you are unable to tap into, as one member of the Fun Squad described it, "the fun person I used to be."

It's possible, however, to reclaim the fun side of your personality (or to develop it for the first time). It's also possible to be a responsible person and citizen (and a force for good in the world) while caring deeply about fun—in fact, I think that, by rejuvenating, inspiring, and connecting us, fun has the power to help us *create* a better world. Also, to be clear, building a more fun-filled life is not about shirking your responsibilities. It's about reorienting yourself toward things that energize and excite you—a process that, in turn, will increase your resiliency and give you more energy for everything else.

I encourage you to give yourself a permission slip to prioritize fun, despite—and perhaps even because of—whatever else might be going on in your life. If you're extremely emotionally evolved and have done a lot of therapy, you may be able to give yourself permission just by reading those words. If you're like the rest of us and could benefit from a literal permission slip, here you go:

> *I give myself permission to think about and prioritize my own*
> *fun without feeling selfish or irresponsible, and I commit to doing*
> *so in a way that feels energizing and enjoyable.*

(signature and date)

PS: I also agree to tell my inner critic to be quiet, and to avoid anything that feels like yet another to-do.

If it seems like it would be useful, please go ahead and sign it.

REDUCE RESENTMENT

If I were to identify a list of universal fun killers, resentment would be near the top of the list. It destroys your ability to have fun with the person you're feeling resentful toward. And in general, resentment is a toxic emotion that, if left unresolved, can poison other situations as well.

Resentment is a common feeling among adults, particularly care-givers. In the case of couples, especially those with children, this is often in part due to the invisible labor (also referred to as the "mental load") that goes into running a household: keeping track of all the things that need to be done and then making sure nothing falls through the cracks. For example, the invisible labor in a typical household might include coordinating everyone's calendars, managing logistics for school and sports, keeping track of doctors' appointments and birthdays (and being sure you have gifts for the latter), stocking the refrigerator, making social plans, keeping track of when to buy toilet paper, and being aware of—and managing—everyone's emotions.

The invisible labor of parenthood was part of the reason that I was scared about having a kid: between my own health (managing type 1 diabetes is like a part-time job) and the stress of being self-employed, I didn't feel like I could take on any other responsibilities. My husband and I talked about this before we even began to try to have a child; I have a clear memory of being stuck in traffic on the highway one evening on our way home from my parents' house and announcing to my husband, seemingly out of the blue, "If we have a baby, *you are scheduling the pediatrician's appointments*." (And he does!)

In fact, my husband took on many of the concrete, visible tasks of parenthood—far more than nearly any other man I know. And yet I sometimes still felt a simmering resentment. He would do anything I asked him, but I was the one doing most of the asking, because I was carrying much of the mental load of managing everyday logistics, keeping track of our family calendar, and planning and organizing new experiences.

I'm not saying that my feelings of inequity were all *justified* (and my husband did plenty of invisible labor, too). But apparently they were real, because when I learned about a book by Eve Rodsky called *Fair Play*, I immediately ordered it, and then devoured it in a day.

The book's basic premise is that, in order to reduce resentment, you should treat your home life like you would a business. You start by defining and divvying up all the responsibilities and labor, visible and invisible, that go into running a household. Then you set aside regular time to check in with your partner, identify what's coming up and what needs to be done, and decide who is going to do it.

Take dinner as an example. Obviously, someone needs to be in charge of making sure your family has something to eat at night. But taking responsibility for dinner doesn't just mean chopping up the ingredients and putting plates on the table. Under the rules of *Fair Play*, if you are in charge of dinner, you are responsible for *all* of dinner—what Rodsky calls Conception, Planning, and Execution (CPE for short)—from figuring out what recipe to make to buying the groceries to cooking the meal. Rodsky points out that much of the mental load comes from the conception and planning, whereas most of the credit goes to the person who completed the execution. This imbalance is one of the main sources of resentment among couples.

I finished the book (which I read when our daughter was about four) right before leaving for my guitar class—and then, in a move that I readily admit was passive aggressive, I left it on top of my husband's pillow. The subtext was not "sub" at all, given its placement, and my husband, not being an idiot, took the hint. The next morning, he brought up the book as we made coffee.

"I read that book you left," he said, attempting to open a conversation. "It was really interesting."

And this is where things get embarrassing for me. Instead of responding to his overture productively, I latched on to the fact that, given the amount of time that had elapsed since I'd placed the book on his pillow—which was to say, about twelve hours, the majority of which we had spent sleeping—it was impossible that he had made his way through all 352 pages.

"There is no way you actually *read* the book," I retorted, with a feeling welling up in me that I now recognize as misdirected rage. "I was only out of the house for two hours."

"Well, I mean, I skimmed it," he said, taking a sip of coffee, oblivious to the hole he had just stepped into. "You know, I didn't feel like I had to read *every anecdote*. If it was like, 'Jessica felt resentful because her husband blah blah blah,' I skipped that part. But I got the gist."

This was not the correct thing to have said. In fact, it was a microcosm of what I later realized was the main source of my frustration. I feel a compulsiveness to be thorough in everything that I do—to anticipate, to review, to leave nothing to chance. My husband, on the other hand, is very good at attending to the big picture without getting too caught up in the details. This often serves him well and is a skill, I will admit, that might be worth me cultivating as well. But in this particular context, I wasn't after the gist; I wanted the details. And I wanted him to want them, too.

I hadn't just read those anecdotes. I had *re*read them. I had related so powerfully to Jessica and her exasperated kin that, as I pored over their stories, I had actually nodded along, so relieved was I to find that my own frustrations—with parenthood, with adulthood, with everything (including many things that had nothing to do with my husband!)—were not unique to me.

"Those anecdotes," I hissed at him, "*are the entire point*."

Then I grabbed the book, stormed upstairs, flopped onto the couch, and burst into tears. And as if that is not embarrassing enough, want to know what I did next? I hurled the book across the room. Yes. I threw it. I was furious.

But even while exhibiting the maturity of a two-year-old, part of my brain was still engaging in the emotional labor of thinking ahead to the possible consequences of my actions. I didn't want to actually *break* anything with my book-hurling. Then I'd have to clean it up, and I was tired of cleaning. So, even though I was blinded by rage, I maintained enough perspective—both metaphorical and literal—to aim toward a pillow. It was much less satisfying than throwing it through a window but did not require me to vacuum.

My husband, listening to my rampage from the kitchen, was confused.

The point of telling you this anecdote is that, while part of my resentment stemmed from the burden of emotional labor, it was also due to the fact that I wasn't having enough True Fun to relieve it. The challenges of early parenthood had made it much more difficult to be social or spontaneous—two important factors in True Fun. And in an ironic twist, the fact that I had recently started my guitar class—and thus reawakened my memory of what True Fun felt like—made me even more ravenous for it. I was like a starving vampire who had gotten a whiff of a paper cut and now was desperate for the taste of blood.

Once I had calmed down and apologized for the book-throwing, I explained to my husband what had made me upset: while I truly appreciated all the execution that he did, I still felt that I was the one bearing the brunt of the conception and planning. He listened to me and shared that he, too, occasionally felt resentful about the invisible work he did that I didn't always acknowledge (e.g., nearly everything involving home repair). He suggested that we have a regular coffee date on Monday mornings to go over our plans for the week and divide up our responsibilities more clearly. Over the months that followed, our levels of resentment lowered dramatically, which in turn created space for both of us—both independently and together—to seek opportunities for True Fun. To me it was proof that even in strong relationships, there may be work to do to create an emotional environment that's conducive to True Fun.

MAKE SPACE FOR
OTHER PEOPLE'S FUN

Speaking of which, when you're building a fun-filled life for yourself, it's very important to create space for the other people in your life to have opportunities for True Fun, too. No matter how close you are with someone, and no matter how many interests and passions you share, you are still going to have some fun magnets and fun factors that do not overlap, to the point that you may not understand how the other person could even find those things appealing, let alone consider them portals to True Fun. *That is fine.*

If a friend or partner or spouse or child has a fun magnet or fun factor that you don't share, don't be a spoilsport. Don't criticize or punish or resent them for spending time on something that they enjoy or that often brings them True Fun, just because you don't share their passion. Instead, help them make space for it. Actively encourage them to engage in it. Give them a permission slip to let go and enjoy themselves without worrying that they'll be scolded later or have to "pay you back."* Chances are, they'll return refreshed—and in a better mindset to have fun with *you*. The more True Fun each person in the relationship is having, the stronger the ultimate relationship is likely to be.

MAKE PHYSICAL SPACE FOR FUN

In addition to comedian autobiographies and books about endocrinology, one of my favorite genres of leisure reading is books about organization and cleaning.† This interest was ignited shortly after college, when I read Julie Morgenstern's *Organizing from the Inside*

---

* Hopefully this is obvious, but True Fun does not involve anything that would hurt the other person or put the relationship at risk. No permission slips for drug abuse, gambling away the family savings, or extramarital affairs.

† I am aware that this does not make me sound very fun.

Out, which encourages you to follow a five-step process known as SPACE—the steps of which are so ingrained in me that I can recite them to you right now without the need for an internet search: Sort, Purge, Assign, Containerize, Equalize. (The fourth step resulted in me going on a binge at the Container Store, where I spent more than two hundred dollars—on the budget of a twenty-three-year-old would-be freelance writer!—on empty boxes.)

Years later, I discovered Marie Kondo's bestseller *The Life-Changing Magic of Tidying Up,* the basic premise of which is that you should touch your possessions one by one and only keep those that trigger a physical jolt of delight—a sensation Kondo refers to as "sparking joy."

In an article about tidying in *The New York Times Magazine,* journalist Taffy Brodesser-Akner describes Kondo demonstrating what it feels like to have your joy sparked: "Her right arm pointed upward, her left leg bent in a display of glee or flying or something aerial and upright, her body arranged I'm-a-little-teacup-style, and a tiny hand gesture accompanied by a noise that sounded like 'kyong.' " Other parts of the KonMari method, as it's known, include kneeling on the floor to greet your space, folding your socks and underpants to give them the respect that they deserve, and verbally thanking your possessions for all they have done for you, occasionally even giving them a hug, before giving or throwing nearly all of them away.

It might sound ridiculous to embrace your favorite T-shirts from college before gently tucking them into a giveaway box, but tidying up actually does change your life. I know this because I've experienced it myself, when I made the bold and perhaps misguided move of reading Kondo's book several months after our daughter was born.

Shortly after finishing it, I found myself awake at 4:45 in the morning possessed by a desperate need to tidy. So powerful was this urge that I begged my husband to take the day off from work and handle baby care duties so that I could put all of my clothing into a heap in the middle of the bedroom and touch my underwear, pair by pair, trying to identify the ones that sparked joy. The process—which resulted in us donating about twenty contractor bags worth of stuff to Goodwill—made me think that the word "tidy" is a brilliant euphemism, along the lines of putting an animal "to sleep" or "disappearing" someone, and that a more accurate title would be *The Life-Changing Magic of Throwing Out Everything You Own*.

But, wow, what a difference! We had hardly been packrats, but over the years our possessions had accumulated like cat hair clinging to a sweater, and it was only in their absence that we were able to fully appreciate how much space, mental and physical, they had taken up. I remember a friend coming over soon after The Tidy and, without knowing that we'd KonMari'd, commenting on how much lighter the house felt—as in not brightness but weight.

I'm not saying that you need to follow in my compulsive footsteps and tidy, well, *anything*. Everyone can tolerate different levels of stuff. But my own experience reevaluating my possessions made me realize something that I had not previously internalized—namely, the influence that our physical surroundings have on our ability to have fun.

It's a well established fact (though one that's often not acknowledged or acted on), that our physical environments have powerful effects on our mental states. As an article in the *Harvard Business Review* puts it, "Our physical environments significantly influence our cognition, emotions, and behavior, affecting our decision-making and relationships with others. Cluttered spaces can have negative effects on our stress and anxiety levels, as well as our ability to focus, our eating choices, and even our sleep. . . . Constant visual reminders of disorganization drain our cognitive resources and reduce our ability to focus."

As the author bluntly concludes, "When our space is a mess, so are we." Cluttered surroundings have also been associated with higher levels of circulating cortisol, which in turn can contribute to feelings of anxiety and depression.* In the case of a messy desk or kitchen table, clutter can also serve as a reminder of our responsibilities and to-do lists (and can itself represent an unfinished item on our to-do lists—namely, reducing clutter!).

This has a direct effect on our ability to have True Fun. Remember: anything that distracts us or causes anxiety will kick us out of flow, and flow is a precondition for fun. True Fun also usually involves a sense of freedom and escape from your normal obligations. This is difficult to achieve if you are literally surrounded by things that remind you of your responsibilities.

The mental effects of clutter may help explain why many of our most fun memories occur in someplace other than our own homes. This makes intuitive sense, given that fun loves novelty, and novelty is harder to come by in familiar surroundings. But it's not just the novelty of new surroundings that is attractive to fun; it's the absence of cues that remind us of the burdens of normal life, even if it's just a pile of junk mail sitting on the counter.

There are also particular characteristics of physical spaces that can be conducive to fun—for example, in the way that they encourage people to gather. The journalism school I attended was a great example of this. The building was nearly entirely one story, with a large courtyard in its middle that was an inviting place to spend time in, thanks to its picnic tables and fragrant, sun-warmed rosemary bushes. The building's main hallway ran around the courtyard's perimeter and had windows that allowed you to see into the courtyard (and to see who was hanging out in it) as you moved between classes.

This design meant that people—both students and professors— often gathered in the courtyard, sometimes to work but more often

---

* The science journalist in me feels it necessary to point out that this could also work in the other direction—namely, that being stressed and anxious could *cause* you to have a more cluttered home and to experience greater feelings of anxiety and depression. But it's pretty easy to run an experiment on yourself to see in which direction the causation lies.

to socialize; many of my most enjoyable conversations in graduate school took place there. The physical layout of the building, in other words, affected the behavior and emotions of the people who spent time in it in ways that fostered closer relationships. I truly believe that if it were not for the courtyard, the school wouldn't have had such a strong sense of community and camaraderie.

The takeaway here is three-fold. First, you may be able to reduce your levels of anxiety and distraction—both of which block flow and therefore fun—by clearing more physical space in your own home. Second, if you want to invite more fun into your life, it can be useful to fully escape your everyday surroundings once in a while—to create space for yourself by physically removing yourself from your normal environment. Lastly, when you do escape, make sure you pay attention to the qualities of the new space that you'll be visiting to make sure that it is conducive to fun.*

The goal isn't to end up living like a monk or to throw out everything you own. It's simply to pay attention to the ways in which your environments affect your behaviors and moods, so that you can create and seek out physical spaces that are welcoming to True Fun.

CREATE MENTAL SPACE FOR FUN

Between the distracting, anxiety-producing, and generally unhelpful thoughts generated by our minds and the constant flow of external information, distractions, and stimulation that we allow into our consciousness, we're often left with no space in our brains to even *think* about True Fun, let alone take steps to create more of it. Compounding the problem, as we discussed earlier, is the fact that there

---

* Ideally, you want a place free from clutter, with a layout that makes it easy for people to gather—for example, a house with a nice living room, or a fire pit, or a deck. At the same time, it's also important to ask yourself how much privacy you need in order to relax. If you're going away with a group of eight friends, is it really worth saving a few dollars per night by renting a place with only one bathroom?

are companies whose entire business models rely on capturing our attention and hijacking our minds. If we want to create more opportunities for True Fun, we need to make space in our own brains.

One technique I find useful is to think about my time and attention as a budget. Just as I have a finite amount of money in my bank account, I also have a finite amount of time and attention. As is the case with money, there are lots of people in the world who would love to take it from me. Unlike money, however, my time and attention can never be replenished; once I spend them, I can never earn them back.

If we want to be sure to save enough of our time and attention for the things that matter to us the most, we need to know what those things are—and to create space for them.

Imagine that you've got a bunch of rocks that you're trying to fit into a bucket. The rocks range in size, with the large ones representing your biggest priorities, and the smaller pebbles representing things that are less important. You also have sand: the stuff that is trivial or unnecessary but that somehow fills your time. The bucket is your day. If you want to fit the big rocks into your bucket, then you're going to need to put them in first. Otherwise, there won't be room. The pebbles and sand can fit around the big rocks, but the big rocks can't muscle their way into space that's already been taken up by pebbles or sand.

You can probably see where I'm going with this. If you know that you have a large task to accomplish—like, say, *writing a book*—you need to carve out time for it. Otherwise, the less important activities, such as (oh, I don't know) checking the news or your email, are going to sap your focus and energy, and you'll have no steam left for your most meaningful tasks. This is a recipe for frustration and exhaustion.

The same principle applies to relationships and opportunities for fun. If you say that your relationships with your friends or children or your spouse are the most important things to you in life, then you need to treat them as such—and put away distractions when you're together. If you know that a particular activity is a fun magnet for you, then you need to make space for it on your schedule.

About two years ago, a friend of mine told me about a daily planner that she was using to help her to identify her rocks and pebbles and to keep her priorities straight. It had, she told me with a completely straight face, changed her life.

She pulled it out one morning when we were having breakfast together, and I had to laugh: it was more of a diary than a planner, chunky, easily half a pound, so large that there was no way to take it out of the house without committing to carrying a bag. It was the opposite of efficiency and streamlined design, this planner, the equivalent of trading in your smartphone's calendar for a brick.

I could not quite imagine how such a thing could be at all practical, let alone life-changing. But I trust this friend immensely, so I ordered one on the spot.

And sure enough, it has changed my life as well, to the point that I feel compelled to tell you about it, too.

The planner walks you through a series of daily exercises that have been designed to help you identify and stick to your priorities, and focus on the positive aspects of your life. After identifying your "most impactful goal for the day," (note: "impactful" should not be a word, but I love this planner so much that I'm willing to let it slide), you write down no more than five goals labeled "important," and five more labeled "nice to get done." In other words, you can have ten to-dos per day, tops, and that *includes* non-work-related items such as exercise and hobbies.

The planner also prompts you to start your day by listing three things you're grateful for, plus three things you're excited about or looking forward to—both of which are techniques that have been proven to boost people's overall sense of well-being. It includes space for you to jot down your schedule for the day and to allocate specific time for each of your important tasks.

Writing in the planner at the beginning of my day helps me identify my "big rocks" and makes it less likely for me to get swept away by distractions. It's worth noting that I try to do this *before* I look at my phone. In fact, I make a point of avoiding my phone (and the internet) as much as possible in the early morning, since it's typically the most productive time in my day. I do so by charging my phone out of my bedroom—I typically charge mine in a closet—wearing a watch, and using a separate alarm clock. (If your phone is your alarm clock, you are guaranteeing that your phone will be the first thing you touch when you get up—and you'll be risking allowing your day to be hijacked by whatever distraction or alert you happen to find on its screen.) I also try to set limits on the number of times per day that I check and respond to email.

Then, before bed, I put my phone into its charging station, pull out my planner, and respond to its evening prompts (yes, it has evening prompts), which include writing a positive sentence to describe the day and listing three accomplishments and three of the day's best moments. This combination of morning and evening exercises helps me to bookend my day with self-reflection instead of unsatisfying scrolling.

As I read through the words I've just written, it occurs to me that I may be coming off as a model of focus and discipline, a person who starts her mornings in a lotus position and glides through the day on a cloud of intention, productivity, and grace while drinking only herbal tea. This is not the case. Take right now as an example: my brain desperately wants me to stop writing this paragraph so that it can get a dopamine hit from checking my email. The only reason I'm managing to resist the urge is that I've promised myself that if I can finish a draft of this section, I can have a piece of chocolate.

If I'm honest, chances are high that I will eat the chocolate before accomplishing that goal. And that's okay. One of the most important messages I want you to take away from this book is that we have to be understanding toward ourselves. Sticking to our intentions and creating balance is hard, especially when it comes to technology. We're trying to create boundaries with devices and apps that are purposely designed to make boundary-setting difficult. We're trying to train ourselves to resist our dopamine-fueled cravings for the sake of ultimately much more satisfying—but also harder to come by—real-life experiences. In other words, we're fighting against powerful forces, including our own brains. So if you mess up, don't wallow in it. Don't hate yourself or decide that you're a failure. Just notice what derailed you and get back on track.

LIMIT YOUR LIST

Another way to create more space for yourself is to make a daily list of your "not-to-dos." This is a chance to clear space in your schedule by preemptively identifying your most time-sucking activities and consciously deciding not to let them hijack your day. (During the SARS-CoV-2 pandemic, the friend who told me about the planner sent me a photo of her own "not-to-do" list for the day: 1. Facebook 2. Zillow 3. Despair.)

This concept—that is, identifying the things on which you do *not* want to spend time—is a form of "limiting your list," which means making space for yourself by saying no to more things. Keeping track of your not-to-dos is almost as important as figuring out what you *do* want to do with your day. Not only does preidentifying your not-to-dos make it easier to notice and say no to them when they tempt you, it also helps you preserve space for spontaneity to occur, as well as for activities that, while they are not crucial to your existence, you might actually enjoy. For example, putting "doomscroll the news" on my not-to-do list can free up at least thirty minutes a day for me to spend on playing the piano or exercising or taking a walk or talking with a friend. (Or on doing nothing. That can be worthwhile, too.)

It's also important to limit your lists by reducing the number of responsibilities and leadership roles that you assume, even if they don't represent a waste of time in the same way as, say, a social media spiral. Many of us have collected commitments in the same way that other people collect bobblehead dolls: we start with just a few, and then over time, they start to accumulate, sometimes seemingly on their own. Eventually we end up with so many of them that they spill out of our tchotchke cabinets and begin to take over the house.

Some of our obligations are things we've proactively decided to say yes to and that we actually enjoy. Others have been offered or handed off to us by other people. In an unfortunate twist, the people who are the most inherently responsible tend to have the *most* responsibilities, because other people tend to think of them whenever something needs to be done. These are the people who are running PTAs and coaching sports teams and serving on nonprofit boards and organizing office birthday parties. If you are one of those people, I'd like you to take a moment and ask yourself: How many of your obligations are mandatory, and how many have you taken on by choice? Of the ones that you have voluntarily assumed, how many do you enjoy?

Then comes the big question: What could you say no to? I know this may sound counterintuitive, given that in general, building a fun-filled life requires being open to new experiences. But we need to be judicious. If you want to have space to say yes to more things you enjoy, you need to say no to those you don't.

So, try scanning through your current commitments and seeing what you might want to discard. And any time you're asked to take on something *new*, ask yourself: Is this absolutely necessary? If the answer is no, do a gut check: Does it *feel* fun? (Or, if that seems too vague, ask, Is it likely to produce feelings of playfulness, connection, or flow?) If so, say yes. If not, say no.

A few years ago, I had a chance to do this myself when I reevaluated my decision to serve on a board. I liked the other people on the board, I cared about the organization, but I noticed that on the evenings of our meetings, I came home feeling drained and exhausted. My participation was voluntary and, while I liked to think that my contributions were valuable, I also knew that the organization would survive without me as a board member. In addition, I already was feeling overwhelmed by other not-fun things going on in my life at the time. When I asked myself, "Is this fun?"—and whether it was likely to lead to further opportunities for playfulness, connection, or flow—the answer was no. So, even though it made me feel awkward to do so, I quit. The organization is still functioning, and I have more space in my schedule.

You can also use a fun gut check to make decisions about people. There are those who make you feel good when you're around them and those who don't. Some degree of interaction with negative people may be unavoidable if they're a close family member or a colleague or a boss. But if you realize that someone is a consistent anti-fun factor for you—they make you feel self-conscious or judged or always seem to throw a wet blanket over things—and you *do* have control over how much time you spend with them, then why not try to minimize it? Life is too short to surround yourself with people who make you feel bad.

When you're trying to limit your people list, it's useful to keep Dunbar's number (or, more precisely, *numbers*) in mind.

Robin Dunbar is an anthropologist and psychologist who has done extensive research about how big groups typically get before they break into smaller groups or collapse entirely, as well as how many relationships people can maintain at any given time. Dunbar, who has studied other primates as well as humans, has concluded that this is dependent on the size of a part of the brain called the neocortex, which is associated with cognition and language. The larger a species's neocortex, the larger the network of social connections the species is able to support.

According to Dunbar's research, the number of social connections the average person can maintain at one time is roughly 150: whenever a group gets bigger than about 150, it tends to break up.* Dunbar's research (and subsequent findings from other scientists) suggests that this is a fixed number, consistent between cultures and over time. He also concluded that the maximum number of people we can maintain close-ish relationships with (with "close-ish" defined as people you might invite to a group dinner) is about fifty. Your intimates—the people you confide in—are likely no more than fifteen; your truest, closest friends are likely limited to about five.[†]

So, why not experiment with making space by limiting your lists? Start by doing a "fun gut check" about the activities and people to which and to whom you currently give time and attention. Then ask what commitments and responsibilities you could jettison so that you have *more* time available for people and activities that you enjoy—or for spontaneity to occur. Your time and attention are zero-sum; use them on one thing and you can't use them on another. If you want to have more True Fun, you need to be ruthless about how—and with whom—you spend them.

BREAK UP WITH YOUR PHONE

Once you've limited your lists of people and activities—in other words, once you've made space in your metaphorical house for fun to occur—the next step is to guard this space by putting locks on the

---

* Dunbar defines "social connections" as casual friends of the sort whom you might invite to a large party. The 150 figure is a rough average; depending on the person, the number can range from around 100 to up to about 200 on the high end.

† Dunbar's findings directly conflict with our approach to social media, where we strive to have as many "connections" (I'm putting that heavily in quotes) as we possibly can. As Dunbar himself told a reporter for *The New Yorker*, "What Facebook does, and why it's so successful in so many ways, is it allows you to keep track of people who would otherwise effectively disappear." (To which I say, maybe there are some people in your life whom you care about so little that they actually *should* disappear.)

doors. This is especially important when it comes to our wireless mobile devices.

To be clear, when I refer to "breaking up" with your phone, I don't mean dumping it. (Nor am I referring only to phones. As mentioned earlier, other devices and technologies have the ability to interfere with our ability to have fun, too; it's just that phones are currently the worst offenders.) Just as breaking up with a person doesn't have to mean never seeing them again, breaking up with your phone doesn't mean never using it again. It simply means giving yourself space to evaluate what's working and what's not so that you can create a new, healthier relationship that keeps what you love and minimizes (or eliminates) what you don't.

After all, our phones—and all of our internet-enabled devices— are an essential and often enjoyable part of modern life. I grew up before smartphones, and I can tell you: it's wonderful to be able to listen to any music I want, learn anything I want, and connect with anyone I want, at any time. (I know what it's like to huddle next to a stereo waiting for a particular song to come on the radio so that you can record it onto a cassette—indeed, you know you're part of my generation if you came out of adolescence with a collection of mixtapes whose songs all start three seconds in.)*

But as we've discussed, many apps are deliberately designed to steal our time and attention from us. This means that when it comes to identifying time that is available for us to reclaim, some of the lowest-hanging fruit is likely to be on our phones.

So, how do you go about breaking up with your phone?† First, you need to figure out what you actually *want* to be doing with your time—otherwise, you're going to be trying to resist your impulses

---

* I understand that technology's benefits extend beyond providing us with easy access to the beginnings of songs. But, wow, that was annoying!

† For anyone looking for a detailed guide, see my previous book, *How to Break Up with Your Phone.*

using your willpower, and relying on willpower is a horrible way to change a habit. (Eventually it'll run out and you'll be right back where you started.) Instead, it's far more effective to focus on identifying and creating space for your fun magnets and other things that matter to you. (The next chapter, on pursuing passions, will help.)

Once you've done that, you'll find yourself with less time to spend on screens—and less of a desire to spend time on them to begin with—because you'll have a long list of things you'd rather be doing instead. Your phone will have been transformed in your mind from a temptation that you must resist to an obstacle that's getting in the way of how you actually want to live.

One of the biggest mistakes I see people making is to assume that all screen time is bad. This is not true. Instead, it's more productive to think about screen time—and, indeed, *all* possible uses of our time—as being like food. Some things we spend time on, such as social media, are like junk food and are very hard to consume in moderation, whereas others, such as using your map app to avoid traffic, are more like oatmeal: practical, boring, and very unlikely to result in a binge. If you were trying to adopt a healthier diet, you wouldn't stop eating food entirely; you'd eat more food that made you feel good and cut back on food that left you feeling gross. You can use this same approach to develop a more nuanced approach toward technology. Simply ask yourself which uses of your screens are necessary and/or enjoyable, and what amount will leave you feeling sated but not stuffed.

I also find it helpful to think about my leisure time—whether with screens or without—as falling into three categories: connection, creation, and consumption. (I call these the three c's.) Then I ask myself which of these feel the most enjoyable, nourishing, or satisfying—and in what doses. I like some forms of consumption (reading, eating, certain movies), but only in moderation. Creation typically feels better to me when it doesn't involve screens, possibly because more of my senses are involved—for example, playing music or cooking feels more enjoyable to me than editing a video on my computer screen. By far, the thing that makes me feel best is connection. And there's a hierarchy there, too. In-person connection leaves me feeling better than phone calls, which in turn leave me feeling better than texts or email. (For me, "connection" via social media is so unsatisfying as to be meaningless, so I try to avoid it.)

When I'm evaluating my screen time in particular, another technique I like to use is what I call "phone feng shui." Feng shui, which literally translates to "wind-water," is an ancient Chinese practice in which you try to create a sense of connection between yourself and your external environment by designing your surroundings in a way that encourages the free flow of qi (pronounced "chee"), which roughly translates to "life energy." (Bear with me here.)

One of the goals of feng shui is to eliminate spots in your physical environment where qi could get "stuck"—for example, rooms should be uncluttered, and you always want to have a clear line of sight to the door. Personally, I'm not convinced that qi always needs a visible escape route, but I do find the idea of "stuck energy" useful, especially when I'm evaluating what I'm doing on my phone. For example, if I am using my phone to check my email or the news, my attention—and thus my energy—is getting stuck within the phone itself. This is not a fun use of my phone. If I'm using my phone to call a friend, however, or look up information—say, a recipe, or chords for a song that I'm trying to learn—then my attention and energy flow through my phone and onto a real-world target.

I recommend playing around with this idea even if you do not buy into the literal concept of qi; it allows you to connect with how your daily activities make you feel on a visceral level. You can even use it to help you evaluate the relationships in your life. Which people do you feel a shared energy with? Who makes you feel drained? Which relationships require the most work?

These are really all just ways to practice mindfulness—which is to say, to become more aware of what you're doing in any given moment and how it makes you feel. It's an essential step in changing a habit, for a reason that's very simple yet often overlooked (at least outside the context of Alcoholics Anonymous): you can't change a habit—or solve a problem—if you haven't acknowledged its existence. It would be like trying to quit smoking if you didn't know that you were a smoker to begin with; you need self-awareness in order to stop. The first step in creating distance from your phone is therefore to identify and acknowledge your habits and reflect on how they're negatively impacting your life.

This is easier said than done, though, because when it comes to our devices, many of our habits are so automatic that we don't notice when we're engaging in them; our phones often end up in our hands without us even knowing how they got there. To make it easier to catch yourself, I recommend a two-step process. Start by putting a rubber band or hair tie around your phone. This way, when you reach for your phone on autopilot, you'll be interrupted by a physical impediment. Part of your brain will wonder, even if only for a split second, "Why is there a rubber band around my phone?" When that happens, the next step is to ask yourself a series of questions that will help you better understand *why* you reached for your phone, which in turn will enable you to proactively decide whether you *want* to be on your phone in that moment.

I call this exercise WWW, which is short for:

What for?
Why now?
What else?

What for? Is an opportunity to ask yourself what you picked up your phone to do. In other words, what was your purpose? (Sending an email? Reading a particular news story?) Did you *have* a specific purpose, or were you just picking it up to see what you might find?

Why now? Is a reminder to ask yourself what, in this moment, caused you to reach for your phone. This is a particularly interesting question because, while it's possible that you may have had a specific reason, in many cases, the trigger is likely to be emotional. You were momentarily bored or feeling anxious. Your focus was waning, and you wanted a distraction. You were feeling lonely, and you wanted a connection.

Once you understand your "why now," you can move on to the final part of the exercise: *What else?* This is where you use your answers to the first two questions to brainstorm possible alternatives and decide what to do next. If you are seeking connection, maybe you could skip social media and use your phone to actually call a friend. If you are feeling anxious, perhaps you could put down your phone and take a walk around the block or do a short meditation.

Your answer to "What else?" might be to do *nothing*—to give your brain a chance to rest. (That's a wonderful way to create space.) And it's also possible that you'll finish the exercise and conclude that you truly *do* want to be using your phone in that moment. That's totally fine. The point of the exercise isn't necessarily to get you to put down your phone. It's simply to make sure that when you engage with your devices, it's the result of a conscious choice.

Once you've gotten in touch with the emotional triggers for your phone habits and begun to practice responding more intentionally, you can then move on to making changes to your phone and physical environment to support new habits that leave you feeling healthier—and that help you have more fun.

The basic idea is to use the concept of "friction" to make it harder to fall into the habits you're trying to change, and easier to engage in the ones you're trying to establish. Friction is a term often used by Silicon Valley types to refer to any sort of impediment that might make it incrementally harder or less convenient to interact with their products. For example, unlocking your phone used to require you to actually type in a code. Then came fingerprint readers, and then facial recognition. Each of these steps reduced friction. Now, instead of having to consciously think, "I want to check my phone," and physically type in a series of numbers, all you need to do to activate your phone is to look at it.

Once you understand the idea of friction, you can use it for your benefit. Say you want to write in your journal before bed instead of scrolling through social media. First, add friction to your current habit by charging your phone out of your bedroom—or at the very least, out of arm's reach. Then reduce friction for the new habit by putting your journal on your bedside table where your phone used to be. That way, when you reach for your phone on autopilot (which you will, because it's an ingrained habit), you'll encounter the journal instead; it will be easier to write in your journal than to get out of bed and fetch your phone. You can use this technique in all sorts of different contexts. For instance, I know that I want to get better at guitar, so I reduce friction by leaving my guitar out of its case and in the living room. Having it out in the open instead of zipped in a bag makes it much more likely for me to spontaneously pick it up to play.

Note that the screen-free alternatives that you provide yourself with do not need be high-energy or help you toward the pursuit of some future goal—especially if you're trying to come up with ideas and options for times when you know you are going to be tired. (Often, easier is better.) At the end of a long day, perhaps your best alternative to phone scrolling would be to read a novel or do a simple crossword puzzle, as opposed to deluding yourself into thinking that you are really going to use your last moments before sleep to teach yourself Japanese.

* * *

The next step in breaking up with your phone is to make your phone as boring as possible—you want it to be a tool, not a temptation. The most effective way to do so? Reduce dopamine triggers.

Start by disabling most notifications. Notifications are designed to hijack our attention and often benefit app makers more than they benefit us; adjust your settings so that you only receive notifications for things you actually care about. (I personally only allow notifications for text messages, phone calls, calendar reminders, and navigation prompts.)

Next, redesign your home screen by moving or deleting problematic apps—a technique that addiction psychiatrists refer to as "reducing ease of access." If you're trying to stop drinking, for example, it wouldn't make any sense to keep your fridge stocked with wine. So if you're trying to cut back on a particular app, then why is that app on your home screen—or, for that matter, on your phone at all?

My biggest digital temptations are email and the news, so to reduce my ease of access, I deleted those apps from my phone and do my best to only check them from my actual computer (and I try to do so only a few times a day). This doesn't mean that I never access email or the news from my phone. I can always get to them through the phone's internet browser if I want or need to; the point is just to create boundaries by assigning specific purposes to each device.* I also engage in what I call "on-again, off-again" relationships: if I decide that I really do want to use a problematic app that I've deleted (or that doesn't work on a desktop computer), I simply reinstall it, use it, and delete it again when I'm done. This

---

* For example, if you have a smartwatch, I recommend using it only for non-distracting purposes *for which it's well designed,* such as tracking your sleep or heart rate or, I dunno, telling the time. If you try to check your email from your watch, or allow it to send you notifications for the news, you are only going to end up more frustrated, scattered, and stressed. (I don't even like getting text messages on my watch.)

only takes about twenty seconds, but it's enough time to give me a chance to notice my impulse before I carry through with it, and to ask myself whether it's really how I want to be spending my time.

TAKE BACK YOUR BRAIN

Lastly, if you want to make space for fun, you also need to reduce the mental clutter in your own brain.

Our minds had a bias against quiet *before* internet-enabled devices like phones were created; learning how to quiet the mind has been a key pursuit of many religions and philosophies, most notably Buddhism, since humanity started having religions and philosophies to begin with. The challenge is not new, in other words—it's just that our phones are making it harder.

So, why is it so important to practice quieting our minds? It's simple: because not all of the random thoughts that our minds generate are worth paying attention to! They're just coming up with new thoughts *because that's what minds do*. If we don't give ourselves any mental space, we'll never be able to decide which ones are actually worthy of our attention and time. Instead, we'll just be dragged along with whatever thoughts and ideas our minds come up with, some of which will be useful or interesting, and some of which may be worthless or downright destructive. I like to think about my mind as a very dear friend who's also mentally unstable. I love her, I couldn't live without her . . . but she's also completely nuts.

One way to quiet your mind is to consciously embrace boredom. When you're waiting for a friend, observe the world around you instead of grabbing your phone. When you're on an elevator, watch the lights indicating the passing floors. When you're traveling, try looking out the window. While you're waiting in line, practice taking slow, deep breaths. (In other words, become that weirdo gazing off into space with a peaceful or bemused look on their face.)* It'll be hard at first—especially if you see other people on their phones—but with time, you may find yourself looking forward to these minivacations from constant stimulation.

If you want to go a step further, try taking longer breaks from screens.† (We'll talk more about how to do so in chapter 10: "Keep at It.") Go for a walk without your phone. Make plans with friends—and then, instead of sending each other minute-by-minute updates about where you are and how late you'll be, simply show up at the predetermined place and time. (I know: crazy.) Try not to look at your screens for the first and last hours of your day. If you're like most people, you'll probably feel twitchy and anxious at first but then may begin to experience an unexpected sense of calm.

Another mind-calming strategy is to try, whenever possible, to do just one thing at a time—which is a precondition for flow, and therefore, True Fun. If you're folding clothes, *just* fold clothes. If you're spending time with someone, *just* focus on them—keep your phone completely away and out of sight. The more you practice this, the easier it will become (and the better your relationships will be).

Indeed, doing just one thing at a time is a great way to rebuild your attention span, which likely has atrophied as a result of being bombarded by constant distractions and stimulation. One technique I recommend is simply to put your phone in a different room, set a kitchen timer (or any timer that is not on your phone), and read a book or magazine article for ten minutes straight. Increase the time

* I am often that weirdo myself. I was once waiting for a friend in a restaurant and passing the time by gazing at an old-fashioned exit sign. She walked in, took one look at me, and just started laughing. (To which I say, yes, admiring an exit sign might be weird—but isn't it *weirder* for us to be perpetually staring down at our phones and ignoring everything around us?)

† You can alleviate your FOMO-induced anxiety by creating email and text message autoresponders telling people that you're away (or not responding as frequently as normal), and that you will get back to them when you are back online.

by five minutes a day till you can maintain your attention for a full hour. (Try not to be depressed and frustrated by how difficult it is at first.)

You could also experiment with mindfulness meditation, which is a secularized form of Buddhist meditation that's been the subject of much scientific study. The basic idea is to choose a point of focus—the most common one being your breath—and to try to maintain your attention on it as thoughts drift in and out of your mind.

And thoughts will definitely be drifting. One of my favorite analogies is to think of your mind as a snow globe that's been shaken up into a miniblizzard. The snowflakes are individual thoughts, swirling around haphazardly and making it difficult to see. When you practice mindfulness meditation, you try to observe the storm—i.e., your thoughts—without judgment, and without trying to change anything. The idea is that eventually, the flakes will settle to the bottom of the globe, leaving the water clear.

I recommend trying it for yourself, but with two caveats. First, you have to adopt an attitude of forgiveness toward yourself; as I alluded to earlier, your brain is filled with thoughts because having thoughts is its job. If you're trying to calm your mind but keep getting distracted, don't beat yourself up about it. That's totally normal. The fact that you *noticed* your thoughts means that you are succeeding.

Second, many of us pack our lives to the brim because stillness and space can be deeply uncomfortable; we stay busy so that our anxieties can't rush in. I think that keeping busy can be a useful coping strategy, to a certain extent (I certainly do it myself!), but many of us have taken this too far, and our busyness has become its own source of anxiety and distress. The challenge is that if you take away that busyness, you may risk another temporary side effect: existential despair.

INTERLUDE: THE RISK
OF EXISTENTIAL DESPAIR

Back in 1946, Viktor Frankl gave a name to this phenomenon when he described what he called "Sunday neurosis"—i.e., "that kind of depression which afflicts people who become aware of the lack of content in their lives when the rush of the busy week is over and the void within themselves becomes manifest."

In 1932, Bertrand Russell made a similar observation. "A man who has worked long hours all his life will become bored if he becomes suddenly idle," he wrote. "But without a considerable amount of leisure a man is cut off from many of the best things."

Frankl and Russell's words are still true today. When we put in the work to create space, the reward is more time for the things we love. But if we don't know what those things *are*, we risk finding ourselves in what Frankl referred to as an "existential vacuum." This has the potential, perhaps unsurprisingly, to result in a lot of angst.

These passages stood out to me for obvious reasons: they both describe what had happened to me during the freak-out moment on my couch that I told you about in the prologue. (The only difference was that my neurosis had struck me on a Saturday.) I had been so busy allowing my time to be filled that I no longer knew how I wanted to fill my own time.

If your experience is anything like mine, the process of creating space may make you realize that you have lost touch with what fun feels like. Or, worse, you may discover that you're having a hard time feeling anything at all. I'm serious! This happens surprisingly often: we've gotten so used to constant busyness, stimulation, and distractions that any deceleration, or break from the digital world, can leave us feeling disoriented and empty.

But don't despair. Learning how to sit and be present with this discomfort (which, somewhat counterintuitively, is often the best way to move *through* it) is a skill that can help us navigate all sorts of challenges, such as disappointment, loss, and fear. Also, a certain degree of angst can actually be useful. Some of the best things in life require effort and discomfort to achieve, and a little existential malaise, while unpleasant, can also be quite motivating. I can say this with certainty because it's what happened to me: my panic on the couch motivated me to figure out what I wanted to spend my time on—a process that I'm still involved in and enjoying today (and that led me to write this book).

The good news is that we all have the ability to build lives that are more conducive to fun. Now that we've taken the first steps by clearing space for activities that enliven us, we get to move on to the fun part: figuring out what those activities actually are.

CHAPTER 7

PURSUE PASSIONS

"The popular assumption is that no skills are involved
in enjoying free time, and that anybody can do it.
Yet the evidence suggests the opposite: free time is more
difficult to enjoy than work. Having leisure at one's
disposal does not improve the quality of life unless one
knows how to use it effectively, and it is by no means
something one learns automatically."
—Mihaly Csikszentmihalyi, *Flow*

WHEN I DECIDED, AT AGE FORTY, THAT I WANTED TO
learn how to row crew, the first challenge I faced was to find someone who was willing to teach me.

This might seem like it should be easy: Philadelphia is famous for
its rowing culture, and I live a ten-minute bike ride away from Boathouse Row, a line of fifteen boathouses perched on the bank of the
Schuylkill River that send out a steady stream of rowers into the
water every day at dawn and at dusk.

It turns out, however, that rowing is a sport that most people start
while young, usually in high school or college; people who row as
adults usually have learned to do so before turning twenty-one. Further raising the barrier to entry is the fact that the boats themselves
are expensive—thousands of dollars for even a basic scull—and a
slight bump or misplaced foot can damage them beyond repair. You

don't want to have them handled by people who don't know what they're doing.

So perhaps it should not have surprised me that out of all the boathouses on the river, only two offered any sort of adult "learn to row" programs, and that even those organizations were not particularly quick to respond to inquiries from someone with no rowing experience. But eventually I managed to find a boathouse that would give me lessons.

My interest in rowing had been piqued by a neighbor, who told me about the magic of seeing the skyline from the water and of experiencing glimpses of nature in the midst of one of America's biggest cities, including baby turtles, lined up on a log, that seemed to watch her as she rowed. This struck me as idyllic. It also seemed like it would be much more engaging than using a rowing machine—a contraption known as an erg—which had been my go-to form of aerobic exercise for years, since I have arthritis in both my knees, and rowing is one of the few activities that don't upset them. Rowing on an erg is a great full-body workout, but it is hard and boring and pretty much the antithesis of flow. One minute on an erg can easily feel like ten.

Physical activity is a fun factor for me, and rowing on the water seemed like a form of exercise that might actually be enjoyable. Instead of staring at a wall in the gym, going nowhere, I'd be outside, moving. I'd hear the swish of my oars. I'd see the baby turtles. Maybe I'd discover a new fun magnet! Rowing intimidated me—people who do it seriously are *intense*—but I wanted to try.

The boathouse coach was a young man named Brian, who had ruddy cheeks and a dry sense of humor. Once we'd reviewed basic techniques on an erg in a room equipped with extra fans so that when the room was filled with sprinting eighteen-year-olds, there wasn't a risk of anyone *passing out from lack of oxygen* (see above comment about intensity), he suggested that we get into the river.

Brian helped me into a boat that he referred to as a "bathtub," a nickname that made me question what kind of baths he was taking, because it was skinnier than a kayak. He climbed into a beat-up pontoon and drove at my side, giving me instructions as I struggled to maneuver the oars, each of which was nearly twice my height.

The Schuylkill River receives Philadelphia's stormwater runoff and other questionable forms of effluent; it is not the type of river you'd want to swim in. And yet, it wasn't long before signs of nature emerged. As I took my first awkward strokes, a fish flopped out of the water in front of me. And sure enough, I soon saw a row of baby turtles sunning themselves on a log, against the humming backdrop of I-76.

I expressed such excitement at the sight of these turtles that they became a running joke between me and Brian, who routinely implored me through his megaphone (which was his primary form of communication when we were on the river and which for some reason I found hilarious) to "do it for the turtles." I took him up on this, to the point where I began to time my strokes using the phrase "baby turtles" as a three-beat mantra, with the first two beats being the recovery and the catch, and the last representing the push. "Bay-bee *turtles*," I muttered to myself as I rowed. "Bay-bee *turtles*."

Over the course of the summer, I biked to the boathouse every Thursday morning for a lesson, gradually becoming more confident on the water. Eventually, I mastered the bathtub to the point where Brian felt I was ready to upgrade to a single scull.

For anyone not familiar with the sport, this is the equivalent of jumping from a tricycle to a racing bike. Take a moment, if you will, to contemplate the width of your own bottom. No matter how thin you are, I can assure you: a racing scull is thinner. It is so narrow that instead of sitting *in* the boat, you are essentially balanced on top of it. It would have been possible to capsize the bathtub, but I would have had to work at it. A scull, on the other hand, is so unstable that the only thing keeping you from tipping over into the water is the stability provided by your oars.

The particular morning that I would like to tell you about was Halloween. It was unseasonably warm, but there were menacing rainclouds; Brian and I exchanged a series of text messages discussing whether to reschedule. We eventually decided to go for it, our logic being that it was likely to be the last opportunity for a lesson that season before the river got too cold.

As I biked to the boathouse, the wind began to pick up; by the time Brian and I were standing at the edge of the dock, boat already in the water, the clouds looked as if they were about to burst.

"What do you think?" he asked.

"I dunno," I said. "What do *you* think?"

"If you were one of the kids," he said, referring to the high school team he coached, "I'd tell you to get in."

"Okay, then," I said, my ego irrationally challenged by the thought of being out-toughed by strangers less than half my age. "Let's do it."

The moment at which I pushed off the dock—which is the point of no return, since the oars are so long that there's no easy way to reverse course—was the moment it started to rain. Hard. What's more, the wind picked up, making Brian look like a fisherman on the TV show *Deadliest Catch*—hood pulled up, eyes squinting as the drops hit his face. The wind added chop to the water, making it even more essential that I not stop rowing; like a bicycle, a scull is most stable when it's moving.

The rain's arrival highlighted a change that had seemed trivial but that proved quite consequential: I was not using my normal set of oars. Another coach had adjusted them in a way that made them no longer fit me, and so Brian had handed me a different pair. The handles of my normal oars had slight grooves for my fingers and a textured material that provided grip. The handles of these oars were totally smooth and, now that they were wet, slick.

"They keep slipping!" I yelled to Brian as he followed me in his pontoon.

"That's because those are the slippery ones," he responded dryly. "Why'd you take that kind?"

As I muttered obscenities and continued to row, I realized something that I wished I'd noticed before launching: while there was normally a steady stream of rowers passing us (since I was nearly always the person being passed), today the river was entirely empty. Brian and I were the only people out. Given the popularity of rowing in Philadelphia, this was truly unusual, and more than a bit ominous—the equivalent of merging onto a major highway to find that you're the only person on the road.

At this point we were crossing the river to get to the invisible "lane" designated for boats going upriver. This was near the log where the turtles usually hung out, though there were none present that morning, because turtles are smart. Without realizing it, I had cut too sharply toward their usual location and now was in danger of rowing myself into the riverbank. Brian called for me to take a stronger stroke with my left arm to steer myself away from the shore.

As soon as I began to reach for the stroke, I could tell that something had gone horribly wrong. My right hand was empty, and I was tumbling sideways. I could see exactly where I was headed—which is to say, into the river—and there was absolutely nothing I could do to stop. I took a breath, closed my eyes, and hoped for the best.

The first thing I said upon resurfacing was "That didn't taste as bad as I expected." And it's true: for a river that routinely has bodies fished out of it, the taste was surprisingly clean. The second thing I said was "I think I just got hepatitis." (Brian thought that tetanus was more likely.) The third was "You'd better get a photo of this for me to send to my husband." (And so it was that our 2019 holiday card featured a photo of me giving a thumbs up as I clung to an over-turned boat.)

"Why did that happen?" I called up to Brian, my breath catching in my throat from the sudden cold.

"You let go of the oar," he replied—a phrasing that I took issue with, given that "let go" suggested a conscious decision on my part, which was not the case, and that the source of the slippery oars was my rowing coach, who was now laughing at me.

But there was no time to argue with him while I was still in the water. "What do I do?" I yelled, still clinging to the capsized boat.

"Swim to me."

I did an awkward breaststroke around the scull, which was surprisingly difficult due to the coldness of the water, the boat's length (nearly thirty feet long), and the fact that I was wearing all of my clothes. Brian helped me climb a short ladder up to the pontoon, which he maneuvered next to the scull so that he could dump out the water and turn it right side up.

The day was so unseasonably warm that once I was out of the water, I felt fine. Nonetheless, I still assumed that falling into the river represented a get out of jail free card and that surely we would call it a day and return to the dock.

But Brian was having none of it. "Get back in," he told me, holding onto my scull with his hand as it floated next to the pontoon.

"Are you serious?" I asked him.

"Oh, yes," he said, devilishly. "Get in."

He helped me slide back into the seat—which I still can't believe I did without re-capsizing—handed me my oars and shoved me away from the pontoon. Then, with him yelling encouragements, the rain still pouring, and me dutifully reciting "bay-bee *turtles*" to myself, we made our way up the river to our normal turnaround point, and then made a wide turn to head back down.

Earlier in the season, I had told Brian about the awkward man in my swing-dancing class—the guy I mentioned to you earlier who had kept repeating "We're having fun, we're having fun" to himself over and over again as we danced. So, as I fought my way back down the river to the boathouse through the rain, Brian and I traded call-and-response rounds:

"This is fun!" he shouted.

"I'm having fun! I'm having fun!" I yelled back, struggling to maintain control of the oars.

Here's the thing, though: I actually *was* having fun. My wet pants clung to my thighs, rain was dripping into my eyes, and with every stroke, I worried that I would capsize again. But I wasn't in actual danger, and when I asked myself, "What's the worst that could happen if I keep rowing?" my answer was "I'll fall into the river"—and I'd already done that. Despite my discomfort and residual anxiety, I couldn't seem to stop laughing.

The entire situation struck me as delightfully absurd—so much so that even now, more than a year later, just writing about it puts a smile on my face. When we got back to the boathouse, where the manager was nervously awaiting our return, I cheerfully announced, "I fell into the river!" even though by that point I could easily have pretended I hadn't; it was raining so hard that Brian was just as soaked as I was. Yes, I was wet. Yes, my confidence had been shaken. But I also felt *alive*.

At that time, I hadn't come up with a definition of fun, but if I think about the experience, all three elements were clearly present. Even though we weren't close enough to consider each other friends, Brian and I had a very playful connection and had spent enough time together to build a repository of inside jokes. The physical challenge of rowing—not to mention my desire not to capsize again—kept me out of my head and engaged with my body. And I unquestionably was in flow: completely absorbed and pushed to the edge of (indeed, one might say *beyond*) my abilities.

I wouldn't *choose* to fall into the river again, but I'm grateful that I did. It gave me a new, if somewhat uncomfortable, memory of True Fun to add to my collection. I didn't get hepatitis. And besides, what else would I have done that morning if I hadn't rowed? Written more emails?

* * *

My tumble into the Schuylkill was the result of my attempt to follow the P in SPARK. It stands for "pursuing passions" (well, actually it's short for "pursuing passions, interests, and hobbies," but I kept it short for the sake of alliteration)—and it's the next step in our process.

We just did a lot of work to create emotional and physical space in our lives. Now we need to identify what we want to *do* with that space; otherwise, we'll be left with a vacuum, and it won't be long before our old habits come rushing back in to fill it. Remember the part in the prologue when I said that building a more fun-filled life is like going on a diet where you get to eat more of the things that you love? We've already identified some of these things—they're our fun magnets. But why stop there? Ideally, each of us would have a long list of enjoyable activities—some big, some small—that put us into flow and that we could turn to any time we encounter an opportunity for leisure. That's what this chapter is designed to help us create.

WHAT IT MEANS TO DO THINGS "FOR FUN"

When I suggest that we pursue passions, interests, and hobbies, what I'm really saying is that we should do more things "for fun." Sometimes these activities will lead to True Fun; sometimes they won't, but they all are enjoyable and rewarding (and, in many cases, easily accessible), and thus are worth our time.

The challenge is that in our everyday speech, we tend to classify *any* activity that we don't do for work as something that we do "for fun"—which means that we often employ the same words to describe everything from passive, low-energy (and possibly draining and soul-sucking) pastimes to active, energizing, truly pleasurable experiences that have the possibility of generating True Fun. In other words, we use the phrase so casually and sloppily that it borders on being meaningless.

So let's get more specific. I'd like to propose that the following activities do *not* count as legitimate uses of the term "for fun," and that we should stop using it to describe them:

- Activities that we compulsively seek out but that are ultimately unenjoyable, draining, and/or unsatisfying (think doomscrolling). These are sources of Fake Fun and obviously shouldn't be described as things you do for fun because, well, they're *not*.
- Things we do to self-medicate, such as binge-watch television shows, mindlessly scroll, or consume drugs or too much alcohol.
- Activities that we don't get paid for and are not enjoyable.
- Things we do *purely* for relaxation or restoration, such as taking naps or baths. These activities are likely soothing and nourishing and enjoyable (and thus worth our time), but they're not technically things we do for fun, because they don't typically generate playfulness, connection, or flow.

In short, if an activity does not generate playfulness, connection, or flow (and our purpose is not enjoyment), *then we should not say that we're doing it for fun.* By becoming more precise about how and when we use the term, we will reduce our chances of accidentally spending our leisure time on things that leave us feeling dead inside.

So what *does* qualify? Our fun magnets, by definition, obviously *do* fall into the category of things we spend time on for fun. So do our hobbies, interests, and passions.

DEFINING INTERESTS,
HOBBIES, AND PASSIONS

Simply put, passions, hobbies, and interests are activities that we enjoy and that get us into flow. They're things that we find so intrinsically interesting, pleasurable, and motivating that we pursue them for their own sake, even though we don't get paid for our effort or receive any type of external reward. Sometimes they lead to connection, sometimes they invite playfulness, but flow is the variable that unites them all—and it is their consistent ability to put us into flow that makes them worthy of being categorized as things we do for fun even if and when they don't result in the magical confluence of all three elements.

In general, interests are subjects that we enjoy *learning about,* and hobbies are things that we like to *do*. (For example, studying Spanish would be an interest; reading a Spanish-language newspaper every Sunday morning would be a hobby.)

The main characteristics that distinguish our *passions* from our hobbies and interests are the pull we feel toward them and the amount of energy that they produce. Whereas hobbies and interests tend to result in relaxation or pleasant engagement, passions *invigorate* us; they're essentially interests or hobbies that have been turbocharged. (The intensity of the energy produced by any particular activity can fluctuate depending on our stage of life and circumstances, which explains why some things that start as interests or hobbies eventually morph into passions, and why some things we once felt passionate about now spark only mild interest.) The greater our passion is for a particular activity, the more motivated we'll be to seek it out, the more joyful energy it will spark, the more alive it will make us feel—and the greater its likelihood will be of generating True Fun.

But that doesn't mean that you should only spend time on things you're passionate about (that's a pretty high bar!) or be disappointed if you "only" have interests and hobbies. *Anything* that makes you feel pleasantly alive is worth your time, and hobbies, interests, and passions *all* have the capacity to help us attract more True Fun.

First of all, the fact that they are voluntary means that hobbies, interests, and passions can all be considered forms of play. (If they get *too* serious, they may still be enjoyable or rewarding, but they'll lose their playfulness and become less likely to lead to True Fun.) Having a wide variety of leisure activities may also allow you to express different parts of your own personality, including perhaps a more playful side that, when you're consumed by daily stresses, usually gets lost.

Interests, hobbies, and passions also foster connection by strengthening preexisting relationships *and* by introducing you to new people and communities. My mother and my mother-in-law are great examples of people whose interests, hobbies, and passions have helped create these types of connections. In my mother's case, some of the people from whom she's taken lessons have become members of our chosen family; her passion for trying and learning new things directly inspired my own. As for my mother-in-law, since her retirement, she's sung in multiple choirs, participated in book clubs, managed a pottery studio, and taken classes in everything from Turkish to the flute. For both of them, every activity in which they've participated has introduced them to new people. Some of these connections have lasted only for the duration of the activity or class; others have developed into longer-lasting friendships. None of them would have happened if they hadn't made it a point to get out into the world and try new things.

Lastly, interests, hobbies, and passions give us skills and knowledge that can help us slip into flow in more contexts—and the more we're in flow, the more alive we will feel.

Mihaly Csikszentmihalyi makes this point in his seminal book on the subject, the aptly titled *Flow*, using the example of a chessboard. To someone who doesn't know how to play chess, it's just a board with a bunch of carved figurines. But for someone who has put in the effort to learn how to play the game, who has the skills and knowledge necessary to engage with it, a chessboard is an opportunity for flow (and possibly even playfulness and connection).

In other words, the more interests, hobbies, and passions that you cultivate, the more knowledge and skills you will have, which in turn will give you more avenues into flow. If you learn to speak a foreign language, you can travel to new places and connect with people in ways that are inaccessible to most tourists. If you learn how to cook, you can host dinner parties. If you put effort into Scrabble, you can tap into an entire subculture of word lovers. If you learn how to play an instrument, you can make music with other people. In fact, my guitar is a perfect example of this concept: before I started taking classes, it was just a large object taking up space in my closet. Now it's a direct portal into playful, connected flow.

Interests, hobbies, and passions also make you more interested and interesting, a term I first heard from my college roommate and have been inspired by ever since. The more of them you develop, the more engaged you'll feel in your own life—and the more you'll have to talk about with other people. As an added bonus, even things you try that do not turn into interests, hobbies, or passions—or that end up being unpleasant or uncomfortable—can turn into good stories. For example, I wouldn't have had nearly as much fun telling you about a rowing lesson that had *not* ended up with me capsizing into the river.

THE VALUE OF SOLITARY PURSUITS

The benefits of passions, hobbies, and interests also extend to activities that you do alone. In fact, I highly endorse the pursuit of solitary interests, hobbies, and passions, because many of our everyday opportunities for leisure—for example, a lunch break, or an hour before bed on a random weekday night—tend to pop up when we're alone, or when it would be difficult to seek out a fun magnet or coordinate an activity with a friend. These are the moments in which we're most likely to reach for our phones, not necessarily because we *want* to passively consume content right then, but because the habit is easy and accessible, and we can't think of anything better to do.

The more solitary interests, passions, and hobbies you have (and the more accessible you make them) the easier it will be to avoid reacting to your free pockets of alone time by automatically turning to a screen—*because you'll have other things you want to do instead.* These pastimes may not be likely to attract True Fun, due to the inherent difficulty of experiencing a sense of connection with another person when you're alone. But they still are likely to be more enjoyable and rewarding—and make you more interested and interesting—than whatever else you would have done.

For example, when the lockdowns of the SARS-CoV-2 pandemic led my husband and me to decamp to my parents' house in rural New Jersey with our daughter, I wanted to find some new interests and hobbies that would help me avoid regressing to my old routines. (Instead of trawling for doorknobs, I was now doing fantasy real estate searches, but the basic motivation—a desire to self-soothe and distract myself from my anxieties—was the same.)

Since we were spending a lot of time outside, I decided I would learn about edible plants. (In retrospect, I may have been in a bit of a survivalist phase.) I bought books about backyard foraging, downloaded a plant identification app, and became the flora-focused equivalent of a bird watcher, unable to take more than a few steps at a time before pausing to identify a leaf that had caught my eye.

Occasionally this hobby produced delicious results, as when my daughter and I found an enormous patch of wineberries growing around the perimeter of my parents' property and filled our bucket to the brim with the sweet, sticky fruit. More often, they were not—as was the case when I forced her to come outside with me during a rainstorm so that I could gather a bag of gingko fruit off a Philadelphia sidewalk. (The smell of raw gingko fruit has been described, accurately, as "cheesy vomit," and when I tried to roast the nuts, following instructions I'd found online, they exploded with such force that it lifted the lid off the pot. They tasted fine—the smell disappears once you've roasted them—but it took much more work than they were worth, and I later learned, thankfully not from personal experience, that the fruits themselves contain the same chemical that makes poison ivy itch, and can be toxic if you eat more than a few at a time. I will not be collecting gingko nuts again.)

My main takeaway from plant foraging is that there is a reason that certain plants have been cultivated for human consumption while others have not. But the end result isn't what matters. What matters is that I tried something new. I did something interesting and active with my leisure time, and found a new way to tap into flow.

As my adventure in plant identification demonstrates, the other great thing about solitary leisure pursuits is that they often *do* lead to connections with other people and thus facilitate True Fun, albeit in a roundabout way. This certainly happened with me and my daughter—we often slipped into playful, connected flow while gathering plants together, and before long, *she* was the one scouring the side of the road for what foragers refer to as "trailside nibbles." And as the social restrictions imposed by the pandemic began to recede and I went for walks with friends, I often found myself excitedly pointing out the edible plants that we encountered.

You'll have to ask my companions how much they appreciated my botany lessons, but my new interest certainly entertained *me*. What started as an enjoyable solitary hobby had blossomed into something with the potential to generate playfulness, connection, and flow. In other words, it had become fodder for fun.

HOW TO IDENTIFY—AND DISCOVER—
INTERESTS, HOBBIES,
AND PASSIONS

One of the many great things about passions, hobbies, and interests is that they are *accessible*. You can't get out of bed in the morning and boldly proclaim, "Today, I shall have True Fun," both because that's vague, and because True Fun is an emotional experience that does not respond well to plans. You *can*, however, say, "Today I will do the crossword" or "Today, I will try a new recipe" or "Today, I'll read a bit of that novel." Unlike fun, you can put hobbies, interests, and passions on your calendar.

But that's not to say that pursuing your passions, hobbies, and interests is necessarily going to be easy. As we've discussed, many of us can't remember what sorts of active pastimes we enjoyed when we had more time, energy, and freedom (that is, if we can remember a time when we had more energy and freedom to begin with).

What's more, our life circumstances may have changed in ways that preclude us from engaging in the things we used to enjoy. For example, one of my favorite things to do in my twenties was to spend Sunday afternoons playing pickup ultimate Frisbee in Prospect Park with friends, and then retreating to their house for a casual barbeque. But that was twenty years ago. Most of us now live in different cities, nearly all of us are married with children, and I can no longer play ultimate to begin with, thanks to the arthritis in my knees. So much for that.

What's more, even if we *are* able to identify things we like to do for fun, many of the activities on our lists likely require time, planning, and other people (and, if you have kids, a babysitter). For example, you might know that you really love going on ski vacations with your college roommates—indeed, you may consider those trips to be nearly guaranteed fun magnets—but that's not exactly the kind of thing you can spontaneously pull off on a random Tuesday night.

Put this all together, and it makes sense that many of us have gotten into the habit of spending most of our everyday leisure time on passive consumption, such as watching television or staring at our phones or computers. Passive consumption takes no planning. It is easy and accessible. And considering how mentally exhausted many of us feel, easy and accessible is often exactly what we're looking for. After a long, busy day, who could be blamed for just wanting to sink into the couch?

And indeed, I'm *not* blaming you. Nor am I saying that every moment of our lives needs to be active. The problem, in other words, isn't passive consumption itself; the problem is what happens when passive consumption is our *default*.

Unfortunately, that's exactly what passive consumption has become. Our levels of stress and burnout are so high—and technology and entertainment companies have made passive consumption so easy—that we turn to it even when it is *not* actually what we want or need.

This is not a new issue. Bertrand Russell wrote about it in 1932 when he pointed out that the amount of energy people were devoting to their jobs was sapping their ability to participate in active leisure activities. "The pleasures of urban populations have become mainly passive: seeing cinemas, watching football matches, listening to the radio, and so on," he wrote. "This results from the fact that their active energies are fully taken up with work."

But while it may not be a *new* problem, technology has made the situation worse—in part because it has eroded the boundaries between home life and work life, and in part because getting us to spend our free time on passive consumption is essential to many companies' bottom lines.* If we want to change our defaults and

---

* As Netflix CEO Reed Hastings once put it, "We're competing with sleep."

take back control of our leisure time, we need to expand our repertoire of passions, hobbies, and interests, and make these activities as accessible as possible so that they have a chance of competing with the easy, passive options available on our screens.

Kids have no problem identifying their hobbies, interests, and passions (or, for that matter, their fun magnets). When I asked my (then-four-year-old) daughter what she found fun, she yelled, "Tap dancing!" and began to twirl around our dining room on her tiptoes, eyes sparkling, a joyful smile on her face. When I asked my friend's eleven-year-old daughter the same question, she rattled off, "Baking, knitting, and soccer," without skipping a beat. When I asked her why, she said, simply, "because I love doing those things."

If you, like those children, already have lots of interests, hobbies, and passions, great: devote more time to them. But if you don't, please don't beat yourself up. Many adults barely remember what it's like to engage in activities that are so intrinsically enjoyable that they light us up inside.

Regardless of which category of grown-up you fall into, I recommend that you start by looking at your fun times journal and lists of fun magnets to see if you're already doing things that would qualify but just haven't yet tagged them as interests, hobbies, or passions.

Next, I suggest that you brainstorm *new* ideas for possible interests, hobbies, and passions. This is important because adults tend to be stodgy. We encourage our kids to try new things, but we refuse to do so ourselves. Instead, we decide at some point in our lives that we do not enjoy particular activities—and then never revisit them. But just as there are certain activities that we enjoyed when we were younger that no longer hold appeal, there are likely to be activities that we did *not* previously find pleasurable (or that we never felt motivated to try) that might hold the potential to become hobbies, interests, and passions, if not full-on magnets for fun. If we want to feel fully alive, it's essential that we try new things.

Speaking of which, novelty itself is such a powerful fun factor that trying new things can often generate fun even if the activity itself doesn't end up being something that you enjoy. (I am quite sure that my husband could provide you with multiple examples of activities I've made him do that would qualify.) There's a reason, after all, that many relationship experts recommend that couples who feel stuck in their routine skip their normal date night routine and instead find a new activity or class to do together, or an experience to seek out.

You might already have some ideas in the back of your mind for things that you're curious about. (That was what inspired me to try rowing lessons.) If so, great! Make a plan to try one. If not, one idea is to pick two or three of your fun factors at random and come up with as many activities or subjects as you can think of that would combine them. You could also call a friend who knows you well and ask them to help you brainstorm things to try (perhaps together!) or do internet searches for activities, meet-ups, and classes going on near you to see if anything strikes your fancy. And make sure that your list also includes ideas for things to do alone, at home, when you're tired.

I find that the following prompts can be helpful:

- I'm interested in learning
  to_____
- I'm interested in learning
  about_____
- I'm curious about_____
- I'd like to try_____
- I'd like to get better at_____
- It might sound silly, but I'd love to

  _____

- When I was a child I
  enjoyed_____
- Things I used to do with my free time but don't
  anymore:_____
- Things I always say I want to do or learn, but supposedly
  don't have time for:_____
- I feel alive when I_____

I recommend that you set a timer for fifteen minutes and write down everything that comes to mind. Keep going until the timer stops; sometimes your most interesting ideas will come after you've exhausted your initial burst. Again, do not self-censor as you do this or set the bar too high. Nothing is too niche or too silly, and anything that sparks even mild interest or curiosity is good enough to write down. Also, don't assume that you actually have to *do* all the things you come up with. We're not trying to overwhelm ourselves with new commitments; we're just trying to open our minds and break out of our normal patterns of thought.

Once you've got a list of ideas, try one! It doesn't matter what you choose, and it doesn't have to be exciting; just do *something*.

Then afterward, ask yourself: Did you enjoy it? Is your curiosity piqued? Would you like to do it again? If it's an experience, notice how it made you feel physically—and don't be put off if it left you a bit nervous or jittery. These can be signs that you pushed yourself out of your comfort zone, which is often a good thing. (They can also be signs that you hated it, in which case, move on to something else.)

If you're not sure how you feel, take a page from parenting guidebooks—the ones that suggest that you require your kid to try a new food three times before they decide they truly don't like it—and give it a few tries before you make a final call.

And also, if you've given something what you consider to be a good college try and you still are not enjoying yourself, *you have per-*

mission to stop. That's the glorious thing about doing things for fun: if they don't feel fun, then you don't have to do them! If you try something new and it doesn't work out, that's great: you just freed up some space and time to try something else.

All of this may sound fine and good on paper, but in reality, trying new things can be hard and scary; whenever people search for new interests, hobbies, and passions, they often encounter similar obstacles. So let's take a moment to talk about how to deal with them.

WHAT TO DO
WHEN YOU *ONLY* GRAVITATE TOWARD
SOLITARY ACTIVITIES

If your goal is just to enjoy yourself, then pursuing solitary activities is totally fine: they'll make you more interested and interesting (and can put you into flow) even if no other people are involved. But if you're looking to generate True Fun, you're going to need to figure out a way to incorporate a sense of playfulness, and perhaps more challengingly, a feeling of connection.

One idea is to ask someone to join you. For example, say you love reading. While reading can legitimately be pleasurable (she writes, hoping that you are enjoying what you are reading right now), it does not often lead to True Fun in our sense of the word, because it's an activity that we do alone. But if you join a book club—or, easier, have a conversation with a friend about what you're reading—it can serve as a springboard into a conversation that produces True Fun.

Classes are another great way to add a social element to solitary activities. If you love doing yoga at home, why not check out a nearby studio? If you like painting, perhaps you could sign up for a workshop. You don't have to talk with anyone if you don't want to. But who knows? Maybe you will.

WHAT TO DO IF YOU'RE TOO BUSY TO MAKE ANY MORE COMMITMENTS

First, as we've discussed, you don't have to make any new commitments; our goal is *not* to add to your list of to-dos. You have full permission to dabble in whatever appeals to you or piques your curiosity in any given moment, and you can do things for fun in bite-sized pieces—say, the random pockets of time that you usually spend scrolling. (And you can even pursue interests, hobbies, and passions *on your phone*. I know: that might sound heretical coming from me. But there are plenty of ways in which our phones and devices can support our interests, hobbies, and passions rather than take time away from them. My plant identification app is a good example of this.)

If you do find something you truly enjoy that requires a bigger time commitment than you feel you can fit into your schedule, then you may want to revisit the last chapter and explore other options for making space. You also may want to have a conversation with the people in your life to discuss ways that they can help take some weight off your shoulders so that you feel less constrained. Speaking of which. . . .

WHAT TO DO WHEN OTHER PEOPLE ARE THE OBSTACLE

It can be challenging to identify and pursue personal passions, interests, and hobbies if you live with someone and spend most of your leisure time together. Over time, you may find that your individual passions have been replaced by shared interests. Shared interests are great and will contribute to the health and longevity of the relationship, but it's also essential to carve out time for things that are just for you.

Eve Rodsky, the author of the aforementioned book *Fair Play* (i.e., the one I hurled into the couch in the last chapter), refers to this as "Unicorn Space," which basically means time set aside for each person in the relationship to pursue their own individual passions. As she puts it, "Whoever you are and whatever you do, you still need time and space to engage in something outside of the work you do for money to make you come alive."

Importantly, Unicorn Space does not refer to the time you spend on passive pursuits, such as following sports or watching television. It's time for active leisure, the things that make you interested and interesting—a term that she uses as well—and that nourish your internal flame. (It's worth noting that if you're in a long-term relationship, these are likely some of the qualities that drew your partner to you in the first place, and vice versa.) It's time, in other words, for your passions.

Creating and protecting Unicorn Space can be especially difficult if you have kids, both because children themselves take up a lot of time (leaving you with less to spend on your own needs) and because prioritizing your own needs when you're a parent is often construed, at least in America, as selfish. Personally, I prefer to think of it in terms of an airplane safety announcement: if you want to assist other people, you've got to make sure you have your own oxygen supply first.

This may require some negotiation with the person you live with—first, to get their buy-in that making time for Unicorn Space is worth it, and second, to figure out how to actually do so logistically and without breeding resentment. One idea? Emphasize how important it is for them to have Unicorn Space, too—and encourage them to take it. Try it for a month and take note of the effects it has on your energy levels, moods, and connection.

WHAT TO DO ABOUT DIFFICULTY
(HOW TO GET OVER THE HUMP)

As we talked about, one of the main benefits of spending time on our passions, hobbies, and interests is that they put us into flow, a state that's so intrinsically enjoyable and satisfying that it serves as its own reward. The more we experience flow, in other words, the more flow we want to experience.

But as we also touched on, achieving flow often requires a certain degree of skill or competence—and developing skill and competence can be hard. You can't just sit down at a piano and start playing Mozart; you're going to have to make it through an initial stage that may include more moments of frustration than fun. (It's worth keeping in mind that the root of "passion" is the same as the root of patient and, for that matter, passive: they both come from the Latin word for "suffer.")

This is why Mihaly Csikszentmihalyi, the psychologist who coined the term "flow," recommends that when you are in the early stages of any new activity, you build in some external rewards for yourself to keep you motivated until you reach a level at which flow is possible and you're able to enjoy the activity for its own sake. For example, if a child is resisting piano lessons, it might make sense to offer some type of reward to motivate them to practice, at least up to the point where they are competent enough to begin to get into flow. At that point, playing the piano may begin to become more intrinsically satisfying; eventually, they may pursue it on their own without the promise of an external reward.

You can try the same approach on yourself any time one of your new pursuits feels challenging or you sense your frustration beginning to build. Say you're learning a foreign language. What could you reward yourself with if you manage to study vocabulary words for thirty minutes every day for a week?

Eventually you'll reach a level of competence where these extrinsic motivators will no longer be necessary—for example, you'll become fluent enough in Spanish that reading the newspaper or carrying on a conversation will feel less difficult and more enjoyable and, therefore, will become its own reward. But the path to that point can be hard, which is why so many of us end up frittering away our free time on meaningless—but easier—activities instead. So whenever you're trying to do something new and it feels hard, take a breath and acknowledge that your frustration makes sense. Then take Csikszentmihalyi's advice and make it easier for yourself by building in some extrinsic rewards—in other words, imagine that you're a dog that you're trying to train, and give yourself some treats.

WHAT TO DO WHEN YOU'RE WORRIED THAT YOU'LL FEEL DUMB

One of the biggest obstacles that prevents people from trying new things may be the most challenging to overcome: fear. Most of us are terrified of looking or feeling stupid or doing something that might be perceived as a failure. As play scholar Stuart Brown puts it, "Probably the biggest roadblock to play for adults is the worry that they will look silly, undignified or dumb if they allow themselves to truly play."

Margaret Talbot captured this sentiment in a piece for *The New Yorker* in which she writes, "Among the things I have not missed since entering middle age is the sensation of being an absolute beginner."

I get why people wouldn't gravitate toward activities that they fear will result in shame. (Uh, who would?) But if you're an absolute beginner at something, why would you feel any shame at all? You're not supposed to be good!

Far from being a trigger for humiliation, being an absolute beginner at something can be *freeing,* because no one *expects* you to be good. It's also an act of bravery. If you're an absolute beginner at something, it probably means that you're trying something new, which can feel scary. And trying new things is the only way to expand your collection of interests, hobbies, and passions and open up more paths to True Fun. We should be embracing that beginner feeling, not running away from it.

That's not to say that being a beginner will feel comfortable. But if you don't give yourself permission to explore, how are you ever supposed to grow? What would happen if babies never tried to walk because they were too worried about falling down?

I thought about this a lot myself during my rowing lessons. I'm a relatively coordinated person, but I didn't feel that way when I got in the boat. My balance was unsteady, the oars seemed too long, and even before I had capsized, every stroke left me feeling like I was going to tip over. The feeling of physical and emotional vertigo was extremely disorienting. It made me think of my daughter, who was then four years old. More specifically, it made me think of how she must experience this vertigo all the time, because so much of her world was new. I decided that if she—despite having only *one-tenth* of the life experience as I did—somehow managed to keep going, I would, too. (And then I fell into the river . . . but I survived to tell the tale.)

One of the unfortunate side effects of our fear of looking dumb is jealousy of people who *do* seem to manage to try new things: they're exhibiting a confidence and bravery that we wish we had ourselves. But since we're too scared to join them (or can't figure out how to do so), we judge them instead. We call them self-indulgent or privileged, or accuse them of being selfish. We refer to them as dilettantes.

As if criticizing other people isn't problematic enough, we also often turn our criticism inward, toward ourselves. But when you're a beginner at something, it's essential to avoid *any* critics who might scare you away by making you feel self-conscious or dumb—including yourself. It reminds me of an essay I read in which the author, who had begun to take voice lessons as an adult, approached her teacher after her first recital and asked for a critique of her performance—perhaps because her own penchant for self-criticism was so strong that she felt driven to seek it from other people, too. The teacher looked at her blankly and said, "You are a beginner. You are right where you are supposed to be in your development. Why would I critique anything?"

This brings us to one of the biggest roadblocks of all: our own perfectionism. It's a huge problem, and not just in terms of our ability to have fun.

In 2017, Thomas Curran and Andrew P. Hill published a study that investigated the rates of perfectionism—defined as "a combination of excessively high personal standards and overly critical self-evaluations"—among American, British, and Canadian college students from 1989 to 2016. The study found that perfectionism is on the rise; as the authors wrote in a description of their findings, "increasingly, young people hold irrational ideals for themselves, ideals that manifest in unrealistic expectations for academics and professional achievement, how they should look, and what they should own." Young people, they continued, are "seemingly internalizing a pre-eminent contemporary myth that things, including themselves, should be perfect." After all, who posts a video to YouTube of their first try?

Some of the rise in perfectionism might be attributable to what the researchers refer to as "our society's emphasis on social comparison, and the sorting, sifting and ranking that follows" a description that seems to perfectly (ha!) describe what we do on social media. But regardless of the cause, the rising rates are a problem because, as Hill and Curran point out, "perfection is an impossible goal. Those who become preoccupied with it inevitably set themselves up for failure and psychological turmoil. They become obsessed with winning the validation of others and demonstrating their worth through flawless performance after flawless performance. They ruminate chronically about their imperfections, brood over what could have been or should have been, and experience considerable anxiety and even shame and guilt about their perceived inadequacies and unworthiness."

Not only can perfectionism prevent you from trying new things out of fear of failure, but it can actually be damaging to your health. Perfectionists have been found to have stronger physiological reactions to stress and perceived failure than non-perfectionists (e.g., higher spikes in blood pressure), and are more susceptible to anxiety, depression, social phobia, anorexia and even suicidal ideation. Curran and Hill point out that "there is growing evidence that the increase in psychological ill-health of young people may stem from the excessive standards that they hold for themselves and the harsh self-punishment they routinely engage in," and hypothesize that perfectionism may be behind what they describe as "almost epidemic levels of serious mental illness in young people."

Hill and Curran's research was specifically about rates of perfectionism in college students, but it has lessons for older people as well. First, we need to put less pressure on our kids, and teach them from a young age that perfection is not an attainable—or healthy—goal.* And second, we need to be better role models by cultivating more acceptance toward ourselves, and not being afraid to put ourselves out there and try new things, even if we might end up feeling (or looking) dumb. As a recovering perfectionist myself, I know this is hard. But if you want to have more fun in your life, it's absolutely essential.

One way to loosen perfectionism's grip is to gently investigate what, exactly, you're afraid will happen if you do *not* perform

---

* I've been trying to do this with my own daughter by resisting the urge to use the word "perfect" as an adjective as much as possible. I felt like my efforts might be working when I accidentally referred to something she had drawn as "perfect" and she responded by looking up at me with a bemused smile and declaring, "Mama. *Nothing's* ever perfect." (This either means that she will be well adjusted, or that she'll need a lot of therapy. Or, perhaps, both.)

perfectly—and then continue to ask questions until you convince yourself that it's going to be okay. (It's what I was trying to do when I asked myself "What's the worst that could happen?" after I fell out of the boat; it's also similar to what parenting experts recommend you do if your kid is scared of monsters.)

And also: start small! When it comes to trying new things, there is nothing that says that you need to do something dramatic, like sign up for a dance troupe or try out for a play. Just find some activity—any activity—that piques your interest or sparks your curiosity (or that you already know that you enjoy but that you're not an expert at) and carve out some time this week to do it. You could even return to something you *used* to be decent at, but for some reason, you've stopped spending time on.

As Margaret Talbot writes, "Being willing to involve yourself in something you're mediocre at but intrinsically enjoy, to give yourself over to the imperfect pursuit of something you'd like to know how to do for no particular reason, seems like a small form of resistance."

So resist. Be a beginner. Pursue passions, interests, and hobbies whenever possible. Make a point to try new things. As you do, keep in mind that far from implying flightiness or irresponsibility, the word dilettante actually comes from the Italian verb "to delight." And "amateur" doesn't refer to a lack of skill. Instead, its root is the Latin word for love.

CHAPTER 8

ATTRACT FUN

"Determine to live life with flair and laughter."
—Maya Angelou

NOW THAT WE'VE MADE SPACE AND IDENTIFIED POSSI-
ble passions, interests, and hobbies, we're ready for the next step of
SPARK: Attract fun. Why "attract"? Because opportunities for playfulness, connection, and flow float around us all the time; the better
we are at attracting and appreciating them, the more fun our lives
will be. We've talked about activities, settings, and people as being
magnets for fun. Now, our goal is to become fun magnets *ourselves*.

We all know people who attract fun. They are the friends whose
presence at a dinner party guarantees that everyone is going to have
a good time. They exude warmth, playfulness, and self-confidence;
they make you feel fully seen and appreciated when you're with
them, and people always seem happy to have them around.

What might not have occurred to you is that it's possible for *you*
to become one of those people—even if you think of yourself as shy
or introverted.

Consider some of the traits that popped up again and again in
people's responses when I asked members of the Fun Squad to describe people in their lives whom they considered fun.

- They're spontaneous.
- They're at ease with themselves and comfortable in their own skin.
- They're not afraid to be silly.
- They're not afraid to try new things and to be a beginner.
- They're not afraid to be vulnerable.
- They're appreciative of the small things.
- They find joy in being alive.

Many people described fun people as being able to laugh at anything. Curiosity and open-mindedness came up a bunch. Being present in the moment did, too

"They have a very positive attitude and seem to be enjoying themselves," wrote one person. Said another, "My mom is fun! She has a wild imagination and can find something new and exciting in every situation. She doesn't think too much about what people think of her, and she surrounds herself with things that make her smile."

Many of the descriptions of fun people also had to do with the way the fun folks made *other* people feel in their presence. For example:

- I never feel judged by them.
- They make everyone feel included.
- They're considerate of others' feelings.
- They get excited with you.
- They create wonderful, shared memories.
- With them, there is always something to do, and they make these events as fun as possible.
- They're generous, give everyone the benefit of the doubt, and are really open to others.
- They always have the time and energy to make people feel special.

When I read through these descriptions of fun people, two things stood out. First of all, very few of the characteristics mentioned were genetically determined. (No one suggested, for example, that blondes have more fun.) And second, while many fun people are indeed extroverts, you don't *need* to be extroverted to be considered fun. For instance, you do not need to be a leader or the life of the party to make other people feel included and comfortable, or to create wonderful shared memories, or to appreciate the small things in life, or to be confident or have a good sense of humor. In fact, many of the qualities people mentioned, such as being considerate of other people's feelings, are things that introverts do naturally.*

The fact that being perceived as a fun person doesn't depend on genetics or an extroverted personality means that being a fun person is not something that only comes naturally to some people and is out of reach for everyone else. Instead, many of the traits that make people seem fun are the result of choices, attitudes, and habits, practiced over days and years. This means that, to a greater extent than we might imagine, being a fun person isn't something that's decided at birth; it's a skill we can develop.

So, let's talk about two ways to do so—namely, by adopting a fun mindset and by learning to recognize and create playgrounds.

ADOPT A FUN MINDSET

The primary thing that separates people who attract fun from their supposedly less fun peers is their *attitude*. Not only do they notice and take advantage of preexisting opportunities for playfulness, con-

---

* This is especially important because many of our personality traits—including whether we're introverted or extroverted, or anxious, or sad—are heavily influenced by genetics and therefore unfortunately *aren't* entirely under our control. As Martin Seligman, the psychologist who helped found the field of positive psychology, writes in his book *Flourish*, "Strong biological underpinnings predispose some of us to sadness, anxiety, and anger. Therapists can modify those emotions but only within limits."

nection, and flow, and make time for their fun magnets, passions, interests, and hobbies, but they approach these activities—and, indeed, life in general—with what I call a Fun Mindset. (A Fun Mindset is a fun-oriented twist on what Stanford psychology professor Carol Dweck has dubbed a "growth mindset.")

Adopting a Fun Mindset doesn't mean becoming saccharine and forcing yourself to be outgoing or ridiculous or constantly cheerful. Instead, having a Fun Mindset refers to the habit of intentionally approaching and reacting to your life in a way that is attractive to fun. (People with fun mindsets are the ones who always seem to be enjoying themselves more than other people, even when they're in exactly the same context.) This boils down to deliberately seeking out as many opportunities as you can to create—or appreciate—humor, absurdity, playfulness, connection, and flow.

BE EASY-TO-LAUGH

One surefire way to cultivate and radiate more of a Fun Mindset is to notice and appreciate the humor in everyday life. This does not require that you develop a side hustle as a standup comedian, or even that you take on the responsibility of pointing out humor or absurdity to other people; you can start by simply noticing them for yourself or expressing your appreciation when *other* people point these things out. In the words of former Twitter CEO Dick Costolo, "The easiest way to have more humor . . . is not to try to be funny—instead, just look for moments to laugh."

My husband and I refer to this as being "easy-to-laugh," and it is one of the *most* powerful ways to nurture a Fun Mindset.* We all enjoy spending time with people who make us laugh and who laugh a lot themselves. The easier you are to laugh (and the more things

---

* My copy editor has correctly pointed out that "easy-to-laugh" is not actually an expression and doesn't even make grammatical sense. (It should be "laughs easily," or "is quick to laugh.") But it's become so much a part of our family lexicon that I'm keeping it.

you can find to laugh about) the more attractive you'll be, both to other people *and* to fun. (And, to point out the obvious, you'll also spend more time laughing, which in itself will make you feel good.)

SAY "YES, AND"

Another way to develop a Fun Mindset is to take a cue from improvisational comedy and master the art of "Yes, and."

Improv comedy, should you not be familiar with it, is the art of making up comedic scenes on the spot. A typical improv show involves the actors (who refer to themselves as "players") asking the audience to shout out a word or idea, and then playing a game in which they construct a humorous scene based on that idea. At its finest, improv can be magical—an experience of playful, connected flow for the players and audience alike. If your fun factors include performance, spontaneity, and uncertainty, then you might enjoy trying it out firsthand.

Given that my fun factors do *not* include these things (particularly performance), you may wonder why I decided, at age twenty-three, to sign up for a class in improvisational comedy at a theater in New York called The Upright Citizens Brigade. The reason was that I was trying to push myself out of my comfort zone (mission accomplished)—but sure enough, it didn't take long before I came to dread Saturday mornings with an intensity I usually reserve for bloodwork or gynecological examinations. At our final show, my performance was so objectively embarrassing that afterward, the few friends who'd shown up simply handed me a bouquet of flowers, made several awkward comments about how brave I was to do something I obviously was not good at, and took me out to lunch. We never spoke of it again.*

I have very few memories that make me cringe, but that class was

---

* I recently brought this up to one of the friends who attended the show. She claimed not to remember the show or the lunch, instead saying she just had a vague memory of being impressed that I had signed up for the class. I do not believe her for one second.

one of them. And yet it introduced me to a tool that has shaped my life ever since: the philosophy of "Yes, and."

"Yes, and" is the basic rule of improv comedy, and the idea is quite simple. Whenever you're on stage with someone and they say something to you or make a pronouncement about the scene, you agree with it (i.e., say yes) no matter how crazy their suggestion might seem—and then build on it. (That's the "and.") For example, if you are in a scene with someone who says that their father is Santa Claus, it is not acceptable to say—as I did in our final performance— "No he's not." Instead, the principle of "Yes, and" means that you accept the idea that their father is Santa and propel the scene forward by adding something new. It doesn't matter what you add, as long as it's open-ended and builds on what they said.

In her book, *Bossypants,* Tina Fey—master improviser and *Saturday Night Live* alum—explains this much better than I can:

"You are supposed to agree and then add something of your own. If I start a scene with 'I can't believe it's so hot in here,' and you just say, 'Yeah . . .' we're kind of at a standstill. But if I say, 'I can't believe it's so hot in here,' and you say, 'What did you expect? We're in hell.' Or if I say, 'I can't believe it's so hot in here,' and you say, 'Yes, this can't be good for the wax figures.' Or if I say, 'I can't believe it's so hot in here,' and you say, 'I told you we shouldn't have crawled into this dog's mouth,' now we're getting somewhere."

Thankfully, you don't have to be an actor to benefit from the *philosophy* of "Yes, and." (Believe me.) Instead, you can use it as a way to strengthen your Fun Mindset by opening yourself to spontaneity and becoming more adaptive. As Mike Myers has written, "[Improv] isn't just a game—it's a way of looking at life."*

In other words, even the nonactors among us can use the princi-

---

* I found this quote in the textbook for our class, which I read in one sitting, hoping that if I studied hard enough, I'd get better at spontaneity.

ple of "Yes, and" to build momentum and attract fun—whether by suggesting new things or by enthusiastically going along with other people's ideas. The more you say "Yes, and," the more comfortable and confident other people will feel in your presence, the more connected with them you'll become, the more opportunities for play will present themselves, and the more often you'll find yourself in flow. And the more you do that, the more often you'll experience True Fun.

SEEK ABSURDITY

Tina Fey's progression of possible responses also highlights another core element of having a Fun Mindset: an appreciation for the absurd. Things that are absurd are illogical and a bit ridiculous, which makes absurdity a welcome escape from our usual goal-driven approach to life. Absurdity makes us laugh, and laughter attracts fun. In short, the more absurdity you can notice, experience, and create, the more True Fun you're likely to have.

One way to do so is to intentionally seek out (and say yes to) situations and activities that have an element of the absurd. For example, I once convinced my husband to join me in an aqua aerobics class in Riga, Latvia. (Why we were in Latvia to begin with is a whole separate story.) Water aerobics itself is inherently absurd, and in this case was made even more so by the teacher, a woman named Olga, whose primary form of communication was not a language at all, but rather, high-pitched yips. Whenever Olga wanted the ladies in the pool to do a different move—and besides my husband, we were all ladies—she got their attention with a sound usually associated with a chihuahua. When demonstrating a favorite exercise—say, extending a ball to one side and your legs to the other—Olga let out an entire series of these yips, occasionally finishing with a blood-curdling "yoooo!" that echoed through the room like a scream.

Adding to the absurdity was the fact that the things Olga expected us to do were, at least for me and my husband, physically impossible. Grinning, she began doing front kicks while simultaneously swinging her arms back and forth at her side, her movements in perfect time with the music's beat. I tried to follow her but failed; not only did the drag of the water make it impossible for us to maintain a speed anywhere close to hers (Olga was demonstrating from outside the pool) but it was difficult to move all of my limbs forcefully through the water without, well, actually *swimming* somewhere. My kicks pushed me backward; the awkward movement of my arms kept throwing me off balance.

Olga did not care. Now perched on a stool, she demonstrated that we were to use two feet at once as we kicked to the side, to the front, to the side, to the front. *Too fast! Too fast, Olga! What do you think we are exercising in? Air?* I felt like I was doing aerobics in a vat of Jell-O. I tried using just one foot and keeping the other on the bottom of the pool so that I could perform both movements without dunking my head underwater. Olga immediately noticed and used her hands to create pretend binoculars. "I see you," she mimed. "Two feet up. Two!"

I had no chance to explain myself, not only because I do not speak Latvian (or the language of yips) but because Olga had added yet *another* layer of absurdity to the situation by pelting us with small rainbow-colored balls. At first I thought that perhaps they were medicine balls—the weighted ones often used for abdominal exercises. But these were simply filled with air and thus seemed like silly accoutrements for a class already taking place in the buoyancy of water.

Oh, Catherine. Yes, it's true that tossing the balls out of the water might have been pointless. But holding the balls under water was a different story. The balls did not want to be submerged. They protested, fighting for the surface as if they were small animals we were trying to drown.

Undeterred, Olga demonstrated that we were to hold them between our thighs while performing two-legged kicks, side to side. This proved impossible—the balls rebelled. The pool began popping with rainbow explosions as, one by one, they escaped.

In short, the whole thing was pretty ridiculous. But perhaps the most absurd part of all was our reaction to the class. Without each other's knowledge, my husband and I had both spent the cooldown entertaining the fantasy of becoming professional synchronized swimmers.

"I was really good," he said, as we walked out of the building together. "Did you see me do those kicks?"

Needless to say, neither of us went on to launch careers as water ballerinas. But there's no question that we had fun. Today, every time we look back on that memory, the absurdity of it still makes us laugh.*

But you don't have to take water aerobics—or, for that matter, travel to Latvia—in order to take advantage of the fun-generating potential of absurdity. It's floating in the air around us; we just need to seek it out.

SPRINKLE IN PLAYFULNESS, CONNECTION, AND FLOW

In addition to seeking and appreciating absurdity, another way to develop a Fun Mindset is to regularly ask yourself, "How could I add a bit of playfulness, connection, or flow to whatever I'm doing or experiencing right now?" You can do this whether you're with other people or alone, and your ideas don't have to be earth-shattering to be effective.

A woman named Helen who was participating in the Fun Squad

---

* Speaking of absurd things that make me laugh: on that same trip, my husband accidentally got a perm.

shared an example from her own life. She told me that after reading an email I sent about Fun Mindsets, she had decided to experiment with the idea while pouring herself some tea.

"I thought, 'How could I make pouring tea more fun?'" she told me in an email. "So I poured tea while standing on one leg, and you know what? It was more fun."

I don't think anyone—including Helen—would argue that her one-legged tea pouring will end up being one of her peak fun memories, but still: it goes to show how approaching life with a Fun Mindset, even in little ways, can affect your moment-to-moment experience and improve your mood.

Adopting a Fun Mindset—and figuring out ways to add even teensy bits of playfulness, connection, and flow to your everyday activities—can also help objectively non-fun activities, such as chores, feel more tolerable. It reminds me of the introduction to the *Mary Poppins* song "A Spoonful of Sugar," in which Mary Poppins matter-of-factly states, "In every job that must be done, there is an element of fun. You find the fun and, snap! The job's a game."

Granted, the ensuing scene involves Mary Poppins performing a whistling duet with an animatronic robin and doing a fair amount of magic; cleaning your room would indeed be more fun if you could snap your fingers and make your clothes fold themselves up and leap into a drawer. And I'm not saying that you're going to turn cleaning your cat's litterbox into a delight. But the point still stands. The more you can cultivate a Fun Mindset in your everyday life, the lighter your everyday life will feel.

STRENGTHEN YOUR PLAY MUSCLES

If you're still drawing a blank on how to strengthen your Fun Mindset, there are concrete—and scientifically validated—exercises you can try.

For example, you could experiment with some of the techniques described in a 2020 paper published in *Applied Psychology: Health and*

Well-Being in which researchers investigated whether people could train themselves to have a more playful attitude. The researchers adapted a series of exercises from the field of positive psychology that have been shown to help people have more positive thoughts, feelings, and behaviors, and used them to try to boost participants' playfulness.

The first exercise was a modified version of a positive-psychology staple called "three good things" (also known as "what went well" or "three blessings"), which has been shown to increase people's sense of well-being and reduce depressive symptoms for up to six months in placebo-controlled studies.

In the traditional version of three good things, you set aside ten minutes before bed for seven days and write down your three best moments from that day, paying attention to these specific details:

- What you did or said and (if others were involved) what they did or said
- How the event made you feel at the time when you experienced it, and how it makes you feel to reflect back upon it
- What you think caused the event—in other words, what made it come to pass

The moments don't have to be big—something like "The barista at the coffee shop remembered my name" would count. Just make sure that you also reflect on *why* that good thing happened, and what role you played in it. (For example: they remembered your name because you had gone out of your way to make conversation the last time you visited the shop.) The point is to begin to shift your mindset toward focusing on the positive events in your life—and to understand your role in making them occur.

The researchers also incorporated a positive psychology exercise known as "using your signature strengths in a new way," which has been shown to have similar effects.

In the traditional version of the exercise, you start by taking a survey designed to help figure out your signature strengths (also described as "character strengths"). These are traits that are essential to who you are and that feel effortless and energizing—for example, kindness or leadership or humor or hope.

Then, once you have a sense of your own signature strengths, you find opportunities to use them in your everyday life and record how doing so makes you feel. It's similar to our practice of using our fun factors to generate ideas for new things to try. For example, if one of your signature strengths is creativity, you might decide to set aside an hour each night to work on a new project.

In the study about playfulness, researchers adapted these exercises (plus a third, in which you simply count the number of kind acts you've performed in a day, every night for a week) to focus specifically on playfulness. Instead of writing down three *good* things, participants were asked to write down three *playful* moments from their day, as well as who had been involved and how they felt as a result. And instead of finding opportunities to use their signature strengths, participants were asked to find opportunities to be playful in new ways, such as "doing something playful at the workplace." (They also asked participants to reflect on the number of playful experiences they'd had each day.)

The results of the interventions, which lasted for a week, suggested that while we each may have different levels of intrinsic playfulness, it is indeed possible to "stimulate playfulness," as they put it, by choosing to focus your attention on it. What's more, given the very short amount of time involved (five to ten minutes, for seven evenings—less than the time you're probably spending on your prebedtime phone scrolls), the effects were "comparatively large."

SEND OUT PLAY SIGNALS

Another way to build a Fun Mindset is to create more moments of everyday connection by sending out more play signals—i.e., things we do to let other creatures know that we are being playful and that our intentions are friendly, and to invite them to respond with playfulness, too. For example, one of the play signals dogs use is the bow they perform when they try to get another dog to play with them (or when they're trying to get a person to throw a ball): they lunge onto their front elbows, stick their bottoms in the air, and wag their tails. An example of a play signal in humans would be brief eye contact combined with a smile, or a comment that invites conversation. Even a playfully sarcastic line can work, such as "Nice weather we're having" when you're in the midst of a snowstorm.

This is one of the many ways in which our interactions with our devices are getting in the way of fun: Instead of sending play signals, we're all staring down at our screens. With no signals, there are no invitations to play, and no play happens. Possible moments of play—and possible connections—are lost. And I'm not just talking about possible *big* connections, like meeting your future spouse (though that could happen, too). When we look down at our phones we also miss out on fleeting connections with strangers—seemingly meaningless interactions that actually have the power to make us feel less isolated and alone.

In one experiment that proves this point, researchers had pairs of students who didn't know each other come to a small waiting room, either with or without their phones. They were then told that the researchers were running late and were asked to wait for ten minutes. Hidden video cameras recorded their facial expressions as they waited, and they were later asked how they felt while waiting and whether they'd interacted with the other student in the waiting room. The videos were also analyzed to measure how often the participants smiled at one another and how genuine their smiles were.

The resulting paper's title—"Smartphones Reduce Smiles Between Strangers"—says it all. The researchers found that the people who had their phones smiled fewer times (and with less genuine smiles) and spent 30 percent less time smiling than the people who didn't have their phones with them.

"Smiling is a really powerful social lubricant," the study's lead researcher, Kostadin Kushlev, said to *Greater Good Magazine*. "When somebody smiles at you, that indicates approachability. Our research suggests that phones might actually be impeding this very important approach-related behavior that serves to create new social ties."

In contrast, making a point to look up from your phone and send play signals is a wonderful way to invite more playful interactions—and ultimately, more fun and joy—into your life.

"What play signals do is invite a safe, emotional connection, if even for an instant," writes Stuart Brown in *Play*. "Even in casual interactions, the sincere compliment, the remark about the hot/rainy/freezing/damp weather, a joke or sympathetic observation opens people up emotionally. It transforms a grim, fearful, and lonely world into a lively one."

PRACTICE PRESENCE

Another related way to develop a Fun Mindset and become more of a fun person is simply to practice being present, both on your own and when you're with other people. In fact, this is one of the easiest ways for people who consider themselves introverted or shy to become more fun. This is true for a number of reasons, the most basic of which is that if you're not present, then you can't be in flow and therefore can't have fun. (You also can't engage in "Yes, and" when you're distracted. Imagine watching an improv show where one player threw out a suggestion and the other player was like, "Hold on, lemme just finish this text.") Also, it feels really good when someone pays attention to you, especially given how distracted everyone is these days. Someone who is fully present is someone people want to be around.

Not only will becoming more attentive make people want to spend more time with you, training yourself to be present and focused can help *you* have more fun and enjoy *your* life more, too. Indeed, researchers have found distraction to be one of the biggest negative influences on our moment-to-moment moods. As one paper put it, "The propensity to experience lapses of attention has been associated with negative consequences in terms of long-term affective well-being." The title of another research paper summarizes this in plain English: "A wandering mind is an unhappy mind." Considering how often we seek distractions specifically *because* we're feeling down and want to boost our mood, this is a very big deal.

As we touched upon when we talked about making space for fun, you can train yourself to be more present through techniques such as mindfulness meditation or getting in the habit of doing just one thing at a time.

You can also learn to attract more fun simply by making a point to pay attention to other people when you're with them. It doesn't matter whether they're a family member, a friend, or a stranger: when you encounter another living, breathing human being, put your phone away and look up. Make eye contact. Smile. Let them know that in that particular moment, they have your full and undivided attention. In our distracted society, this is a powerful and generous gift. Notice how people react when they receive it.

SEEK DELIGHT

One of my favorite ways to notice—and attract—potential fun is to deliberately seek out sources of delight—an idea that was sparked a year or so ago when my friend Vanessa told me about a book called *The Book of Delights*, by a poet named Ross Gay. The book is the result of a project in which Gay challenged himself to write an essay about something that delighted him every single day for a year.

Throughout the book, when he describes something that delights him, Gay marks it by including a parenthetical that says, simply, "Delight!" Examples of delights: Pecans. Strong espressos. Cuttings from a fig tree. Pretty much anyone who calls him "sweetie." People's reactions when he carries a tomato plant onto a plane. A young TSA worker at the airport who mishears Gay say the word "poems" and announces to a coworker, "That guy's being flown to Syracuse to read palms!"

Having read the book myself and heard Gay speak on the subject, I can assure you that he is not a Pollyanna. Many of the essays touch upon decidedly undelightful things, such as racism, mortality, and the loss of loved ones. And yet according to Gay, the more he focuses on noticing delight, the more he finds himself surrounded by it.

As he writes, "It didn't take me long to learn that the discipline or practice of writing these essays occasioned a kind of delight radar. Or maybe it was more like the development of a delight muscle. Something that implies that the more you study delight, the more delight there is to study. . . . [As I continued the project], I felt my life to be more full of delight. Not without sorrow or fear or pain or loss. But more full of delight. I also learned this year that my delight grows—much like love and joy—when I share it."

This revelation—the more you focus on delight, the more delights will reveal themselves to you—echoes the same philosophy we've been talking about throughout this book: that our lives are what we pay attention to. If we train ourselves to notice delights— the everyday beauties and kindnesses and amusing absurdities, the things that make us laugh or that we feel grateful for—we will feel more positive. If we pay more attention to sources of playfulness, connection, and flow, we'll have more fun. And once we get started, it's easier than we may think. As Jennifer Aaker and Naomi Bagdonas write in their book, *Humor, Seriously,* "When you walk around on the precipice of a smile, you'll be surprised how many things you encounter that push you over the edge."

On the other hand, if we train ourselves to focus on disappointments, failures, and sadness, then we will experience our lives as a series of disappointments, failures, and occasions to feel sad. And if we spend our time consuming content that makes us anxious and upset, the more anxious and upset we will be.[*]

The practice of noticing and labeling delights stands in stark contrast to our usual approach to life, which for many of us involves a lot of time spent ruminating on past mistakes and dwelling on anxieties. Indeed, this is part of the reason that practices like gratitude have proven to be so effective in boosting our sense of well-being: they offer a structured way to reframe our reactions. But until I read Gay's work, I'd never heard of anyone doing the same thing with delight. I immediately wanted to try it for myself.

So Vanessa and I started our own delight practice, which I invite you to join as well. When we encounter something in our lives or environment that sparks delight, no matter how small, we take inspiration from Ross Gay, and we label it. By which I mean, we point a finger at the thing in question—or, if it is not a physical "thing," we raise a finger in the air—and announce, out loud and enthusiastically, "Delight!" (The out loud part is important, even if you are alone.)[†]

For example, I just heard a flutter of wings, and a little brown bird with polka dot speckles on its belly landed on the roof outside my window, peered in at me for a moment, and then flew away. Delight!

It's a humid morning, so much so that the mere act of touch typ-

---

[*] Whenever I see a car with a bumper sticker that says, "If you're not outraged, you're not paying attention," I am tempted to point out that I actually *am* paying attention; I'm just choosing not to only pay attention to things that would outrage me.

[†] It makes intuitive sense that focusing on the positive would boost your mood, but if you don't believe that such things would make a difference, try spending an hour doing a twisted version of the delight exercise in which, instead of noticing and labeling delight, you respond to negative thoughts and stressful environmental cues by pointing your finger in the air and announcing, "Anxiety!" (or, depending on the context, "Fear!" or "Cause for despair!"). Then switch back over to labeling your delights and notice what a difference it makes.

ing has left me sticky, but there is a fan blowing cool air onto my back, tickling my skin. Delight!

I'm drinking coffee from my favorite cup while eating a bowl of fresh strawberries. Delight!

Gay was right: the more attention you pay to the delights in your life, the more delights will reveal themselves to you. It's almost like tuning in to a frequency on a radio dial. And the better attuned you become to everyday delights, and the more actively you seek them out, the more likely it will be for one of your delights to cross the line into fun. (And even when this does not happen, you'll still be delighted, which is a lovely state in which to spend your time.)

Focusing on delight will also help you cultivate a Fun Mindset by rekindling your inner playful spirit, the part of you that knew how to have fun when you were a child, and coaxing it a little bit further out of its grown-up shell. Not only will you attract more delight to yourself, but you yourself will become more delightful—which in turn will transform you into an even more magnetic force, both to other people, and to fun itself.

What I love about the concept of noticing delight is that, compared to many other similar exercises, it feels easy and accessible. Noticing delight is essentially a gratitude practice, served in a tiny teacup. And tiny teacups are themselves delightful. So there you go.

SAVOR WHAT'S GOOD

The more I thought about delight, the more it reminded me of a psychological technique called "savoring": the practice of deliberately paying attention to and appreciating the positive things in your life. Fred Bryant, a social psychologist at Loyola University Chicago who's the world's leading expert on the subject, describes savoring as "swishing the experience around . . . in your mind" (which makes savoring sound a bit like mouthwash, but you get the point). When practiced over time, savoring has been shown not only to reliably boost people's happiness but also to strengthen relationships, increase creativity, and even improve physical health.

If you read descriptions of the most effective techniques for savoring, you'll immediately see the similarities they share with Gay's practice of noticing delights.

For example, researchers who study savoring suggest focusing your attention on your present positive experience—in other words, catching yourself in a pleasant moment so that you can savor it on the spot. They also recommend tuning in to your senses and taking a mental photograph of the thing you're trying to savor.

Positive psychologists have also found that, when you're trying to savor something, it's helpful to engage in what they call "behavioral displays": expressing positive emotions with nonverbal behaviors, such as smiling—or, I'd argue, jutting a finger in the air as you label something a delight. What's more, experts who study savoring have found that telling other people about your positive event, a practice they call "capitalizing," has an additional beneficial effect on your mood.

I tried a delight-oriented version of this technique during the SARS-CoV-2 pandemic, when I felt desperate for something, *anything*, to help me maintain a positive mindset. I started by focusing on personal delights. Then I mentioned the practice to friends. Then I included it as an exercise for the Fun Squad and offered a month-long "December Delights" challenge to people on my mailing list. Before long, I started to receive messages back from strangers cataloguing their delights. Here are a few examples:

- Brisk fall days
- Tiny boxes
- Making my kids laugh
- Warm coffee
- Super crispy bacon

- Ripe peaches
- Frost that makes the grass sparkle like diamonds
- Building a snow woman
- Good lunch salads

Friends also began to text me photos with the caption, "Delight!" For example, one friend sent me an article about wearable sleeping bags (not just delightful but also *genius*);* another sent a series of videos of mornings at his bird feeder. Eventually, some group text chains developed, including one between me, my husband, and some of our closest friends from California whom we no longer regularly see now that we've moved back to the East Coast. Every few days I would look at my phone to see a new delight sent by someone from that list—a fifth-grade school portrait of my friend Steve, complete with gold necklace and red V-neck sweater; a playlist someone on the internet had dug up of the precise songs that had played in dressing rooms at the Gap on June 6, 1992 (an artifact whose specificity I find both delightful and absurd); a video of my friend Natalie and her husband Simon performing a highly choreographed dance for her niece's tenth birthday. Every time I saw one of these texts, I smiled.

In short, what started as a lark turned into a real source of, well, *delight*. It gave my friends and me something to talk about other than the pandemic and the news, and it created a collection of delights that I could turn to any time I needed a boost. (Looking back on your pleasant experiences is referred to as "positive mental time travel" and is another proven technique for improving your mood.)

---

* As one reviewer described the concept, "The idea is that you can stay warm around a campfire while your arms remain free to hold your beer or s'more (or, let's be honest, both). Then you can hobble/stumble over to your tent and pass out for the night—no need to climb into your sleeping bag because you're already wearing it."

PUT YOURSELF IN FUN'S WAY

As the metaphor of "attracting" fun makes clear, the potential for fun is all around us (or, if not full-on fun, then some combination of playfulness, connection, and flow). Another way to attract fun and hone your Fun Mindset is simply to become more attuned to pre-existing opportunities for fun and put yourself in more situations where fun is likely to occur. (This is a great technique for introverts or people who do not like planning or hosting things.) In other words, you're trying to find ways to allow fun to find *you*.

If you know that you typically have fun at a particular friend's parties, and they are throwing a party, then get yourself to that party! If you become aware of a preexisting, fun-sounding event that you could attend, make it a priority to do so! This may sound completely obvious, but often we feel so overwhelmed (or paralyzed by inertia) that we say no even to things that we might actually enjoy.

For example, I, your resident fun cheerleader, almost did not sign up for swing-dancing camp—the one that I rhapsodized about earlier. I knew that I loved swing dancing, I knew that I loved summer camps, and yet the logistics of it (getting there, finding childcare, et cetera) just seemed so *hard*. It was my husband (who does not have a dance background and *never* would have sought out this camp on his own) who convinced me that we should give it a shot. I believe his exact words were "I don't understand why you're hesitating. You know you'd have a good time." Sure enough, it's now one of the highlights of the year.

In short, the more you understand your own personal fun magnets and fun factors, and the more you adopt a Fun Mindset, the easier it will be to identify events and opportunities that are likely to attract fun, and thus are worth making an effort to participate in—and the more likely you are to become a magnet for fun yourself.

Also, I encourage you to make a habit of seeking out any situation in which you know that there will be a lot of playful energy, especially if you are not feeling full of playful energy yourself, because being around other people who are in good moods can be contagious. (It can also be annoying, but still is usually worth trying.) We've all had experiences where a friend has dragged us kicking and screaming to something, and then we've ended up having a fantastic time.

BE ABLE TO LAUGH AT YOURSELF

Just as it's important to be someone who laughs easily (but never cruelly), it's also important to be able to laugh at *yourself.* Laughing at yourself is a way to feel more confident about putting yourself out there and trying new things. It's a very specific form of self-assuredness and confidence and, indeed, bravery that popped up again and again in the Fun Squad's descriptions of people whom they considered fun. Fun people were described as being "not afraid to be silly" or "not afraid to try new things and to be a beginner" or "not afraid to be vulnerable."

Being able to laugh at yourself is a talent that comes naturally to some people; for others, it's a skill that has to be developed. But all of us have the ability to do it, and it is worth the effort. The ability to poke fun at yourself is a form of playfulness, and a powerful signal that you're comfortable in your own skin. It will create a protective force field that insulates you against your own insecurities and draws people closer and, in so doing, attracts fun.

BUILD PLAYGROUNDS

Once you've begun to cultivate a Fun Mindset, the next step in becoming someone who attracts fun is learning how to recognize and build playgrounds. Don't worry: I'm not (necessarily) talking about a place with monkey bars. I'm talking about structures, either metaphorical or literal, that foster fun by encouraging playfulness, connection, and flow and that signal to people that it's okay to let down their guard.

These structures are helpful because, as play scholar Miguel Sicart has pointed out, "play requires a certain element of design, material or contextual or both, so we know we can play, or be playful." Well-designed playgrounds do just this: they invite playfulness, they offer clear rules and guidelines for how to behave within their walls, and they repel anti-fun factors such as self-consciousness and spoilsports—thereby protecting the people inside.

Just as there are often opportunities for playfulness, connection, and flow floating in the air, there are playgrounds all around us, even if we haven't labeled them as such. As Johan Huizinga explains in his book *Homo Ludens,* "The arena, the card-table, the magic circle, the temple, the stage, the screen, the tennis court, the court of justice, etc., are all in form and function playgrounds, i.e., forbidden spots, isolated, hedged round, hallowed, within which special rules obtain. All are temporary worlds within the ordinary world, dedicated to the performance of an act apart."

As an example of an everyday playground, consider the party game pin-the-tail-on-the-donkey. In normal circumstances, it would be extremely weird to volunteer to have someone blindfold you, spin you in a circle, hand you a tack, and demand that you use it to pin a fake tail on a paper donkey as a group of people laugh at your attempts.

Arguably, this is *still* weird; I hate pin-the-tail-on-the-donkey. But when this occurs in the context of a birthday party, no one bats an eye. We all know the goal of the game (it's right there in the name), and we all know how to play it. If you agree to let someone blindfold you and hand you a donkey tail, you have also tacitly agreed to enter the "playground" created by the game. Once you're inside its walls, you have given yourself a permission slip to do things that would otherwise be ridiculous. This leaves you free to immerse yourself in the game's absurdity with no need to feel self-conscious or dumb about it (unless you're like me, in which case you probably shouldn't play the game to begin with—it's important to know the playgrounds that don't work for you).

Once you start thinking about the concept of playgrounds, you'll notice them in all sorts of different contexts. Games and sports are obvious examples. So are rituals and celebrations, such as wedding receptions where everyone knows that there will be dinner, drinks, and a toast from a drunk relative or two, followed by a night of dancing. What all playgrounds have in common is a structure, either explicit or implicit, that guides our behavior and gives us permission to behave in a playful way.

A twenty-seven-year-old member of the Fun Squad told me about a particularly creative playground that attracts fun for her: an elaborate yearly Pie Madness tournament that she organizes with friends. (Their Facebook group now has more than two hundred members.) As the official description of the tournament explains, "In March 2017, a wonderful tradition based off of pie was created. Some people made lasting friendships based on their favorite pie flavor and some people who had been friends for years now despise each other. Beautiful."

Modeled after the March Madness basketball tournament, Pie Madness pits different flavors of pie against one another. In 2019, for example, mocha cream upset banana cream in the first round to become the first-ever eighth seed to win a matchup, and maple bourbon brown butter peach "burst onto the scene and took the pie world by storm."

In 2020, an in-person competition was impossible due to the global pandemic, but this didn't stop the contest from happening. Instead, the organizers simply adapted the structure—and, in so doing, created a different type of playground for fun.

"The 'flavorful four' celebration took place over Zoom, and instead of baking and tasting the pies, official representatives of the four pies participated in a presidential-nominee-style debate," the Fun Squad member explained to me. This adversarial (but playful) structure resulted in people breaking into factions—e.g., the #CreamTeam and the antiestablishment "cruster movement"— which in turn gave them more playgrounds for fun.

As the Fun Squad member continued, "I had a ton of fun debating the representative of the Oreo-Nutella pie over their corporate connections and their failure to address how the palm oil in Nutella is directly contributing to massive deforestation and habitat loss. . . . Even though the debate got heated (like an oven) it was a lot of fun to escape the craziness going on this year through sheer absurdity."

If you take a step back, you can see that all the elements of a playground are present. The tournament provided the structure and scaffolding; everyone knew what was expected of them, and how the brackets would be run. Participation was entirely voluntary— playgrounds don't usually work if they're forced—and participants knew not to cross the line from playful ribbing to personal attacks. They also knew that if you wanted to be a part of Pie Madness, you were expected to go all in; no spoilsports were allowed.

There were also clear boundaries between the world of Pie Madness (in which giving an impassioned speech about Oreo-Nutella pie and its effects on global deforestation was welcomed and appreciated) and the external world (where such a speech would be, well, bizarre). The absurdity of the underlying premise—that pie is a subject worthy of serious debate—only added to the fun.

Pie Madness also illustrates one of the paradoxical things about playgrounds that professional bringer-together-of-people Priya Parker points out in her excellent book, *The Art of Gathering*— namely, that "rules can create an imaginary, transient world that is actually more playful than your everyday gathering." By providing structure, playgrounds create room for spontaneity. By establishing boundaries, they foster creativity. In short, well-constructed playgrounds create a sense of safety and belonging that allows us to let go and be playful. And whenever that happens, we're more likely to attract fun.

HOW TO BUILD A PLAYGROUND

As noted earlier, the easiest way to experience the fun-generating potential of playgrounds is to participate in playgrounds that already exist. You can do this by simply seeking out situations or activities that have some sort of built-in scaffolding that provides them with a structure that's attractive to fun. (Classes or group activities are often good places to start.) In fact, depending on your personality, this may be perfectly sufficient: you may be able to find plenty of playgrounds to spend time in without having to build your own.

But if you'd like to experiment with building a *new* playground by organizing a gathering or event, the first step is to recognize why so many of our events and gatherings do *not* end up feeling fun. In the words of Priya Parker, "Most of us remain on autopilot when we bring people together, following stale formulas, hoping that the chemistry of a good meeting, conference, or party will somehow take care of itself, that thrilling results will magically emerge from the usual staid inputs. It is almost always a vain hope."

Instead, she writes, "Gatherings crackle and flourish when real thought goes into them, when (often invisible) structure is baked into them, and when a host has the curiosity, willingness, and generosity of spirit to try." They succeed, in other words, when their host has built a playground.

Playful competitions and games are good ways to create playgrounds, but if you're not up for hosting your own Pie Madness tournament (or hate competitions or games), don't despair: there are lots of other ways to create them. As Miguel Sicart writes in *Play Matters,* "Almost any space can become a playground."

Indeed, there are as many different possible playgrounds as there are ways to have fun, and I suggest mining your list of fun magnets and fun factors for ideas that might be particularly appealing to *you*.

For example, Stuart Brown highly recommends any activity that involves movement (he's got a soft spot for Twister)—an obvious good choice for anyone whose fun factors include physicality. Music is also a fantastic playground. As Johan Huizinga wrote, "Making music bears at the outset all the formal characteristics of play proper: the activity begins and ends within strict limits of time and place, is repeatable . . . [and] transports audience and performers alike out of 'ordinary' life into a sphere of gladness and serenity, which makes even sad music a lofty pleasure."

For people whose fun factors include intellectual stimulation, conversations can be playgrounds; conversations have natural structures (i.e., beginnings, middles, and endings) and the ones that feel the most fun often involve bantering or riffing on a theme—the conversational equivalent of playing on monkey bars. They also have built-in rules, even though they're implicit. Most people know, for example, what topics are off-limits, and would be unlikely to begin a conversation by saying something like "Wow, looks like you've gained weight!" Also, conversations are a part of nearly every gathering, which means that if you can figure out how to bring a playful structure to these interactions—in other words, if you turn them into playgrounds—you'll be making them much more likely to attract fun.*

---

* I have a friend who is engaged in a running conversation/debate with her friends about whether they would choose to buy a Manhattan penthouse or brownstone if they were suddenly to become extremely wealthy. Mind you, they are *not* extremely wealthy, and they live in Mississippi, not Manhattan—which adds to the playground's absurdity and, therefore, the fun. (As she put it, "It's something that involves creativity and fantasy and lets you get into ridiculous exchanges, such as whether a doorman is more important than a garden.") Not into real estate? This type of playground works with any two subjects that inspire strong opinions and provide fodder for playful debate. For example, you could ask people whether they are on Team Lake or Team Beach.

If you're not sure where to start or what type of playground best suits you, don't obsess too much over the details. Just try *something*. For example, a friend of mine told me about a playground she and her husband had created (though they didn't call it a playground in their invitation, lest no one show up) in which they invited two other couples over for an extremely informal tasting of wines that all came from a particular region of the world. Each guest brought a different type of wine, as well as a dish typical of the area where the wine was made. Then they conducted a blind taste test in the form of a playful competition, to see if they could identify the wines. Importantly, no one who attended these dinners knew very much about wine. As my friend put it, "We were *bad*." But the point wasn't to become sommeliers; it was to attract fun. And it did.

As the Pie Madness tournament demonstrates, when a playground is successful, it is likely to turn into a tradition—and traditions themselves can spawn additional playgrounds that attract fun. For example, my husband once had a colleague who organized an annual croquet party for everyone at his law firm. People dressed in white and wore silly hats, and at the end of the day, awards were handed out. Everyone bought into the idea that for one morning a year, they were going to abandon their professional roles and play along with the game. Over time, people developed reputations—so and so always cheated, or so and so always wore that particular hat—which gave everyone things to banter and talk about leading up to and after the event (thereby creating opportunities for conversational playgrounds). There was playful trash talk. There were theme cocktails. What started as a one-off event turned into a tradition that people looked forward to all year.

Traditions can be particularly potent playgrounds because, in addition to attracting fun in the moment, they hold the potential to create a "play community" that, in the words of Johan Huizinga, "generally tends to become permanent even after the game is over." In the case of the croquet party, the playground created stronger bonds between people who already knew each other. In the case of my guitar class (which is a form of minitradition, since we meet each week), the playground created a community out of strangers.

"Of course, not every game of marbles or every bridge-party leads to the founding of a club," Huizinga acknowledges. "But the feeling of being 'apart together' in an exceptional situation, of sharing something important, of mutually withdrawing from the rest of the world and rejecting the usual norms, retains its magic beyond the duration of the individual game."

CHOOSING THE RIGHT SETTING AND PROPS

When you're trying to develop your ability to notice (and create) potential playgrounds for fun, it's also worth paying attention to your physical surroundings; as we touched on earlier, our environments can powerfully affect the way we behave and feel, to the point that particular settings can actually function as fun magnets. Consider, for example, how differently people act when they're in an opera house compared to an amusement park or a sports field, or how much better your mood is when you are in a garden full of flowers as opposed to an office cubicle.

In her book *Joyful: The Surprising Power of Ordinary Things to Create Extraordinary Happiness,* Ingrid Fetell Lee explores how the physical world influences our emotions and why certain objects spark a feeling of joy. In her research, she noticed that particular things popped up again and again when she asked people what brought them joy, to the point that she concluded that they weren't joyful for just a few people but rather for nearly *everyone.* For example: rainbows and beach balls. Fireworks, swimming pools, and treehouses. Hot-air balloons, googly eyes, and ice-cream sundaes with colorful sprinkles.

"We all have an inclination to seek joy in our surroundings, yet we have been taught to ignore it," she writes. "What might happen if we were to reawaken this instinct for finding joy?"

I had her words in mind as I read through the Fun Squad's memories of True Fun—and sure enough, I noticed that several settings were mentioned repeatedly, to the point that I began to wonder if perhaps there was something larger to be extrapolated. For example, many of people's memories of True Fun involved the elements, especially water. Countless people mentioned fun moments that involved pools, waterslides, rain, snow, and, yes, beaches. Fire also seemed to facilitate fun—give people a campfire to gather around, and chances are high that they'll slip into playful, connected flow. Wind and earth were less common, but they still did appear in activities that people identified as personal fun magnets, such as flying kites, paragliding, camping, and gardening.

I also noticed that, as Lee observed, certain *objects* tend to facilitate fun. This suggests that while in general, accumulating material possessions is not a pathway to fun, there is value in stocking your environment with particular *types* of possessions—namely, things that people can interact with and that encourage playfulness. By transforming an environment into a playground, these props can give adults permission—you could even say an excuse—to get back in touch with a more playful part of themselves.

Some fun-generating possessions can be expensive, such as nice cooking gear or a set of skis or a new bike. But money isn't necessary. For example, I have gotten a lot of fun out of a tool consisting of two pieces of rope strung between two handles that enables me to make giant bubbles, which my daughter loves to chase. Any type of musical instrument can be a great prop. The same is true for Hula-Hoops, lawn games, and sleds. And you should never underestimate the fun-generating potential of things that you can throw and catch.

I'm serious. For example, one summer my husband bought foam

balls and submergible hoops for my parents' pool. We found that when friends came over to use the pool, they gravitated toward these props and started making up spontaneous games with them. In fact, one of my most fun memories from that summer was an afternoon spent jumping off the diving board over and over again with a group of friends, trying to catch two balls at one time. When my husband finally did so—he was the first and only one of us to succeed—the rest of us threw our arms in the air and cheered, as if he were a figure skater who'd successfully landed a quadruple axel. It was a moment of pure delight.

PROTECTING YOUR PLAYGROUND

If you have put in the work to build (or find) a playground for fun, there is one more absolutely essential step that you must take—and that's to protect it from spoilsports.

Everyone has experienced a spoilsport or wet blanket (and most of us have probably felt like or been one ourselves). Spoilsports are people who refuse to fully enter the playground and play along with its rules. Sometimes, a person will deliberately destroy your playground—in which case, please do not invite that person to a party again. But often people don't *mean* to be spoilsports; they're just not particularly into the activity, or they have some sort of underlying insecurity that makes it difficult for them to let go of their own self-consciousness and enter the playground themselves.*

The problem is that, whether it's intentional or not, this can ruin the fun for everyone else.

---

* As a very shy child, I inadvertently ended up being this type of spoilsport many times myself, including one incident in second grade when I refused to wear a paper crown during a class party. I wasn't trying to ruin anyone's fun; I was just painfully self-conscious, and festive headwear has always made me feel dumb. If you ever find yourself witnessing a similar situation, I do *not* recommend that you do what my teacher did and loudly proclaim, while pointing at the embarrassed child, that "every party has its pooper." That will not help your party and certainly will not help the second-grader.

As Huizinga explains it, "the spoil-sport shatters the play-world itself. By withdrawing from the game he reveals the relativity and fragility of the play-world in which he had temporarily shut himself with others. He robs play of its *illusion*—a pregnant word which means literally 'in-play.'"

In other words, the problem with spoilsports is that, even if they're not *trying* to put a damper on things, their refusal to participate will make other people feel self-conscious about their own participation—and self-consciousness is like kryptonite to fun. Once people become self-conscious, fun is destroyed. Your carefully built playground will crumble.*

When you're organizing an event or building a playground, it's important to go out of your way to make your guests feel comfortable and welcome. As you may recall, the ability to make other people comfortable was a common characteristic of people whom Fun Squad members described as "fun." This means that if you're organizing a gathering, you need to be careful about whom you include.

In other words, not only should you make a point to invite people whom you consider fun magnets, but you should reflect on who might be a possible spoilsport (or just not a good fit for the particular group or activity), and consider *not* inviting them. We're trained to assume the attitude of "the more the merrier," lest we risk being rude or hurting people's feelings. But when you're building playgrounds to attract fun, in some cases, more is *not* merrier; protecting your gathering from spoilsports—or, really, anyone who you think won't add positive energy—is an act of generosity toward your guests.

---

* If this section makes you realize that you are often a spoilsport yourself, you may want to engage in some reflection on *why* you find it so hard to let go. (It probably has to do with a fear of looking foolish.) Maybe, like me, you'll just conclude that you want to avoid parties with donkey tails and hats, but it's also possible that this exploration will lead to other useful insights.

* * *

By emphasizing the importance of playgrounds, I'm not suggesting that you can only have or attract fun in highly structured situations, or that playgrounds need to be elaborate in order to be effective. There are plenty of times when fun does emerge organically or in situations that have just the slightest bit of scaffolding, and many people might instinctively rebel against the idea of "structured" fun.

But if you analyze your past experiences of fun, you may be surprised by how many of them *do* involve some sort of playground, even if it's subtle, and how often your fun magnets are activities that, upon reflection, are not as loosey-goosey and organic as they might at first have seemed. You don't need to obsess over this idea; trying too hard will scare away potential fun. But understanding the concept of playgrounds—and experimenting with ways to create or facilitate or participate in them—is another tool you can use to construct a life that is more attractive to fun.

It will also help you help other people. As bestselling author Michael Lewis points out, "People don't want to have a boring life, or even a boring conversation. They're just risk averse. If you create an environment where there's no reason to be afraid, all of a sudden things loosen up." In other words, if someone is standing awkwardly on the sidelines, whether metaphorically or literally, it's probably not because they don't *want* to have fun. They're just waiting for an invitation.

CHAPTER 9

REBEL

"The need of feeling responsible all the livelong day
has been preached long enough."
—William James, "The Gospel of Relaxation"

WHEN I LOOKED THROUGH THE ANECDOTES THAT FUN
Squad members had shared about their past experiences of True
Fun, I noticed that a lot of them involved people taking part in activities that were, if I may say so, mildly naughty. People described
doing things that broke the rules (even if barely). They committed
acts of playful deviance. They deliberately behaved in ways that
were unexpected, or unusual, or mildly taboo.

They engaged, in other words, in rebellion.

Here are a few examples:

I was about nine, and my best friend and I used to leave school
in the middle of the day to go eat lunch in the park and climb
trees. I think we each got a note from our parents giving us
permission to "go home" for lunch. But then we'd go to the park
and play. I can't remember if we were deceiving the school, our
parents, or both. It didn't last long, but it was magical.

A few girls I was friends with lived together in an apartment in Minneapolis. We were probably around the age of twenty-two, just hanging out one hot summer night, when one of the girls, apropos of nothing, grabbed a plastic laundry basket and started gathering random items. She urged us to grab stuff, too, that we would need for our adventure. I don't recall everything we brought, but I do recall that nothing made sense; for some reason I think one of the items was a colander. . . . We ended up at the definitely closed kiddie pool, hopping the fence with the laundry basket, splashing around in the water, making use of the laundry basket items in as absurd a way as possible. It was so random, so silly, so illegal (in the tamest way), and spontaneous.

For a few years in a row in my late thirties/early forties, I hosted friends for an International Ice Cream for Breakfast gathering in the middle of winter at a local park. Ice Cream for Breakfast Day is a thing (look it up!) and it comes at what can be a really gray and bleak time of year in Seattle. My family and I gathered at a large picnic shelter on the shore of the Salish Sea that had a giant stone fireplace and lots of tables. We made a big fire and provided a few different types of ice cream—some traditional, some fancy or "exotic"—and a variety of fun toppings, as well as hot cocoa, tea, coffee, donuts and bacon (which are both quite good with ice cream). The celebration was sort of incongruous given the typical weather, but that's part of what made it fun. Lots of people dropped in whom I might not otherwise see, and people enjoyed the low-key decadence (ice cream, with all sorts of crazy fixings, for breakfast!) and the sense of "we're in this together"-ness of standing around in the cold weather, bundled up while indulging their inner child with a treat not usually partaken in at that hour.

Some of my best holiday memories are from times I blew off the holiday and my husband and I did something together, like camping in Baja in a tent surrounded by a bunch of elderly retirees who must have thought we were destitute because we woke up the morning after Christmas to discover that they had left food and bottles of ungodly cheap champagne outside our tent, or the time we celebrated New Year's while freezing our butts off on the rim of the Grand Canyon.

I was about eleven, I think, and a girlfriend and I (she was a bit older) dressed up in weird clothes from the dress-up box—old hats and tiny sequined vests, wide pants. . . . We put our hair in braids and pinned them on top of our heads and painted our faces white like mimes. We walked around our neighborhood and my sister took pictures of us in unusual poses. I think we may have even gone downtown like that, walking barefoot, getting lots of stares. So, so, so *fun*! And I think it was fun because we were transgressing boundaries of what's nice for little girls to do.

As these examples make clear, I'm not talking about rebellion that would hurt you or anyone else or put you in jail—or even that gives you an adrenaline rush, if that's not your thing. I mean committing acts of harmless rebellion in which you deliberately step outside the bounds of your "normal" life and do something different just for the fun of it.

Before reading the Fun Squad's anecdotes, it had never occurred to me to think of rebellion in this way, even though I've engaged in (and enjoyed) a lot of examples of it myself. But if you look at the literature on play, you'll notice a lot of overlaps between the deviance that's associated with rebellion and the escape from "normal" life that's associated with play.

Indeed, not only can rebellion be a form of play, but play itself is often a form of rebellion. As play expert Stuart Brown writes, "Play, by its very nature . . . is about stepping outside of normal life and breaking some normal patterns. It is about bending rules of thought, action, and behavior." Similarly, Johan Huizinga wrote that "play is not 'ordinary' or 'real' life. It is rather a stepping out of 'real' life into a temporary sphere of activity with a disposition all its own."

This suggests that finding ways to deliberately *rebel*—and doing so regularly—might be a tool we can use to become more playful (and, for that matter, more connected and in flow) in our everyday lives. And the more we do that, the more likely we will be to have True Fun.

If you're a rule-following adult, the idea of being more rebellious might make you clench up. Deviating from the norm? Abandoning your duties? Doing things just for yourself? It just seems irresponsible and indulgent—maybe even a little bit scary.

But here's the thing: In the proper doses, irresponsibility and indulgence (and pushing ourselves out of our comfort zones) are *very good* for us. In fact, they're absolutely essential to our well-being. Having too many responsibilities makes us feel heavy and burdened. Always prioritizing other people's needs over our own leads to resentment and burnout. As journalist Jennifer Senior puts it in her book about modern parenting, *All Joy and No Fun,* "All of us crave liberation from our adult selves, at least from time to time."

She continues: "I'm not just talking about the selves with public roles to play and daily obligations to meet. (We can find relief from those people simply by going on vacation or, for that matter, by pouring ourselves a stiff drink.) I'm talking about the selves who live too much in their heads rather than their bodies; who are burdened with too much knowledge about how the world works rather than excited by how it could work or should; who are afraid of being judged and not being loved."

This is the exact type of liberation that playful acts of rebellion can provide.

The word "rebellion" itself means to wage war against something, which is a little violent for our purposes but highlights an important point: in order to rebel, you need to have something to rebel *against*. If you grew up in a nudist colony, for instance, skinny-dipping wouldn't feel rebellious because swimming naked would be the norm. (Swimming in a bathing suit—now *that* would be rebellious!) The feeling of deviance is what makes rebellion fun.

So, how do you fill your life with more everyday acts of playful rebellion? The first step is to identify what type of rebellion you enjoy. Just as each of us has different fun magnets and fun factors, each of us also has different preferred forms of rebellion; if something makes you *truly* feel uncomfortable or goes against your values or your fun factors—say, if it involves a loss of control, and you hate losing control—then it's not the right kind of rebellion for you. You should feel empowered, in other words, to rebel against other people's definitions of rebellion.

Here are some ideas for how you can playfully rebel.

You can rebel against habits and routines. Doing so will help you fight back against what Senior calls "the dirty secret about adulthood"—namely, "the sameness of it, the tireless adherence to routines and customs and norms." It will also bring you back to the present, help you temporarily escape your daily responsibilities, and encourage you to try new things—all of which will help you feel more alive. (This is what a Fun Squad member was getting at when they wrote that "[fun] makes me forget about the outside world and really focus on the present. If I've had a 'fun' day out, I haven't been thinking about other things in my life.")

After all, habits and routines make our lives easier, but they also make things boring. Consider your commute, or your weekly run to the grocery store: you've probably traced and retraced the same route so many times that you no longer have to think about it. That's convenient and efficient, but when you're on autopilot, you're not really present. You could walk out your front door and end up at your desk or in the produce aisle with absolutely no memory of how you got there. (This is even more true if you've spent the trip there staring at your phone.)

Not only will navigating your life on autopilot leave you with fewer memories, it will actually make time seem to speed up. William James described this in his classic 1890 text, *The Principles of Psychology*, when he wrote that "as each passing year converts some of [our] experience[s] into automatic routine which we hardly note at all, the days and weeks smooth themselves out . . . and the years grow hollow and collapse." (Way to twist the knife, William.)

Psychologists refer to this phenomenon as "dissociation," and screens are a particularly powerful trigger for it. According to tech addiction expert David Greenfield, that's what's happening when you look up from your phone and have no idea where the last forty-five minutes of your life have gone. As James alluded to, when you fill your schedule with routines, habits, and passive consumption, your memories will arrange themselves in a smooth chain of indistinguishable links, with very little to help you tell where one day ended and another began.

The best way to fight back and to slow down time is to focus on creating more opportunities for what scientists call "pattern separation"—in other words, finding ways to break up monotony. A life filled with new experiences and small rebellions can do just this. Instead of a long, smooth chain, you'll end up with the equivalent of a necklace made of colorful beads, each of which holds the potential to become, in the words of Johan Huizinga, "a treasure to be retained by the memory." The more distinct these beads are (and the more beads you collect each day), the more time will seem to slow down.

As an example, think of your four years of high school. Chances are that you have distinct memories from freshman, sophomore, junior, and senior years, and that, for better or for worse, those four years seemed to pass relatively slowly. Compare that to how many distinct memories you have from the last four years of your adult life.

Interestingly, rebellion's ability to create pattern separation has a lot to do with dopamine, the same brain chemical that is so problematic in the context of drugs and compulsive technology use but that also plays a major role in our perception of fun. The fact that novelty is a dopamine trigger—and that rebellion often involves trying new things—means that rebellion itself is a dopamine trigger.

As you know, dopamine is a tool our brains use to form memories and record things that are worth doing again—in other words, it's a salience indicator. Dopamine focuses our attention on the present moment, helping us to tune in to sensory details and experience things more intensely. This means that every time we rebel against our routines and habits and have an even slightly positive experience, not only will we be creating a vivid memory to look back on but the ensuing dopamine jolt will reinforce the idea that trying new things is worth repeating in general. This can help boost your confidence and motivate you to try new things in the future. In other words, it's a biochemical feedback loop that, unlike other feedback loops such as those associated with anxiety and rumination, actually makes us feel good.

I'd be remiss not to point out that too much rebellion-fueled dopamine may encourage you to engage in forms of rebellions that are actually dangerous or destructive, like reckless driving or doing harmful drugs, or shirking your responsibilities to the point that it becomes a problem. More (or more intense) is not necessarily better. But if you're intentional about it, you can use rebellion against routine to harness dopamine's *positive* effects and bring more novelty and fun into your life.

So, *how* do you rebel against habit and routine? The first step is to commit to embracing the Fun Mindset we discussed in the last chapter. Next, scan your life and take note of the things you do regularly out of habit—in other words, identify the areas of your life in which you're on autopilot. Then you ask yourself a few times each day how you could mix things up.

These changes do not have to be dramatic; you can come up with ideas just by adopting a more curious attitude toward your own life. Start by getting in the habit of asking *Why?*, *What if?*, *and What's the worst that could happen?* For example: Why do you do the same type of exercise every day? What if you tried something new? What's the worst that could happen? You may conclude that it's because you genuinely love your routine. But in some cases, the answer might simply be that you've never considered switching things up, or that you've gone on autopilot without even noticing, or that you've been holding back because you're scared.

In addition to deliberately brainstorming ways to shake up your routines, you can also rebel against habits simply by being flexible and saying "yes"—being the type of person often referred to as laid-back or easygoing (two words that are not often associated with me). For example, this past summer my husband, who played a lot of badminton as a child, bought a set of badminton birdies with tiny rainbow LED lights in them that light up when you hit them. One evening, he brought them out and invited me to play badminton with him at dusk. Even though I am not good at racquet sports, and even though this was not what I had *planned* for the evening (my plans had probably involved reading an academic book about play or looking through my tree-bark identification guide), I decided to say yes. We then spent a half hour laughing and running around barefoot in the grass as we swatted the birdie in the dark.* And you know what? It was fun!

Habits and routines are a great place to start, but they're hardly the only things you can rebel against.

For example, you can rebel against **convention**. As my grandmother used to say to me, "If everyone else jumped off the Brooklyn Bridge, would you?" (To which I say: Why does everyone use the Brooklyn Bridge for this particular rhetorical question? She lived in Queens.) Just because everyone else likes talking about politics, or following sports, or watching a particular television show, or sharing photos of their children on social media, why do you have to? Being a contrarian is a form of rebellion—and getting in the habit of only following trends that you *want* to follow will leave you with more space in your life for fun.

You can also use a rebellion against convention to surprise and delight people—and thus, add to *their* fun (as well as your own). I stumbled across my favorite personal example of this on a very cold January day in the early 2000s, as I was waiting for the subway in Manhattan. As the train pulled in, I caught sight of a pair of bare legs, and realized, to my surprise and dismay, that the person standing next to me wasn't wearing pants.

My inner New Yorker jumped into action (her motto is "avoid weirdos") and I made a split-second decision to get into a different car. But just as the doors slid shut—and before I could even congratulate myself on my quick thinking—I noticed that several of the

* Not a euphemism.

people already on the train weren't wearing pants, either. Boxers and underpants, yes. (I even recall a thong.) Pants, no.

As I looked around me in confusion, I heard snippets of conversations taking place between some of these pantless people. "I just forgot them," one person said with a shrug.

Said another: "I have a routine. I brush my teeth, and then I put on my pants. I guess this morning, I didn't brush my teeth."

Then, before I could figure out what to do next, someone began walking down the aisle with a large bag stuffed with clothing. "Pants! Pants!" this person was yelling. "One dollar for pants!"

"Oh, thank God," said one pantless rider to another as he waved a bill in the air. "I didn't know what I was going to do."

I later figured out that this was the work of a group called Improv Everywhere, which organizes a No Pants Subway Ride every January (this is one of the very few instances in life in which I actually encourage you to do an internet image search). The event was so popular that it spread to other cities around the world; in 2013, the No Pants Subway Ride had 4,000 participants *in New York alone.* (Can you imagine?!)

The No Pants Subway Ride was so surprising and absurd to encounter that I still remember its details more than fifteen years later; just witnessing the spectacle produced a jolt of unexpected fun. I've since learned that this was precisely the point. In a segment about Improv Everywhere that aired on the radio show *This American Life,* the group's founder, Charlie Todd, explains that his goal in creating "missions," as he calls them, is to "make people happy." And as the reporter who narrates the segment explains, in Todd's view "happy means fun, and fun means making strange things happen in boring locations."

In other words, it means staging playful rebellions.

* * *

You can rebel against **traditions**.

Traditions can be a powerful tool for building connections. They can bring people closer, and when they're playful, they can create scaffolds and playgrounds for fun. But traditions can also be stifling—in fact, the word "tradition" is derived from words meaning "surrender."

The best traditions are the ones that you have consciously chosen or created. Some might be natural fits from the start. But creating traditions that are meaningful to *you* might require you to rebel. For instance, my friend Marie does not celebrate Thanksgiving on Thanksgiving Day itself. She realized that the traditional schedule—rushing home on Wednesday to prepare, waking up early on Thursday and cooking like crazy to get Thanksgiving dinner on the table, was stressful to everyone involved. So she and her family decided to rebel.

They started by identifying their goal: to have a relaxed, enjoyable holiday. They then identified the problem: getting an elaborate feast on the table in less than twenty-four hours was neither relaxing nor enjoyable. And then she and her family came up with an idea: *What if they celebrated Thanksgiving on Friday instead?*

So now that's exactly what they do. On Wednesday night, instead of rushing, she and her husband have a festive cocktail and do a tiny bit of Thanksgiving prep, such as baking a pie with their kids. On Thursday, they wake up when they want to and spend the day getting ready for Thanksgiving together at a relaxed, leisurely pace. Instead of turkey, that night they order dim sum. Then on Friday, they invite friends and family over to share a traditional Thanksgiving feast.

There are many rebellious elements at play in this new tradition. The most obvious is the choice to celebrate Thanksgiving on a different day from everyone else. Not only does this lead to a more relaxed celebration; the act of rebelling as a group is an effective way to make the members of the group closer, and therefore, helps them achieve the elusive goal of family bonding. It creates a fundamental characteristic of play: the sense, in the words of Johan Huizinga, that "this is for *us,* not for the 'others.'"

Another element of rebellion that adds to their fun is the decision to replace Thursday's traditional Thanksgiving meal with a different type of *special* food—dim sum. This, in effect, creates a *new* tradition, one that further bonds them as a family, because it's another mini-rebellion. The specialness and specificity are very important: consider how much less fun it would feel if they just ate random leftovers on Thursday.

Lastly, the fact that they *do* eat a traditional Thanksgiving meal, but on a day that is not Thanksgiving, is another form of playful rebellion, and this highlights an interesting fact: it's fun to do things outside of their normal context. It's an example of what play scholar Miguel Sicart was talking about when he wrote that "to be playful is to appropriate a context that is not created or intended for play." This is why kids love pajama days, why breakfast for dinner is a thing, why the Fun Squad member's winter ice-cream party became a treasured tradition, and why it can be fun to celebrate Christmas in July.

You can rebel against **beliefs**—even your own. To do so, ask yourself *why* you believe something, and then question the validity of that belief. Doing so might shift your mindset in a way that sparks ideas or opens up opportunities.

For example, one member of the Fun Squad told me that she had automatically assumed that intellectual stimulation was a fun factor for her—but when she questioned that assumption, when she rebelled against automatically accepting her own beliefs, it led to a realization. She explained that she had packed her schedule with hobbies and activities, such as attending lectures, that she'd categorized as "fun" but that, upon further reflection, would actually be better described as growth opportunities. They were things she valued, but they were more about enrichment than joy. As she put it, "For the past few years I've loaded my social calendar with things like this, and I had been feeling *very* burned out. I was frustrated because I thought I was doing things I enjoy. I've never been able to figure out why until just now."

In her case, rebelling against her own beliefs allowed her to obtain a much more precise understanding of why she was engaging in particular leisure activities, and what she wanted to get out of them. This in turn helped her to become much more intentional about what she put on her calendar, and to get more out of her leisure time.

You can rebel against **formality**. Sure, it can serve a purpose—and sure, there are times when it's required—but formality is rigid and can be extremely boring. It also creates distance. We often shield ourselves with formality in order to avoid feeling vulnerable. But our vulnerability makes us human, and our humanity is what brings us closer to other people and helps us have more fun.

Rebelling against formality means becoming more comfortable with who you actually are (and with sharing your authentic self with other people). In a way, this also represents a rebellion against **perfectionism**—which can be extremely freeing, not to mention good for our mental health. You can start by scanning your life for situations in which you present an idealized version of yourself. How often do you answer honestly when someone asks you how you're doing? How often do you post photographs to social media that reflect how you are actually feeling in that particular moment, as opposed to presenting a curated image of how you would like to be perceived? I'm not saying you should go through life without a filter (or that you should spend lots of time posting *anything* to social media). But rebelling against perfectionism and formality is a great way to help yourself become more comfortable in your own skin—which in turn is likely to draw people closer to you, attract fun, and help you feel more connected and confident.

It can also help you deal with anxiety and cope with stressful situations. For example, at some point during the SARS-CoV-2 pandemic, I was asked to give a virtual presentation for a corporate retreat. I was told that there would be about a thousand people on the call, stationed all over the world, but I wouldn't be able to see them on my computer screen—there would be no visual or auditory feedback from the audience. What's more, thanks to a quirk of the platform they used for the conference, I wouldn't even be able to see *myself*. I'd be speaking into the green light of my computer's camera, totally alone.

Adding to the challenge, my husband and I had spent much of the pandemic holing up at my parents' house so that they could help us care for our daughter as I worked on this book. I was sleeping in my childhood bedroom, which was making me feel more like a teenager than a fully grown, (somewhat) mature adult. The house in general was an environment that did not lend itself well to professional backdrops, and there was a risk that my father's sneezes, which have been known to silence entire restaurants, or my parents' dog, who is psychotic, could interrupt my presentation at any time.

Recognizing all this, I decided that instead of cloaking myself in formality and pretending things were normal and that I was a Professional Adult (which I hardly ever feel like anyway), I would lean in to the fact that everything about my life in that moment was a bit absurd. I also decided that I would do my best to focus less on making the presentation perfect and more on making it feel fun—both for my audience and for myself.

After introducing my professional self, I showed a slide that revealed who I *actually* was in that particular moment in time, using a bullet-pointed list:

- Forty-one years old
- Living in parents' house
- Running home school with husband
- No haircut in seven months
- Trying to manufacture video-ready background in a room filled with assorted toys and small plastic dogs
- Highly likely to be wearing pajama pants

There were other elements in my presentation that rebelled against formality and perfectionism, to say the least. At one point, I announced to my faceless audience that while I had successfully managed to change out of pajamas before the talk, I was wearing spandex pants under my dress in hopes that I could sneak in a workout before dinner. In another moment I became flustered from trying to keep track of where I was in my printed notes, and so I decided to cast them aside and wing it. (The recording that the organizers sent me afterward shows papers fluttering to the ground as I announce, "Look at me! I'm *throwing away my notes!*")

While I can't guarantee that everyone in attendance appreciated my approach—or that discarding my notes was the *best* idea I've ever had—it certainly made it more interesting for *me*. Rebelling against perfectionism and formality, and showing who I truly was in that moment, made me feel more comfortable in my own skin and loosened me up in a way that I like to think made my presentation more engaging. Or at the very least, much less predictable.

You can rebel against **adulthood**. This is a particularly effective form of rebellion if you're a parent, given how much of modern parenting involves standing on the sidelines and watching your *children* play.

One way to do so is to join your children in play—to run through a fountain with them, or hop on a swing, or sign up for a class that you can do together. You also can make a point to seek out experiences that make you feel like a kid (in a good way). For example, my friend Kristy and her husband recently celebrated their wedding anniversary by going away for a weekend without their children to a lakeside resort that offered the opportunity to be pulled behind a motorboat on a tube. This, Kristy told me, was her favorite part of the trip. She sent me a photo of her floating in said tube at the end of a ride, and I can confirm: she looked exuberant, so much so that when I saw the photograph, I wanted nothing more than to be plopped into some sort of flotation device and dragged around a lake myself.

You can also rebel against adulthood by doing (harmless) things that would delight your teenage self. One way to start is to notice habits, such as listening to the news or educational podcasts while you're in the car, that you engage in because you're a responsible adult, and at some point in your life you decided that responsible adults do those things.

But who made that rule? And even if you *do* enjoy listening to the news and podcasts, what would it be like instead if you spent your next car trip listening to music that you loved when you were sixteen, maybe a little louder than you should? (Maybe even while singing along?)

You can rebel against **expectations**, by doing something that contradicts your professional persona or that seems out of character—in other words, by taking to heart Walt Whitman's famous line in "Song of Myself":

Do I contradict myself?
Very well then I contradict myself.
(I am large, I contain multitudes.)

A friend told me about an acquaintance of hers, a linguist, who is an avid consumer of romance novels. "She goes through three or four a week," my friend wrote. "Total rebellion against what a female professor is supposed to read."*

You can also rebel against your expectations *for yourself.* For instance, if you are someone who lives mostly in their brain (i.e., if you're like me), you can rebel by saying "no" to opportunities for yet more intellectual engagement, and instead do things that get you out of your head and back in touch with your senses. For example, in the social dancing circles I'm involved in, you don't need to identify as male to be the leader. As someone who enjoys mastery, I used to think this meant I *should* learn to lead the Lindy Hop, just to acquire another skill.

But I've since realized that I don't actually *want* to do so. I am a leader in nearly every other area of my life; one of my favorite things about dancing is how it gets me out of my own head and into my body. I *love* the feeling of responding to another person's movements in real time, without conscious thought. Not learning to lead is a form of rebellion against my own expectations for myself—and it makes dancing much more fun.

Speaking of perceived "shoulds," you can rebel against your **responsibilities and obligations** and make a point of regularly doing things that are totally selfish.

If you are like many people, that last sentence may have made you recoil. We've been conditioned, after all, to think of selfishness as a vice, not a virtue. But why? I think there is an interesting conversation to be had about why the idea of doing something purely for yourself feels like rebellion, instead of something that you deserve

---

* This same friend, who is a journalist, also told me about one of her own minirebellions: a secret game she used to have with a newspaper colleague in which they tried to get the word "tumbleweed" into as many stories as possible.

and that is important for your mental health. After all, as we've noted, you cannot take care of other people if you do not take care of yourself first.

And besides, I'm not talking about quitting your job and running away from your family. (There are forms of selfishness that *are* destructive.) I'm simply talking about using some of your hard-earned free time to do something totally for *you.*

Some of these things might cost money or require planning or logistics, such as signing up for a class in something you've always wanted to try or going on a weekend trip with some of your best friends. Others might be spontaneous, free, and small, such as eating cookies for dinner (an example shared with me by someone in the Fun Squad) or spending an afternoon playing hooky without your phone. (The fact that we are expected to constantly be on call makes *any* activity in which you leave your phone behind—even a walk!—feel rebellious.) At first it may be hard to convince yourself to invest time, effort, and money in things that seem self-indulgent, but once you've tried it, you may be shocked by the long-lasting positive effects.

I feel this way every time I get together with friends to play music. For a few blissful hours, I am not thinking about work or parenting or any of my adult responsibilities. Instead, I am doing something purely for my own enjoyment, something that usually leads to the elusive state of playful, connected flow—and that always gives me a feeling of escape. The sense of lightness and release is intoxicating; it buoys my spirits throughout the week. Far from making me a slacker, having this regular opportunity for fun makes me a *better* wife, mother, worker, and friend—and a much more enjoyable person to be around.

You may also want to ask yourself how you could create a rebellious experience *for someone else.* Could you cut work with a friend or partner and play hooky for an afternoon? If you're a parent, is there a way to create an opportunity for playful, harmless deviance for you and your kids? While describing their memories of experiences that were truly fun, a *lot* of participants in the Fun Squad mentioned special outings with their parents that made them feel like they were breaking the rules by doing something out of the ordinary together. The stepping-out-of-normal-life, the *rebellion,* made these memories precious.

These "rule-breaking" experiences do not have to be dramatic, or even involve the breaking of any official rules at all; one person mentioned a favorite fun memory that simply involved going out into the rain with their grandfather, without umbrellas, and deliberately allowing themselves to get soaked. Anything you do with a child that makes you not seem like an adult is likely to delight them. And seeing their delight can help you realize how wonderful, rejuvenating, and important this type of rebellion can be—for children *and* adults.

The more you approach life from this perspective, the more opportunities for playful rebellion you are likely to find. So ask yourself: Where in your life can you rebel? Is there a habit or belief you could question? A routine or convention from which to deviate? A tradition you could create or reinvent? A way to embrace informality, to abandon perfectionism, to get out of your head, to reconnect with your childhood self, to defy expectations, or to escape your responsibilities, even if just for a little bit?

Experimenting with these types of rebellion can help us express our independence and autonomy, which is something that, ironic though it may seem, many adults do not often get a chance to do (especially the "responsible" ones). It can also help us internalize the fact that being conscientious people, citizens, and/or parents does not have to mean making ourselves miserable.

In short, it's like Walt Whitman said: we contain multitudes. We can be silly *and* serious, responsible *and* rebellious, mature *and* childlike—and in fact, the more we harness the positive powers of rebellion and allow our playful streaks to shine, the more energy we'll have for everything else.

CHAPTER 10
KEEP AT IT

"We do not quit playing because we grow old.
We grow old because we quit playing."
—Oliver Wendell Holmes

ORIENTING YOUR LIFE AROUND FUN IS LIKE EXERCISE: it's not something you can do once and then forget about. It reminds me of something Alex Soojung-Kim Pang says in his book *Rest*. He argues that rest, which he broadly defines as things that restore our energy or ignite new creativity, is something that we must actively work to claim.

"Rest is not something that the world gives us," writes Soojung-Kim Pang. "It's never been a gift. It's never been something you do when you've finished everything else. If you want rest, you have to take it. You have to resist the lure of busyness, make time for rest, take it seriously, and protect it from a world that is intent on stealing it."

The same is true of fun.

Throughout this book, we've worked on many ways to manufacture more opportunities for True Fun, from identifying our fun magnets and fun factors to creating space, pursuing passions, finding ways to attract fun, and exploring rebellion. We're now at the final step of SPARK, "Keep at it," and the basic goal is simple: we need to continue to prioritize fun so that the pursuit of fun doesn't become lost in the sea of all the other things competing for our attention and time—and we need to commit to doing so not just for the next day or the next week but for the rest of our lives.

Here are some ideas for how to do this.

FIND YOUR FUN SQUAD(S)

The most basic definition of a fun squad is simply people with whom you tend to have fun—in other words, they're your human fun magnets. You probably have several fun squads in your life already—a particular group of friends, for instance, or people with whom you share a passion, or coworkers whose company you especially enjoy. The more time you can spend with your preexisting fun squads, the more fun you're likely to have, and the greater sense of community you're likely to feel.

If you're looking for additional ones, you can try inserting yourself into preexisting fun squads by, for example, joining an interest group or a team. You can also create a fun squad specifically for the purpose of finding *new* ways to have fun—sort of a *meta*-fun squad. You can think of this type of fun squad as being like a fantasy football team, except instead of star athletes, you're stocking it with fun-loving seekers of playfulness, connection, flow.

There are no rules about who can or should be in this sort of fun squad, though you should obviously focus on people whom you consider fun, and who you think would be interested in exploring ways to have more of it. (Spoilsports are *not* allowed.) You should not feel *obliged* to invite anyone to participate no matter how close you are to them, nor do you need to know all the people you invite particularly well. (With that said, you do want to put thought into the potential group dynamics to make sure that the energy feels right.)

Your new squad can be as small as just you and a friend, or as big as roughly six people; according to Priya Parker, author of *The Art of Gathering*, this size is particularly conducive to intimacy and high levels of sharing, which can be good ways to attract fun. I also recommend asking people to make a commitment of six months. That's long enough for real change to happen but short enough not to feel overwhelming. (The group can always continue past six months if it's going well.) You can think of it—and describe it to possible participants—as an opportunity to spend six months having more fun. Who would want to say no to that?

In terms of purpose and structure, there are two main types of fun squads: the ones that meet to *talk* about fun and support each other as they reorient their lives around its pursuit, and ones that actually *do* stuff together.

That sentence may have made it seem like I'm hating on fun squads based on talking instead of doing. I'm not at all. If your squad members live far away from each other, or if you're organizing a fun squad out of people who don't know each other (or whom you think would enjoy talking and brainstorming together more than they would doing things together), then this is an excellent option. For this kind of group—which actually works really well with just two people and can be a great way to maintain closeness with a friend who lives far away—I suggest starting by laying out the squad's purpose, learning about why each person is participating and what they hope to get out of the experience, and discussing the definition of fun, along with anything that jumped out at you from this book. Then go through the exercises in "The Fun Audit" and "Find Your Fun" (including keeping a fun times journal), so that everyone is able to identify their fun magnets and fun factors. Devote part of each gathering or call to deciding what each person will try between meetings, so that everyone leaves with a plan.

Figure out a regular time for your group to meet (whether in person or over video)—say, once every month—and use the time to

share stories, come up with new ideas, and hold each other account-
able. I recommend creating some ground rules to keep things focused on fun, such as making certain topics of conversation—work?
politics?—off-limits. (Remember: you're trying to escape daily life.)
You also may want to rotate responsibilities in terms of who is offi-
cially in charge of leading the conversation when you meet.

A fun squad that *does* stuff together is exactly what it sounds like,
and can be a good choice for people who live relatively close to one
another and who have similar fun factors. I recommend starting
these squads in the same way I described above (getting to know
each other, setting intentions, defining fun, identifying fun magnets
and factors, etc.), and establishing a schedule and ground rules.
Next, brainstorm activities that you'd like to try or do *together* (and
that are feasible). To establish a feeling of inclusion and gather a
wide range of ideas, you may want to have each squad member
come up with several ideas and then choose one idea from each person. Then . . . go do one! You may want to consider alternating your
meetings between trying something new as a group and simply getting together to hang out and talk, but feel free to experiment with
formats and rhythms that fit your squad.

When you first recruit your fun squad—or propose doing something different with a group you're already a part of—don't be surprised if you encounter some resistance. Most people are not as
enlightened as you now are and don't fully recognize the importance
of having fun (or understand the difference between True Fun and
Fake Fun). They may wonder why you are rambling on about fun to
begin with and react to your ideas as if you are crazy. For example, a
friend of mine regularly goes on trips with three friends from high
school. Feeling inspired by the idea of creating opportunities for
True Fun, she proposed that instead of just getting together to hang
out, they find a way to *do* something together (she suggested surfing
or signing up for a workshop in improv comedy—both of which

could be hilarious but, let's be honest, are aggressive opening gambits). "It went over like a lead balloon," she told me.

If this happens to you, don't be deterred. But do be prepared to do some convincing or to start with some easier asks. Or, as an alternative, *just make it happen*. I have a friend who hosted a workshop for teachers that included a session where a woman showed up with Hula-Hoops and scarves and gave a hands-on (and mandatory) lesson on how to use them. Some people were skeptical at first, but it ended up being one of the highlights of the event.

PRIORITIZE YOUR FUN MAGNETS

You went through a lot of effort to figure out activities, settings, and people that are conducive to fun for you, so don't let that hard work go to waste. Your leisure time is limited. Prioritize your fun magnets.

PLAN FOR FUN

I know, I know. Planning for fun sounds extremely unfun—and perhaps ineffective, given how elusive fun can be, and how often fun seems to involve an element of spontaneity. But it's actually essential.

First of all, if you don't plan and protect opportunities to engage in your fun magnets, passions, interests, and hobbies, the rest of life will rush in and fill your time. Second, one of the main goals of "keeping at it" is to always have something on your calendar that you're looking forward to, definitely every week and ideally every day. Not only are these future experiences likely to be enjoyable when they arrive but looking forward to things is a form of what psychologists call "anticipatory savoring," which is pleasurable, boosts resilience, and lowers stress. (Having something to look forward to can also make you more productive in the moment. I, at least, find it easier to finish a task if I know there's a reward on the other side.)

So, how do you make sure that you always have something to look forward to? You put opportunities for fun on your calendar. And how do you do *that*? You use your list of fun magnets, hobbies, interests, and passions to create microdoses and booster shots of possible fun.

MICRODOSES

Microdoses are small, everyday pleasurable experiences that result in a feeling of playfulness, connection, and/or flow. Maybe they cross the line to full-on fun, maybe they don't, but they're enjoyable, they're energizing, and they leave you rejuvenated when you're done. I recommend aiming to microdose on a fun-related activity at least several times a week, if not once a day.

It's possible to microdose spontaneously. I think of this as a *carpe diem* kind of fun. For instance, you could make a spur-of-the-moment decision to take a drive on a summer afternoon with the windows down and the music turned up, or to eat dinner on a picnic blanket instead of at the table. (Playful rebellion!) This is yet another reason to focus on reducing distractions: the more present you are in the moment, the more opportunities to microdose on playfulness, connection, or flow will reveal themselves—and the more likely you'll be to say yes to them.

To *plan* for microdoses, I recommend looking at your lists of fun magnets and seeing if you can regularly incorporate a few of them into your schedule. My guitar gatherings are a good example of this: they're fun magnets that I participate in every week. I also suggest that you set aside a time each day (even if it's just ten minutes before bed) to indulge in a hobby, interest, or passion. These are all things that you know you enjoy—which makes them worthwhile uses of your time regardless of whether or not they blossom into playful, connected flow—and are particularly practical and easy to schedule because you can do them on your own, in relatively small pockets of time.

Another way to microdose on fun is to deliberately seek out (and keep room on your schedule for) moments of playful rebellion, like making a weekly date for yourself where you sneak away from your desk in the middle of the day to go for a walk or meet a friend for lunch. Novelty can also help: some people microdose on fun by making a commitment to themselves to regularly try something new. And please: keep up your practice of noticing delights.

You can also work microdoses into your life by scheduling opportunities for connection. Can you set up a standing weekly phone call or coffee date with a friend? Are there any rituals you can create with your family, like going for a hike every Saturday morning? This might feel forced at first, but it will likely pay dividends; as Caroline Adams Miller explains in her book *Creating Your Best Life*, "happy families have regular playtimes."

BOOSTER SHOTS

Booster shots are larger fun-oriented experiences, such as vacations or annual gatherings or events, that take more effort to schedule and plan for but that fill up your fun tank and replenish your energy for a longer period of time. (One of my own booster shots is the swing-dancing camp that I've mentioned to you before. The experience is so joyful, so *fun*, that I look forward to those five days all year.) Ideally, I recommend aiming to have at least one booster shot for every season, so that you always have one on the horizon.

You can start by identifying booster shots that you already have in your life. Does taking vacations to new places fill your fun tank? Do you regularly attend a gathering that brings you joy? Do you have any traditions that reliably fill you up, such as a yearly reunion with a particular group of friends? Make these things priorities. Next, mine your list of fun magnets and fun factors to see if you can come up with some ideas for a few more.

INVEST IN FUN

The pursuit of fun does require an investment in time and attention, but there's no rule that says that fun has to be expensive, or even cost any money at all. Consider the Pie Madness tournament: It takes creativity, but the financial cost is limited to the price of the ingredients for a pie. Fun, whether in the form of a microdose or a booster shot, does not necessarily require lots of cash.

With that said, sometimes creating opportunities for fun—especially booster shots—does cost money. Vacations aren't free; hosting gatherings often incurs expenses; and in the case of the dance camp, my husband and I have to pay for a flight and a car rental, as well as for the camp itself. In these cases, saying yes to fun may require saying no to something else, such as a new television or a round of retail therapy. But doing so is worth it, because spending money on experiences—especially those that involve other people—has been repeatedly proven to be a *much* more effective way to boost your sense of well-being and happiness than spending the same amount of money on objects or possessions.

Leaf Van Boven, a neuroscientist and psychologist at the University of Colorado Boulder who has studied the effects that different types of spending have on happiness, hypothesizes that this might be in part due to the fact that, whereas possessions tend to encourage people to compare themselves to one another (e.g., who has the nicest car or television) and thus divide them, experiences bring people *together*. They're "a better source of entertaining conversation than material possessions," according to Van Boven, and they lead to more enduring pleasure and satisfaction.

Speaking of investments, if you ever have the choice between spending money on an object and spending money on an opportunity to connect with other people, choose the latter. Similarly, if you have limited leisure time, prioritize anything that gives you time with friends.

USE TECHNOLOGY FOR GOOD

As I alluded to earlier, there are many ways in which technology can actually *help* foster playfulness, connection, and flow and support your interests, hobbies, and passions. By adding to my knowledge of the natural world, my plant identification app has given me a different way to enjoy my time outside; my guitar tab app helps me learn new songs. While videogames are not fun magnets for *me*, I know many people who regularly have True Fun—lots of it!—playing multiplayer games with other people. The trick is to make sure that you're using technology in a way that facilitates playfulness, connection, or flow—and that makes you feel engaged, rather than empty.

One idea that might sound obvious but that I, at least, often forget about is to use your phone . . . *as a phone*.

Before I "broke up" with my phone, I only spoke to a small circle of people on it, and the number of people I would call without some sort of scheduling text message exchange first was even smaller. But as I cut back on texting and emailing, I began to call friends in the same way as members of my parents' generation do: with no warning or discernable purpose, and occasionally on speakerphone. I'd go out for a walk and just start dialing numbers until someone picked up.

Since I am not actually part of my parents' generation, this felt very awkward. Casually calling someone without advance warning felt radical, even rude. And also, not many people answered. Whereas in the olden days one could assume that if a friend didn't pick up, they were sitting down to dinner or running an errand out of the house, now everyone has their phone with them at all times. If they didn't pick up, it wasn't because my call had been missed; it was because I'd been silenced.

It was hard not to take this personally at first, but then I realized that while sometimes my friends truly did not want to talk, they were often suffering from the same mild anxiety that I myself felt when my phone rang. I was so out of practice on the telephone that I avoided it. But the more I did it, the more people picked up—and the more friends began to pick up their own phones to call *me*. Eventually, phone calls began to feel more casual—the equivalent of running into a friend on the street and spontaneously grabbing coffee, as opposed to making plans for a dinner party months in advance. I like both, but the latter requires advanced planning and involves some degree of formality, whereas the former feels spontaneous and relaxed—the type of interaction I had all the time in my college years and young adult life but that had faded as my friends and I had gotten older.

Even as I got better at this new (or rather, forgotten) skill, the "phone call," I was continually amazed that I could take this metal rectangle out of my pocket, poke its screen a few times with my finger, and then hear the actual voice of a friend. I felt like I'd discovered something new, as if I were a scientist who'd just had a *eureka* moment: did you know that this slot machine in your pocket, this box of infinite distraction, can actually *call* people? Did you know that it can enable you to have a conversation with a friend while you are going for a walk? And that it works even if they are *thousands of miles away*? How come everyone isn't taking advantage of this all the time? Why the heck is everyone texting?

COMMIT TO SCREEN-LIFE BALANCE

While technology can help foster fun, part of "keeping at it" also requires you to maintain your boundaries with your screens. This is already challenging and is likely to become more so in the future, as the internet becomes faster and more pervasive and we transition from devices we hold in our hands to technology that is implanted in our bodies.

One of my favorite ways to avoid falling prey to the worst parts of technology is to regularly take breaks from my devices. To do so, my husband and I often borrow a tradition from many of the world's religions and spend Friday to Saturday nights disconnected from screens—the practice I mentioned to you earlier that's sometimes called a "technology shabbat," or "digital sabbath." This disconnection helps create space and time that we can then use on activities and traditions that leave us nourished and refreshed.

Tiffany Shlain is a master at this. As a filmmaker and the founder of the Webby Awards, Shlain is no technology hater, but she's been taking digital sabbaths with her family for more than ten years; her daughters, now teenagers, have grown up with the tradition. In her book *24/6: Giving Up Screens One Day a Week to Get More Time, Creativity, and Connection,* Shlain explains how it works. On Friday, she and her family bake loaves of homemade challah and invite friends over for an informal dinner party. (To make it easier, they always serve the same thing.) On Saturdays, they engage in leisure activities that they didn't have time for during the week like gardening, or art projects, or playing games, or going on hikes. By the time they plug back in, they're refreshed—and newly grateful for the positive aspects of technology.

Every time my husband and I take a digital sabbath, we have the same experience: we spend the first evening consumed by cravings and anxiety, desperate to check, well, *anything* as our brains jerkily shift into a lower gear. (I find it helpful to keep a pad of paper on hand to keep track of all the ideas and to-dos that suddenly start popping up in my brain.) But when we wake up the following morning, time seems to slow down, and by midday, our cravings have been replaced by a sense of relief. The sensation is physical, as if we've put down a burden we didn't realize we had been carrying. By Saturday afternoon, we often find that we're enjoying our freedom so much that we don't *want* to turn our screens back on.*

Since the publication of *How to Break Up With Your Phone*, many other people have told me that they've had similar experiences while taking a twenty-four-hour break. In fact, Google itself reached the same conclusion in a report titled "Toward 'JOMO': The Joy of Missing Out and the Freedom of Disconnecting." It found that when people were first separated from their devices, they experienced cravings and anxiety, especially if the separation hadn't been by choice. (Say, if they accidentally left their phone at home.) But if people "reached a point of acceptance" about being disconnected, "they began to enjoy the break from their phone."

CONTINUE YOUR
FUN TIMES JOURNAL

You don't have to write in it every day, but continuing the practice of jotting down experiences that brought you some combination of playfulness, connection, and flow can be a great way to keep the pursuit of fun a priority, track your progress, and identify new fun magnets (not to mention give you something screen-free to do before bed). And while we're on the subject of self-reflection, you may also want to periodically retake the fun frequency questionnaire that you filled out earlier in the book as a way to monitor your fun levels over time.

---

* Curious but scared? I have a free digital sabbath survival guide available on my website, ScreenLifeBalance.com.

BUILD A FUN TOOLKIT

In addition to continuing to write in your fun times journal, I suggest that you create a "fun toolkit": a collection of ideas, prompts, and souvenirs that you can turn to any time you need inspiration or a pick-me-up.

Your toolkit could just be a list of ideas that you keep in your mind, or perhaps on paper—but I personally recommend creating an actual, physical toolkit for fun. It's an idea that was inspired by a "friendship toolkit" that my daughter made with her kindergarten class, which contains tools, such as "optimism glasses" and an "I-statement" microphone, that the children use to build and repair their friendships. (It's something that many adults could benefit from, too.)

If you like this idea, get yourself some sort of aesthetically pleasing container. Next, collect your tools for creating, experiencing, and savoring moments of connection, playfulness, and flow.

For example: you could include your fun times journal, a jar containing scraps of paper on which you record delights, or souvenirs of fun times you've experienced in the past, like a scrapbook or photo album or ticket stubs or other ephemera—basically anything that brings to mind memories that you'd like to savor.

You could create a grab bag filled with objects or books that remind you of interests, or of hobbies or passions you'd like to pursue, or that represent activities you already know give you a feeling of playfulness, connection, or flow. You could also include physical props for fun, such as a Frisbee or a board game you enjoy, or a list of songs you love to dance to, or things that remind you of the members of your fun squad. You could keep a running list of potential fun booster shots for you and your friends or family—trips you'd like to take, events you'd like to attend, or activities you'd like to try. You could include a collection of greeting cards that delight or amuse you, or a list of the kind things people have done for you or that you could do for someone else; practicing random acts of kindness is a proven way to boost your own mood (and who doesn't love receiving a handwritten card from a friend?). You could make a grab bag of ideas for rainy-day activities, or create a collection of framed photographs of past fun experiences that you display in your house on a rotating basis, switching them out every few months to keep them fresh. (Seeing them should spark a moment of delight; once this stops happening, it's time to swap in some new photos.)

Regardless of what you decide to include, make a point of adding to your fun toolkit regularly. Then, whenever you're having a down day—or any time you're looking for inspiration or a boost—open it up and see what you find.

PUT WORK INTO FUN . . .

This might sound counterintuitive or ironic, but sometimes fun takes work. Vacations and parties don't just happen on their own. Childcare doesn't show up unrequested. Trips don't pack for themselves.

This work can feel especially daunting given how fickle True Fun can be; there's no way to guarantee that your efforts will be successful. And the fact that we've conditioned our brains to expect instant gratification and nonstop dopamine hits from our devices only makes it more likely for us to forgo the work of creating opportunities for fun in favor of sinking even further into the couch.

But that's a horrible decision to make if you want to feel more alive.

"Some of the really transforming acts of play aren't pure fun," writes play expert Stuart Brown. If you only do things that are easy, "you will be shortchanging yourself."

Also, let's take a moment here to recognize that some of this work may be emotional: you may need to continually convince or remind the other people in your life that fun is worth the investment, or even work with yourself to minimize your own anxiety and change your negative self-talk. The last two challenges may be the most difficult—but valuable—of all.

. . . BUT DON'T TURN FUN INTO WORK

While prioritizing and creating opportunities for fun does often require effort, it's important not to make it feel like a job. It's all too easy to turn the pursuit of fun into a homework assignment.

A Fun Squad member was getting at this when she wrote, "When I try to make space for or plan fun, I start getting too obsessed about it and anxious, like it's just another thing on my to-do list that I will ultimately resent."

This is why it is so important that you let go of the idea of quantifying or tracking fun in the same overachieving way that many of us count our steps—as Ashley Whillans explains in her book, *Time Smart,* "Whenever we 'track' our leisure . . . we become hyperfocused on time efficiency. Instead of savoring our time, we worry about getting our money's worth from our leisure time." Sure, some level of self-monitoring can lead to useful insights, which is why I recommend that you continue to keep your fun times journal. But don't take the monitoring too far. The point of seeking fun is to *enjoy* your life, not to get a gold star.

BE KIND TO YOURSELF

And that brings me to my last point: please be kind to yourself.

Do not beat yourself up if, despite having followed every single suggestion in this book and having dutifully done every exercise, your life does not always feel fun. *No one's* life is nonstop fun (including my own), and we all go through rough patches where even getting out of bed in the morning can feel like a challenge. It's important to meet yourself where you are, acknowledge what *is* going well, and treat yourself with compassion.

Some days you will have the energy and inspiration to create new opportunities for fun; some days you won't. During the latter, focus less on the idea of creating fun and more on simply becoming more open and receptive to opportunities for playfulness, connection, or flow that happen to come your way. (And see if you can notice a few delights.)

As you "keep at it," you may notice that many of your everyday moments of playfulness, connection, and flow are small, fleeting, and unmemorable, to the point that you may wonder how much they matter. Rest assured: *they do.* These moments will slip by just as surely as any other; after all, we can't stop the passage of time. But unlike many of the other things that fill our hours, they *enliven* us before they disappear. So, instead of focusing on intensity, seek abundance. Try to fill your life with so many tiny moments of playfulness, connection, and flow that it becomes impossible for you to remember them all. In a way, what could be better than that?

Lastly, it's also worth remembering that even in the most ideal of circumstances, developing a more fun-filled life isn't going to happen overnight. Instead, it will blossom over time. In that way, it's a lot like planting seeds: you feed them with light and water, you protect them from predators and weeds, and eventually, if you keep it up, you'll find yourself living in a garden.

CONCLUSION

THE POWER OF FUN

"Doing one thing differently is often the same
as doing everything differently."
—Matt Haig, *The Midnight Library*

I WROTE THIS BOOK DURING THE **SARS-CoV-2** PAN-
demic, a time when the opportunities for playfulness, connection,
and flow felt scarcer—and my own levels of anxiety were higher—
than at nearly any other point in my life.

I was fortunate enough not to have tragedy strike me or my family, and in addition to making me grateful for my privileges, the
disruption caused by the pandemic helped me appreciate things
that are easy to take for granted, including the many positive aspects of technology. But it wasn't long before I became exhausted
from spending so much time in front of screens and longed to see
my friends in their three-dimensional forms; as it did for many people, months of monotony and isolation left me frustrated by the
feeling that I was languishing, caught in a state of emptiness and
ennui.

In some ways, it was a bad time to spend hours each day researching and thinking about fun (and my relative lack thereof). But it was
also, oddly, one of the best: it shifted my focus, clarified my priori-

ties, strengthened my belief in fun's importance, and inspired me to put my own ideas into practice as a way to keep myself sane.

Larger opportunities for fun, such as vacations or visits with friends, were obviously off the table, thanks to travel restrictions and social distancing requirements. But breaking fun down into playfulness, connection, and flow made me realize that there were still ways to incorporate microdoses of fun into my life. There were delights to notice. There were friends to call. There were interests, hobbies, and passions that I could pursue. I had greater control over manufacturing fun than I'd previously assumed, even in circumstances that made doing so feel difficult.

The more I took my own advice and searched for ways to create playfulness, connection, and flow, the more often I found myself in one of these three states. I noticed myself in flow as I practiced guitar and took walks outside to identify clouds and plants and trees. I noticed how connected I felt when I had a phone conversation with a friend, or even just caught the eye of a stranger above their mask. I noticed the playfulness between me and my husband when we joked around after our daughter went to bed. I even noticed myself having moments of full-on True Fun—as my daughter and I did a science project, for example, or when playing socially distanced live music with friends, or when my daughter led a family game of catch, or during a car ride on a warm spring day when we rolled down all the windows and sang along to "Do-Re-Mi" from *The Sound of Music* as loudly as possible.

Many of these experiences were not particularly dramatic—I may not be able to recall their specifics a month from now, let alone in a year. And yet, the more I tuned into and appreciated these microdoses of fun, the more their effects added up. These fleeting fun sessions rejuvenated me. They reduced my anxiety and lifted me out of my emotional rut. And they clarified for me something absolutely essential that I hope by this point you have internalized as well: there are opportunities for everyday True Fun—or at the very least, for individual moments of playfulness, connection, and flow—floating around us all the time. We each have the ability to discover, experience, and create them. And every time we do so, we will feel a little bit more alive.

When I tried to distill what I learned from writing my last book, *How to Break Up With Your Phone*, one phrase said it all: our lives are what we pay attention to. It's a reality that I try to remind myself of as often as I can.

But what I've come to realize since then is that if our goal is a meaningful and joyful existence, both in the long-term and in the day-to-day, understanding the importance of our attention is only the first step. Next, we must answer the question that inspired this book: *What* do we want to pay attention to? If our attention is like a spotlight, crisp-edged and narrow, for which life provides an infinite number of possible targets but only a finite number of days, then where do we want to focus it?

It's a simple question, but its implications could not be more profound. In any given moment, there are countless things competing for our attention—not just external distractions such as those generated by our devices, but all the thoughts and emotions produced by our own brains: our anxieties, our obsessions, our cravings, our self-criticisms, our insecurities, our hopes and dreams and fears.

Our natural tendency is always going to be to pay attention to the negative, to scan the horizon for potential attacks. It's a survival strategy that serves us well when our dangers are physical and real. But now that many of the perceived threats we encounter are emotional and abstract, this bias often hurts rather than helps us, raising our risks for stress-related disease and possibly shortening the very lives that it evolved to prolong.

It also affects our *experience* of our lives: we pay far more attention to correcting what's wrong—and finding problems that need to be "fixed"—than we do to enjoying and nurturing what is going right. (How many people do you know who see a therapist so that they can talk about the things in their life that are going *well*?) Just ask yourself which you gravitate toward: ruminating or savoring? How much time do you spend hashing out your problems versus celebrating what's good? How does the energy you put into fulfilling your obligations or engaging in conflicts compare to the energy you put into creating opportunities that might lead to fun?

It's not that we don't care about the positive. We *do* care, deeply so. We all want lives that are filled with meaning, happiness, satisfaction, and joy—but we don't know how to get there; these are nebulous destinations for which there is no clear path. So instead, we spend our time chasing, striving, and competing, dwelling on the past as we sprint toward future goals, like drivers who are so focused on the road ahead that the scenery rushes by them in a blur. We listen to talks and podcasts about success. We read books about productivity and install time-tracking apps on our phones. We pursue control and agency through endless attempts at self-improvement, hacking away at our supposed problems so that some distant day, we might be happy.

But we are not problems that need to be fixed. We are lives that want to be lived. And living does not suddenly start happening when we achieve inbox zero, or win an argument with someone on social media, or earn a promotion. It happens in every moment. It is happening *right now*.

Deciding what to *do* in this now is another way of asking ourselves what we want to pay attention to in the moment. My life changed dramatically for the better when I decided that my answer to this question would be True Fun—and I encourage you to explore what might happen if you did the same.

★　★　★

One of the many ironies surrounding fun is our assumption that, because it feels so good, it must be frivolous. (How many things in life come with no strings attached?) But maybe the fact that it feels good means that fun *is* good—deeply so. Maybe it means that instead of categorizing fun as unnecessary self-indulgence, we should add it to our list of requirements for happiness and health.

If you think about the factors that make us feel good in the moment *and* that benefit our long-term well-being, it would be difficult to identify three that are *more* potent than playfulness, connection, and flow. Our most fulfilling relationships, our biggest accomplishments, our strongest passions, our fondest memories, all involve some combination of these three states. Once our basic needs have been met, fun can help us achieve our full human potential.

Indeed, it does not seem like an exaggeration to me to say that if we all were to prioritize playfulness, connection, and flow, the world would be a better place. Imagine what would happen if we—as citizens or as leaders or as lawmakers—focused on the factors that connect us rather than those that drive us apart. Imagine how things might be different if, instead of reflexively responding to difficult situations by attacking other people and building walls of self-defense, we instead sought ways to defuse tension with playfulness. Imagine how much we would learn and create, and how we would flourish, if we all had adequate opportunities for flow.

This doesn't need to be a thought experiment; you can start right now. Notice delight. Follow your curiosity and experiment with new interests, hobbies, and passions. Make space for activities that you enjoy. Spend time with people who make you feel alive. Commit to doing something every day *for fun*—not in the cheapened sense with which we so often use the word but in the way we've defined it in these pages: as something that is absolutely vital to our wellbeing. Seek opportunities for playfulness, connection, and flow as if doing so were urgent and essential—because it *is*.

If I have convinced you of nothing else, I hope it is this: fun isn't just a result of human thriving; it is a *cause*. Fun encourages engagement with the world. It invigorates us and nourishes us. It brings us together. It reminds us of who we used to be—and who we *want* to be. Put it all together and my daughter was right: True Fun *is* sunshine. In its purest form, it is a distillation of life's energy, and the more often we bask in it, the more our lives will blossom in its light.

ACKNOWLEDGMENTS

Thank you to my agent, Jay Mandel, for receiving my initial email about the idea of a book about fun (subject: "A Random Idea") and responding seven minutes later with three words—"I like it"—that led to me meeting an amazing professional fun squad: Annie Chagnot and Whitney Frick at the Dial Press. Thank you, Annie and Whit, for loving this idea from the very beginning, for sharing my enthusiasm, and for helping to shape this book into what it is today. Working together has been a delight and, yes, truly *fun;* I finally feel I've found my publishing home.

Thank you also to everyone else at the Dial Press and Penguin Random House who has worked on this book, including Rose Fox, Donna Cheng, Debbie Aroff, Sarah Breivogel, Madison Dettlinger, Maria Braeckel, Avideh Bashirrad, Andrea Henry, Katie Horn, and Virginia Norey, as well as all the people at WME, Endeavor, and Harry Walker who help make my ideas into realities, including (but not limited to!) Elizabeth Wachtel, Jenna Praeger, Marissa Hurwitz, Janine Kamouh, Don and Ellen Walker, Shivanie Gosai, Emma Christensen, Elizabeth Hernandez, Fiona Bard, and Caitlin Mahony.

Thank you to the Screen/Life Balance community—and the readers of *How to Break Up With Your Phone*—for your feedback, support, and ideas. And a huge thanks to the Fun Squad in particular for taking the time to share your stories, insights, and suggestions; reading through your memories of fun is a guaranteed way to make me light up *and* tear up (in a good way!) at the same time. You made this book possible, and I am forever grateful for your help.

Thank you to all the people in my life who provided laughter, delight, suggestions, sanity, and support as I wrote this book, including (but not limited to!) Marie Szuts, Bonnie Hamilton, Al Hanssen, Brooke and Adam Benforado, Nell Stoddard, Galen Born, John Roderick, Ellie Johnson, Miriam Stewart, Sarah Hipkens, Christie Aschwanden, Anne Liska, Ben Herbstman, Jennifer Kahn, Anne Taylor, Steve Korovesis, Stet Sanborn, Natalie Kittner, Simon Tucker, Liz Filios, Derek Walker, Kristin Rising, Liana Ottaviani, Terri Hennessy, Mike Wolmetz, Debora Brakarz, Shaleigh and Jon Cochran, Kristy and Loren Kittilsen, Adrianne Koteen, Carl Shephard, Alex Boxer, Felicia Caviezel, Emily and Henrik Westin, Tim Kendall, Brigitte, Bentele, Carol Christmas, Judy Cuthbertson, Patrizia Magni, John Rose, and Charlotte Esposito. Thank you to Karen Pritzker, Lynn Waymer, the members of BLING, and the teams at Headspace and Miraval for your enthusiasm and partnership, to Laurie Santos, Dan Harris, Adrianna Huffington, Charles Duhigg, A. J. Jacobs, Adam Grant, Kevin Roose, and Jill Harlow for being early cheerleaders for this project, and to Amy Jo Martin, Regan Walsh, Nikki Brafman, and the rest of the renegades for your encouragement and advice.

Thank you to my in-laws, Hannah and Jim, for always being so supportive of my projects (and for placing what I'm pretty sure were this book's first two preorders), and to Nina Newby for being a lifelong role model for what fun looks like. And a special thanks to Todd Rice for giving me my foundation in music, and for having been a source of inspiration to me and my entire family for nearly four decades. (Two notes for five-year-old Catherine, as she hides her Dozen-a-Day finger exercise books behind the piano in hopes that Todd will believe her when she says that she has once again "lost" them in her own home: First, he knows where they are. And second, *it will all be worth it.*)

A huge shoutout to Jenn Treado for formatting my citations, bringing my vision for ScreenLifeBalance.com into existence, helping build our collection of courses, and holding down the fort so that I could complete this book—and to Don't Panic Management for introducing me to Jenn.

Thank you to John Francisco (aka "Mister John") for bringing his magic to Philadelphia; you've created a musical community that has truly changed my life. To all my teachers and classmates: I am so excited to be making music together again.

Emily Soffa, Ben Feldman, and Mark Herczeg, thank you for the songs, the harmonies, the dance moves, the laughter, and most of all, the camaraderie. Playing together is my definition of True Fun; when Johan Huizinga described music as having the ability to transport people "out of 'ordinary' life into a sphere of gladness and serenity," I'm pretty sure he was referring to Ben and Emily's backyard.

Thank you, as always, to Josh Berezin: your edits were particularly appreciated, given the fact that you read my manuscript while in the throes of early parenthood. You've been an essential contributor to all of my books, but the thing I value the most is your friendship: I am so grateful for all of the fun that we have shared and look forward to all the experiences (and piano duets) that are yet to come.

Vanessa Gregory, what can I even say? Who would have thought that our month in Seoul Tower Ville would have blossomed into this? Thank you for reading everything I ever write, and always making it better, for being there to commiserate about—and celebrate!—adulthood, parenthood, and writing, and for inspiring my interest in delight. I truly cannot express how much our friendship means to me.

I could never have written this book without the help of my parents, who not only have encouraged me to pursue writing since I was a child, but who also helped care for *my* child during the pandemic (and allowed us to ~~invade~~ *join them in* their home for more than a year). I am grateful for the unexpected time that we've all had together, and I love and appreciate you more than words can express, both as parents and as grandparents. Speaking of grandparents, I wish that I could share this book with my own grandmother, who bought me my guitar, and whose love of music and dancing inspired my own.

Most of all, thank you to Peter and Clara for inspiring this book, making it possible for me to write it, and being my most important fun squad of all. You are my sunshine. I love you both so very much.

NOTES

EPIGRAPH

ix **If you get in the habit** Jennifer Aaker and Naomi Bagdonas, *Humor, Seriously: Why Humor is a Secret Weapon at Work and in Life* (New York: Currency, 2020), p. 234.

CHAPTER 1: WHAT *IS* FUN?

23 **"Conceptualizing fun is not straightforward"** I. C. McManus and Adrian Furnham, "'Fun, Fun, Fun': Types of Fun, Attitudes to Fun, and their Relation to Personality and Biographical Factors," *Psychology*, 1, no. 3 (2010): 159–68.

24 **The *Oxford English Dictionary* defines fun** Definition of *fun*, Lexico .com and Oxford University Press, accessed July 17, 2020.

25 **"Roast a turkey"** Katia Hetter, "50 Fun Things to Do in the Fall (Take Your Pick)," CNN (website), "Health," September 22, 2020.

25 **A similar list from *Real Simple*** Lisa Millbrand, "33 Fun Things You Can Still Do This Fall (Even During a Pandemic)," *Real Simple* (website), August 18, 2020.

25 **According to Huizinga** Johan Huizinga, *Homo Ludens* (Mansfield Center, Conn.: Martino Fine Books, 2014), p. 3.

26 **"maddeningly elusive"** Bruce C. Daniels, *Puritans at Play: Leisure and Recreation in Colonial New England* (New York: St. Martin's Griffin, 1995), p. xiii.

26   **In a 2017 paper** Harry T. Reis, Stephanie C. O'Keefe, and Richard D. Lane, "Fun Is More Fun When Others Are Involved," *The Journal of Positive Psychology* 12, no. 6 (August 16, 2016): 547–57.

26   **"The psychological literature on fun is very limited"** I. C. McManus and Adrian Furnham, "'Fun, Fun, Fun.'"

26   **"Putting the *Fun* in Fungi"** Adrienne Lindbald, Stacy Jardine, and Michael R. Kolber, "Putting the *Fun* in Fungi: Toenail Onychomycosis," *Canadian Family Physician* 65, no. 12 (December 2019): 900.

28   **Next, I asked people** The fact that I launched the Fun Squad in the midst of the SARS-CoV-2 pandemic (late summer of 2020) made these responses particularly poignant.

36   **"Comparison is the thief of joy"** "Comparison is the Thief of Joy," Quote Investigator (website), February 6, 2021.

CHAPTER 2: WHY YOU FEEL DEAD INSIDE

41   **"When Facebook was getting going"** Sean Parker, "Sean Parker, Chamath Palihapitiya—Facebook is 'Ripping Apart Society,'" Ewafa, recording of November 8, 2017, Axios event in Philadelphia, YouTube video.

43   **This is why philosopher Simone Weil** Maria Popova, "Simone Weil on Attention and Grace," Brain Pickings (website), August 19, 2015.

44   **Clifford Nass** Sofie Bates, "A Decade of Data Reveals That Heavy Multitaskers Have Reduced Memory, Stanford Psychologist Says," Stanford University website, "News," October 25, 2018.

45   **"with the dust bunnies on the power-waxed tile floor"** Tom Vanderbilt, *Beginners: The Joy and Transformative Power of Lifelong Learning* (New York: Knopf, 2021), pp. 11–12.

45   **Much has been written about the mental health problems** For example:

Lucy Dwyer, "When Anxiety Hits at School," *The Atlantic* (website), "Health," October 3, 2014.

Linda Flanagan, "Why Are So Many Teen Athletes Struggling With Depression?" *The Atlantic* (website), "Health," April 17, 2019.

47   **our need for play is intrinsic** For more on play (both human and animal), see:

Stuart Brown, *Play: How it Shapes the Brain, Opens the Imagination, and Invigorates the Soul,* with Christopher Vaughan (New York: Avery, 2010).

Gordon M. Burghardt, *The Genesis of Animal Play: Testing the Limits,* (Cambridge, Mass: The MIT Press, 2006).

48 **"actually had time to sit around a fire"** Celeste Headlee, *Do Nothing: How to Break Away from Overworking, Overdoing and Underliving* (New York: Harmony Books, 2020), p. 20.

50 **"The transformation this idea caused in the world"** Ibid., p. 40.

50 **"Many of us are exhausting ourselves"** Ibid., pp. xviii–xix.

51 **high rates of depression and anxiety** Daniel Markovits, "How Life Became an Endless, Terrible Competition," *The Atlantic,* September 2019.

51 **participation in community organizations has steeply declined** Robert Putnam, "Social Capital: Measurement and Consequences," *Isuma: Canadian Journal of Policy Research* 2, Spring (2001): 41–51.

52 **an epidemic of loneliness** Julianne Jolt-Lunstad et al., "Loneliness and Social Isolation as Risk Factors for Mortality: A Meta-Analytic Review," *Perspectives on Psychological Science* 10, no. 2 (March 2015): 227–37.

52 **A 2018 survey by the AARP Foundation** G. Oscar Anderson and Colette Thayer, "Loneliness and Social Connections: A National Survey of Adults 45 and Older," AARP, "AARP Research: Life and Leisure," September 2018.

52 **a survey of more than twenty thousand American adults** Ellie Polack, "New Cigna Study Reveals Loneliness at Epidemic Levels in America," Cigna (website), "News Releases," May 1, 2018.

52 **The problem is not just an American one** Manuela Barreto et al., "Loneliness Around the World: Age, Gender, and Cultural Differences in Loneliness," *Personality and Individual Differences* 169 (February 2021), web edition.

52 *a minister of loneliness* National Academies of Sciences, Engineering, and Medicine, *Social Isolation and Loneliness in Older Adults: Opportunities for the Health Care System* (Washington, D.C.: The National Academies Press, 2020), p. 2.

53 **In the words of one caller** Emily Buder, " 'The Voices of the Loneliness Epidemic,' a video by Alice Aedy," *The Atlantic* (website), "*The Atlantic* Selects," March 10, 2020.

53 **In a 2017 cover story** Jean M. Twenge, "Have Smartphones Destroyed a Generation?" *The Atlantic*, September 2017. Twenge is also the author of a fascinating book called *iGen: Why Today's Super-Connected Kids Are Growing Up Less Rebellious, More Tolerant, Less Happy—And Completely Unprepared for Adulthood (And What That Means for the Rest of Us)* (New York: Simon & Schuster, 2017).

53 **It showed the percentage** Jean M. Twenge, *iGen*, p. 97. This data is drawn from the Monitoring the Future survey, funded by the National Institute on Drug Abuse. According to Twenge, it is designed to be nationally representative, and has asked twelfth-graders more than a thousand questions every year since 1975 and queried eighth- and tenth-graders since 1991. The graphs in *iGen* show data stretching from 1991 to 2015.

53 **passively scrolling through people's feeds** Katherine Hobson, "Feeling Lonely? Too Much Time on Social Media May Be Why," NPR (website), "Shots: Health News from NPR," March 6, 2017.

53 **It can make people feel bad** Kaitlyn Burnell et al., "Passive Social Networking Site Use and Well-Being: The Mediating Roles of Social Comparison and the Fear of Missing Out," *Cyberpsychology: Journal of Psychosocial Research on Cyberspace* 13, no. 3 (2019) (web-based journal).

53 **less accepted and more left out** Ashley V. Whillans and Frances S. Chen, "Facebook Undermines the Social Belonging of First Year Students," *Personality and Individual Differences* 133 (2018): 13–16.

53 **the experience of *physical* pain** Giovanni Novembre, Marco Zanon, and Giorgia Silani, "Empathy for Social Exclusion Involves the Sensory-Discriminative Component of Pain: A Within-Subject fMRI Study," *Social Cognitive and Affective Neuroscience* 10, no. 2 (February 2015): 153–64.

53 **"The greater the proportion of face-to-face interactions"** Stephen Marche, "Is Facebook Making Us Lonely?" *The Atlantic*, May 2012.

55 **the preexisting epidemic** Maria Elizabeth Loades et al., "Rapid Systemic Review: The Impact of Social Isolation and Loneliness on the Mental Health of Children and Adolescents in the Context of COVID-19," *Journal of the American Academy of Child and Adolescent Psychiatry* 59, no. 11 (November 2020): 1218–39.

Catherine E. Robb et al., "Associations of Social Isolation with Anxiety and Depression During the Early COVID-19 Pandemic: A Survey of Older Adults in London, UK," *Frontiers in Psychiatry* (September 17, 2020) (web-based journal).

58 **upward of four hours a day** "How Much Time Do People Spend on Their Mobile Phones in 2017?" Hacker Noon (website), May 9, 2017.

58 **the number is now even higher** "How much time on average do you spend on your phone on a daily basis?" *Statista Research* (website), July 7, 2021. The survey on which this statistic is based took place from February 5–8, 2021, had 2,028 respondents (all of whom were eighteen or older), and did *not* count work-related time. (The question was phrased as, "How much time on average do you spend on your phone on a daily basis (not work-related)?")

59 **what some experts call "polluted time"** Celeste Headlee, *Do Nothing*, p. 53.

59 **"time confetti"** Ashley Whillans, *Time Smart: How to Reclaim Your Time and Live a Happier Life* (Cambridge, Mass: Harvard Business Review Press, 2020), p. 16.

I also recommend checking out:

Brigid Schulte, *Overwhelmed: How to Work, Love and Play When No One Has the Time* (New York: Sarah Crichton Books, 2014).

59 **they claim that most people have more time** Ashley Whillans, *Time Smart*, p. 15.

59 **"People end up enjoying their free time less"** Ibid., p. 19.

59 **As defined by *Psychology Today*** "Working Memory," *Psychology Today* (website).

63 **part of what's known as the "attention economy"** Ally Mintzer, "Paying Attention: The Attention Economy," *Berkeley Economic Review* (website), March 31, 2020.

"Attention economy" was coined by economist and psychologist Herbert A. Simon, and "surveillance capitalism" was coined by Shoshana Zuboff, professor emerita at Harvard Business school and author of *The Age of Surveillance Capitalism: The Fight for a Human Future at the New Frontier of Power*.

63 **a four-person family could be entitled** Jaron Lanier and Adam Westbrook, "Jaron Lanier Fixes the Internet," *The New York Times*, September 23, 2019.

64 **"What might once have been called advertising"** Jaron Lanier, *Ten Arguments for Deleting Your Social Media Accounts Right Now* (New York: Henry Holt and Co., 2018), pp. 6–7.

64 **"Your specific behavior change"** Ibid., p. 28.

64 **"algorithms behind companies"** Ibid., p. 91.

65 **But according to Roger McNamee** Roger McNamee, *Zucked: Waking Up to the Facebook Catastrophe* (London: Penguin Press, 2019), p. 219.

65 **This information can be gathered** Jaron Lanier, *Ten Arguments for Deleting Your Social Media Accounts Right Now,* pp. 32–33.

66 **"It is deeply creepy"** Roger McNamee, *Zucked,* p. 219.

67 **a 2012 study** Adam D. I. Kramer et al., "Experimental Evidence of Massive-Scale Emotional Contagion Through Social Networks," *PNAS* 111, no. 24 (June 17, 2014): 8788–90.

67 **"Look around you"** Kartik Hosanagar, *A Human's Guide to Machine Intelligence: How Algorithms are Shaping Our Lives and How We Can Stay in Control* (New York: Viking, 2019), p. 34.

68 **"Imagine bookshelves, seminars, workshops"** Tristan Harris, "The Slot Machine in Your Pocket," *Der Spiegel* (website), "International: Zeitgeist: Technology," July 27, 2016.

Another great euphemism for "engagement" is "persuasive design." Many of the people who designed the most problematic apps trained at the Stanford Persuasive Technology Lab, where they learned how to use design elements to nudge people toward particular behaviors. It's worth noting that today, the Persuasive Technology Lab's website says that its purpose has moved on from persuasive technology to focusing on designing for "healthy behavior change" and makes a point of highlighting the work its researchers have done in regards to the *ethics* of design.

68 **"The thought process"** Mike Allen, "Sean Parker Unloads on Facebook: 'God Only Knows What It's Doing to Our Children's Brains,'" *Axios*, "Technology," November 9, 2017.

69 **"The gambling industry is designing"** "Slot Machines: The Big Gamble," reported by Lesley Stahl, produced by Ira Rosen, *60 Minutes,* aired January 9, 2011.

69 **"My Not-So-Silent Retreat"** Miriam Stewart, "My Not-So-Silent Retreat," *What Begins with M* (website), February 18, 2018.

69 **The basic definition** "What Is a Substance Use Disorder?" American Psychiatric Association (website), accessed July 16, 2021.

70   **"internet gaming disorder"** "Internet Gaming," American Psychiatric Association (website), accessed July 16, 2021.

71   **a report from Google, of all places** Julie H. Aranda and Safia Baig, "Toward 'JOMO': The Joy of Missing Out and the Freedom of Disconnecting," *MobileHCI '18: Proceedings of the 20th International Conference on Human-Computer Interaction with Mobile Devices and Services* (September 2018): 1–8.

73   **"We give you a little dopamine hit"** YouTube, "Facebook is 'Ripping Apart Society.'"

75   **Jaron Lanier sums up the situation** Jaron Lanier, *Ten Arguments for Deleting Your Social Media Accounts Right Now,* p. 94.

76   **Chamath Palihapitiya . . . described this** He subsequently walked some of his comments back, but if you watch the video of the talk, his manner is so passionate and heartfelt that it is hard to believe that he did not mean what he was saying. YouTube, "Facebook is 'Ripping Apart Society.'"

76   **In a 2018 report** Nicholas Confessore et al., "The Follower Factory," *The New York Times,* January 27, 2018.

78   **our brains release more dopamine** Robert Sapolsky, *Why Zebras Don't Get Ulcers* (New York: Henry Holt and Co., 2004).

78   **"phantom vibrations"** Michelle Drouin et al., "Phantom Vibrations among Undergraduates: Prevalence and Associated Psychological Characteristics," *Computers in Human Behavior* 28, no. 4 (2012): 1490–96.)

80   **"You have one brain"** YouTube, "Facebook is 'Ripping Apart Society.'"

80   **Steve Jobs himself** Nick Bilton, "Steve Jobs Was a Low-Tech Parent," *The New York Times,* September 10, 2014.

81   **"continuous partial attention"** Linda Stone, "Beyond Simple Multi-Tasking: Continuous Partial Attention," Author's website, November 30, 2009.

81   **the mere presence of a phone** Shalini Misra et al., "The iPhone Effect: The Quality of In-Person Social Interactions in the Presence of Mobile Devices," *Environment and Behavior* 48, no. 2 (2014): 275–98.

81   **"It literally changes"** Mike Allen, "Sean Parker Unloads on Facebook: 'God Only Knows What It's Doing to Our Children's Brains,'" *Axios,* "Technology," November 9, 2017.

82   **The process of transferring short-term memories** Eric R. Kandel, "The Molecular Biology of Memory Storage: A Dialog Between Genes and Synapses," in *Nobel Lectures, Physiology or Medicine 1996–2000*, ed. Hans Jörvell (Singapore: World Scientific Publishing Co., 2003), pp. 393–439.

83   **As Greg McKeown writes** Greg McKeown, *Essentialism: The Disciplined Pursuit of Less* (London: Virgin Books, 2014), p. 68.

85   **Among other things** Brian K. Lee et al., "Associations of Salivary Cortisol with Cognitive Function in the Baltimore Memory Study," *Archives of General Psychiatry* 64, no. 7 (2007): 810–18.

86   **Indeed, it's well established** "Stress effects on the body," American Psychological Association (website), "Psychology Topics: Stress," November 1, 2018.

87   **But when I wrote an article** Catherine Price, "Putting Down Your Phone May Help You Live Longer," *The New York Times*, April 24, 2019.

CHAPTER 3: WHY FUN—TRUE FUN— IS THE ANSWER

88   **"I'm going to keep having fun"** Randy Pausch, "Randy Pausch Last Lecture: Achieving Your Childhood Dreams," Carnegie Mellon University, lecture delivered on December 20, 2017, YouTube video.

89   **Feeling chronically anxious and stressed** "Stress effects on the body," American Psychological Association (website), "Psychology Topics: Stress," November 1, 2018.

89   **Not feeling confident** Jason Castro, "A Wandering Mind is an Unhappy One," *Scientific American* (website), "Mind," published November 24, 2010.

89   **Not being able to find humor** Solfrid Romundstad et al., "A 15-Year Follow-Up Study of Sense of Humor and Causes of Mortality," *Psychosomatic Medicine* 72, no. 3 (April 2016): 345–53.

89   **Not laughing** Kaori Sakurada et al., "Associations of Frequency of Laughter with Risk of All-Cause Mortality and Cardiovascular Disease Incidence in a General Population: Findings From the Yamagata Study," *Journal of Epidemiology* 30, no. 4 (2020): 188–93.

89 **Being socially isolated** Julianne Holt-Lunstad et al., "Loneliness and Social Isolation as Risk Factors for Mortality: A Meta-Analytic Review," *Perspectives on Psychological Science* 10, No. 2 (2015): 227–37.

89 **Feeling lonely** Ibid.

89 **Not spending time in nature** Gregory N. Bratman et al., "Nature Reduces Rumination and sgPFC Activation," *Proceedings of the National Academy of Sciences* 112, no. 28 (July 2015): 8567–72.

89 **Being physically inactive** Kathy Katella, "Why is Sitting so Bad for Us?" *Yale Medicine* (website), August 28, 2018.

89 **Being perpetually distracted** Jason Castro, "A Wandering Mind."

89 **Feeling purposeless** Mara Gordon, "What's Your Purpose? Finding a Sense of Meaning in Life is Linked to Health," NPR (website), "Shots: Health News from NPR," May 25, 2019.

89 **Feeling like we don't have control** Suzanne C. Thompson and Michèle M. Schlehofer, "Perceived Control," website of the National Cancer Institute, "Program Areas: Behavioral Research," last modified September 24, 2020.

89 **"The times we feel most alive"** Stuart Brown, *Play: How it Shapes the Brain, Opens the Imagination, and Invigorates the Soul,* with Christopher Vaughan (New York: Avery, 2010), p. 6.

90 **"absorbing [and] apparently purposeless"** Ibid., p. 60.

91 **"It's not just an absence of games"** Ibid., p. 7.

91 **"When we stop playing"** Ibid., p. 73.

91 **play is "an integral part of life"** Johan Huizinga, *Homo Ludens* (Mansfield Center, Conn.: Martino Fine Books, 2014), p. 9.

91 **"Play cannot be denied"** Ibid., p. 3.

91 **In the words of British psychoanalyst** D. W. Winnicott, *Playing and Reality* (Oxfordshire: Routledge, 2005), p 2–73.

91 **Brown elaborates on this idea** Stuart Brown, *Play,* p. 107.

91 **It may be a smarter and healthier self** Robin Marantz Henig, "Taking Play Seriously," *The New York Times,* February 17, 2008.

92 **and Brown cites research** Stuart Brown, *Play,* p. 71.

92 **Scientists have also found that the periods in life** Robin Marantz Henig, "Taking Play Seriously."

92   **the cerebellum, a part of the brain** Hyo Jung De Smet, "The Cere-
      bellum: Its Role in Language and Related Cognitive and Affective
      Functions," *Brain and Language* 127, no. 3 (2013): 334–42.

92   **According to Caroline Adams Miller** Caroline Adams Miller, *Creat-
      ing Your Best Life: The Ultimate Life List Guide* (New York: Sterling,
      2011), p. 172.

93   **"an absorption, a devotion"** Johan Huizinga, *Homo Ludens,* p. 8.

93   **"a string with which we tie"** Miguel Sicart, *Play Matters* (Cam-
      bridge, Mass: The MIT Press, 2017), p. 18.

93   **"The feeling of being 'apart together'"** Johan Huizinga, *Homo
      Ludens,* p. 12.

94   **according to a 2010 meta-analysis** Christopher M. Masi et al., "A
      Meta-Analysis of Interventions to Reduce Loneliness," *Personality
      and Social Psychology Review* 15, no. 3 (2011): 219–26.

95   **"loneliness somehow penetrated"** John Cacioppo, *Loneliness:
      Human Nature and the Need for Social Connection* (New York: W. W.
      Norton & Company, 2009).

95   **an even bigger risk factor** Julianne Holt-Lunstad, Timothy B. Smith,
      and J. Bradley Layton, "Social Relationships and Mortality Risk: A
      Meta-Analytic Review," *PLoS Medicine* 7, no. 7 (July 27, 2010) (web-
      based journal).

95   *fifteen cigarettes a day* Website of the U.S. Department of Health
      Resources and Human Services, "The 'Loneliness Epidemic,'"
      "eNews," January 2019.

95   **"fertilizer for other diseases"** "Social Isolation, Loneliness in Older
      People Pose Health Risks," National Institute on Aging (website),
      "Featured Research," April 23, 2019.

      Perhaps unintuitively, the increase in the risk of dying early is espe-
      cially pronounced for people *under* sixty-five. And while you'd think
      that people would get lonelier with age, the Cigna survey found (and
      other research backs this up) that Generation Z—adults who at that
      point were eighteen to twenty-two years old—was the "loneliest gen-
      eration" and "claim[ed] to be in worse health than older generations."

96   **Social isolation and loneliness are associated** National Academies
      of Sciences, Engineering, and Medicine, *Social Isolation and Loneli-
      ness in Older Adults: Opportunities for the Health Care System* (Washing-
      ton, D.C.: The National Academies Press, 2020), p. 1.

96 **50 percent increase in the risk** Ibid., p. 1.

96 **Loneliness is a risk factor for inflammation** "Social Isolation, Loneliness in Older People," National Institute on Aging.

96 **It increases the levels of stress hormones** Stephen Marche, "Is Facebook Making Us Lonely?" *The Atlantic*, May 2012.

96 **more attention to negative feedback than positive** "Social Isolation, Loneliness in Older People," National Institute on Aging.

96 **things that will make our loneliness worse** Stephanie Cacioppo et al., "Loneliness and Implicit Attention to Social Threat: A High-Performance Electrical Neuroimaging Study," *Cognitive Neuroscience* 7, no. 1–4 (2015): 138–59.

96 **"High-quality social relationships are vital"** National Academies of Sciences, Engineering, and Medicine, *Social Isolation and Loneliness in Older Adults: Opportunities for the Health Care System* (Washington, D.C.: The National Academies Press, 2020).

96 **"Joy is connection"** Jennifer Senior, *All Joy and No Fun: The Paradox of Modern Parenthood* (New York: Ecco, 2015), p. 243.

97 **The Grant Study** The study is part of the Harvard Study of Adult Development, and only included men partly because, at the time, Harvard was all-male; the most recent version of the study now includes women, as well as the original participants' offspring.

97 **a 2015 TEDx talk** Liz Mineo, "Harvard study, almost 80 years old, has proved that embracing community helps us live longer and be happier," *The Harvard Gazette*, April 11, 2017.

98 **strong close relationships had a bigger impact** Liz Mineo, "Good Genes Are Nice, but Joy Is Better," *The Harvard Gazette*, April 11, 2017.

98 **As George Vaillant summarized** Liz Mineo, "Good Genes Are Nice."

98 **Human connection also helps** Nicholas Epley and Juliana Schroeder, "Mistakenly seeking solitude," *Journal of Experimental Psychology: General* 143, no. 5 (2014): 1980–99. (See also: Ashley Whillans, *Time Smart: How to Reclaim Your Time and Live a Happier Life* (Cambridge, Mass: Harvard Business Review Press, 2020), p. 56.

99 **Exchanging genuine smiles with someone** Rebecca Joy Stanborough, "Smiling with Your Eyes: What Exactly Is a Duchenne Smile?" Healthline, physician review by J. Keith Fisher, MD, June 29, 2019.

99 a "fleeting relationship" Gillian M. Sandstrom, "Social Interactions and Well-Being: The Surprising Power of Weak Ties," PhD diss., University of British Columbia, Vancouver (2013).

99 **Interactions with nature** K. L. Wolf and K. Flora, "Mental Health and Function—A Literature Review," *Green Cities: Good Health* (website affiliated with the University of Washington, College of the Environment), December 26, 2020; updated September 16, 2015.

99 **nature has so many positive psychological benefits** Kari Leibowitz, "What Scandinavians Can Teach Us About Embracing Winter," *The New York Times,* October 15, 2020.

99 **"Collective effervescence happens"** Adam Grant, "There's a Specific Kind of Joy We've Been Missing," *The New York Times*, July 10, 2021.

100 **Flow can even be contagious** Arnold B. Bakker, "Flow Among Music Teachers and Their Students: The Crossover of Peak Experiences," *Journal of Vocational Behavior* 66, no. 1 (2005): 26–44.

100 **during a period of flow** Mihaly Csikzentmihalyi, *Flow: The Psychology of Optimal Experience* (New York: Harper Perennial Modern Classics, 2008), p. 12.

100 **"stronger self-concept"** Ibid., p. 12.

101 **"we feel a sense of exhilaration"** Ibid., p. 3.

101 **"the secret to a happy life"** Ibid., p. 14.

101 **The characters** Héctor García and Francesc Miralles, *Ikigai: The Japanese Secret to a Long and Healthy Life* (New York: Penguin Life, 2017), p. 11.

101 **There they noticed "an uncommon joy"** Ibid., p. 4.

101 **"the happiness of always being busy"** Ibid., p. 2.

102 **"the closer you will be to your *ikigai*"** Ibid., p. 86.

102 **"We didn't see a single old grandpa"** Ibid., p. 118.

102 **"Spending time together"** Ibid., p. 113.

103 **Laughter reduces levels of cortisol** Lee S. Berk et al., "Neuroendocrine and Stress Hormone Changes During Mirthful Laughter," *The American Journal of the Medical Sciences* 298, no. 6 (December 1989): 390–96.

See also: Richard Schiffman, "Laughter May Be Effective Medicine for These Trying Times," *The New York Times,* October 1, 2020.

104 **lower risks for cardiovascular disease** Kaori Sakurada et al., "Associations of Frequency of Laughter With Risk of All-Cause Mortality and Cardiovascular Disease."

104 **Good-humored, genuine laughter** Michael Miller and William F. Fry, "The effect of mirthful laughter on the human cardiovascular system," *Medical Hypothesis* 73, no. 5 (2009): 636–39.

104 **in his 1946 book** Viktor E. Frankl, *Man's Search for Meaning* (Boston, Mass.: Beacon Press, 1992), p. 54.

104 **In addition to lifting our moods** Richard Schiffman, "Laughter May Be Effective Medicine for These Trying Times," *The New York Times*, October 1, 2020.

104 **As we touched on in the last chapter** Gurinder Singh Bains et al., "'The Effect of Humor on Short-Term Memory in Older Adults: A New Component for Whole-Person Wellness," *Advances in Mind-Body Medicine* 28, no. 2 (2014): 16–24.

See also: Brian K. Lee et al., "Associations of Salivary Cortisol with Cognitive Function in the Baltimore Memory Study," *Archives of General Psychiatry* 34, no. 7 (2007): 810–18.

104 **Laughter also releases endorphins** R.I.M. Dunbar et al., "Social Laughter is Correlated with an Elevated Pain Threshold," *Proceedings of the Royal Society B: Biological Sciences* 279 (2012): 1161–67.

105 **Researchers also believe** Ibid.

105 **This is likely why humor** Kari A. Phillips et al., "Humor During Clinical Practice: Analysis of Recorded Clinical Encounters," *The Journal of the American Board of Family Medicine* 31, no. 2 (March 2018): 270–78.

105 **increase people's satisfaction with their relationships** Doris G. Bazzini et al., "The Effect of Reminiscing about Laughter on Relationship Satisfaction," *Motivation and Emotion* 31 (2017): 25–34.

105 *anticipating* **what researchers call "mirthful laughter"** American Physiological Society, "Anticipating a Laugh Reduces Our Stress Hormones, Study Shows," ScienceDaily (website), April 10, 2008.

105 **"When we laugh"** Jennifer Aaker and Naomi Bagdonas, *Humor, Seriously: Why Humor Is a Secret Weapon at Work and in Life* (New York: Currency, 2020), p. 43.

105 **as comedian John Cleese has observed** Ibid., p. 168.

Or, if you'd prefer a more historical perspective, "One hearty laugh together will bring enemies into a closer communion of heart than hours spent on both sides in inward wrestling with the mental demon of uncharitable feeling," wrote ninteenth-century psychologist William James in his essay "The Gospel of Relaxation." (William James, *Talks to Teachers on Psychology: And to Students on Some of Life's Ideals* (New York: Henry Holt and Company, 1899), pp. 199–28.)

105 **laughter is thirty times more likely** R.I.M. Dunbar et al., "Social laughter is correlated with an elevated pain threshold."

106 **"By seeking out positive experiences"** American Physiological Society, "Anticipating A Laugh Reduces our Stress Hormones, Study Shows," ScienceDaily, (website), April 10, 2008.

107 **As Barbara Fredrickson** Barbara L. Fredrickson, "The Broaden-and-Build Theory of Positive Emotions," *Philosophical Transactions of the Royal Society* 359 (2004): 1367–77.

107 **50 to 80 percent of it** Caroline Adams Miller, *Creating Your Best Life*, p. 67.

107 **S(et point) + C(ircumstances)** Ibid., p. 19.

107 **It's the opposite of languishing** Barbara L. Fredrickson, "The Broaden-and-Build Theory of Positive Emotions," *Philosophical Transactions of the Royal Society* 359 (2004): 1367–77.

108 **the more you will flourish** Martin Seligman, *Flourish: A Visionary New Understanding of Health and Well-Being* (New York: Atria Paperback, 2011), p. 24.

110 **"There was formerly"** Bertrand Russell, "In Praise of Idleness," *Harper's Magazine*, October 1932.

110 **a paraphrased version** Kristi Martin, "The price of anything is the amount of life you exchange for it," *Thoreau Farm* (website), February 28, 2017. The actual quote is from Thoreau's essay "Economy" and says that "the cost of a thing is the amount of what I will call life which is required to be exchanged for it, immediately or in the long run." (To me, the paraphrased version is much snappier.)

111 **Psychologists find that** Adam Grant, "There's a Specific Kind of Joy We've Been Missing," *The New York Times*, July 20, 2021.

111 **"Few of our daily activities are focused"** Celeste Headlee, *Do Nothing: How to Break Away from Overworking, Overdoing, and Underliving* (New York: Harmony Books, 2020), p. xvii.

111 **"We've cut out expressions"** Ibid., pp. xvii–xviii.

113 **research done by Adele Diamond** Martin Seligman, *Flourish*, p. 112.

113 **the "undo" hypothesis** Barbara L. Fredrickson, "The Broaden-and-Build Theory of Positive Emotions."

114 **"balance busy lives with deep play"** Alex Soojung-Kim Pang, *Rest: Why You Get More Done When You Work Less* (New York: Basic Books, 2018), p. 14.

115 **"when we stop and rest properly"** Ibid., p. 11.

115 **dopamine, which is our brain's way** I first heard this description from Ramsay Brown, cofounder and former COO at a tech startup called Boundless Mind.

115 **Laughter is also a dopamine trigger** Jennifer Aaker and Naomi Bagdonas, *Humor, Seriously,* p. 49.

116 **In 2008, researchers did a fascinating** Charles J. Limb and Allen R. Braun, "Neural Substrates of Spontaneous Musical Performance: An fMRI Study of Jazz Improvisation," *PLoS ONE* 3, no. 2 (February 27, 2008) (web-based journal).

116 **As an article in *National Geographic*** Claudia Kalb, "What Makes a Genius?" *National Geographic Magazine,* May 2017.

117 **Put this all together and it's not surprising** David Epstein, *Range: Why Generalists Triumph in a Specialized World* (New York: Riverhead Books, 2019), p. 273.

CHAPTER 4: THE FUN AUDIT

121 **"If you don't prioritize your life"** Greg McKeown, *Essentialism: The Disciplined Pursuit of Less* (London: Virgin Books, 2014), p. 10.

CHAPTER 5: FIND YOUR FUN

140 **"Men would not know"** Bertrand Russell, "In Praise of Idleness," *Harper's Magazine,* October 1932.

142 **many psychological studies have found** Seth Margolis and Sonja Lyubomirsky, "Experimental Manipulation of Extraverted and Introverted Behavior and its Effects on Well-Being," *Journal of Experimental Psychology: General* 149, no. 4 (2020): 719–31.

142 **One such paper says so** Harry T. Reis, Stephanie D. O'Keefe, and Richard D. Lane, "Fun is More Fun When Others Are Involved," *Journal of Positive Psychology* 12, no. 6 (2017): 547–57.

143 **"When was the last time you laughed"** Martin Seligman, *Flourish: A Visionary New Understanding of Health and Well-Being* (New York: Atria Paperback, 2011), p. 20.

CHAPTER 6: MAKE SPACE

157 **"The notion of free time"** Stanley Aronowitz and William DiFazio, *The Jobless Future* (Minneapolis, Minn.: University of Minnesota Press, 1994), p. 336.

161 **a book by Eve Rodsky called *Fair Play*** Eve Rodsky, *Fair Play: A Game-Changing Solution for When You Have Too Much to Do (and More Life to Live)* (New York: G. P. Putnam's Sons, 2019).

162 **Under the rules of *Fair Play*** Ibid., pp. 114–16.

166 **In an article about tidying** Taffy Brodesser-Akner, "Marie Kondo, Tidying Up and the Ruthless War of Stuff," *The New York Times Magazine*, July 6, 2016.

167 **As the author bluntly concludes** Libby Sander, "The Case for Finally Cleaning Your Desk," *Harvard Business Review*, March 25, 2019.

175 **Robin Dunbar is an anthropologist** Maria Konnikova, "The Limits of Friendship," *The New Yorker*, October, 2014.

176 **"What Facebook does"** Ibid.

187 **Back in 1946** Viktor E. Frankl, *Man's Search for Meaning* (Boston, Mass.: Beacon Press, 1992), p. 112.

187 **In 1932** Bertrand Russell, "In Praise of Idleness," *Harper's Magazine*, October 1932.

CHAPTER 7: PURSUE PASSIONS

204 **Bertrand Russell wrote about it** Bertrand Russell, "In Praise of Idleness," *Harper's Magazine*, October 1932.

210 **"Unicorn Space"** Eve Rodsky, *Fair Play: A Game-Changing Solution for When You Have Too Much to Do (and More Life to Live)* (New York: G. P. Putnam's Sons, 2019), p. 102.

212 **As play scholar Stuart Brown puts it** Stuart Brown, *Play: How it Shapes the Brain, Opens the Imagination, and Invigorates the Soul*, with Christopher Vaughan (New York: Avery, 2010), p. 211.

212 **Margaret Talbot captured this sentiment** Margaret Talbot, "Is it Really Too Late to Learn New Skills?" *The New Yorker,* January 11, 2021.

213 **It reminds me of an essay** Jenny Hansell, "Perspective," *Yale Alumni Magazine* LXXXIV, No. 3 (January/February 2021).

214 **In 2017, Thomas Curran and Andrew P. Hill** Thomas Curran and Andrew P. Hill, "Perfectionism Is Increasing, and That's Not Good News," *Harvard Business Review,* January 28, 2018.

215 **Perfectionists have been found** Thomas Curran and Andrew P. Hill, "Perfectionism is Increasing Over Time: A Meta-Analysis of Birth Cohort Differences from 1989 to 2016," *Psychological Bulletin* 145, no. 4 (2019): 410–29.

215 **Curran and Hill point out** Ibid.

216 **As Margaret Talbot writes** Margaret Talbot, "Is it Really Too Late to Learn New Skills?"

CHAPTER 8: ATTRACT FUN

219 **"Strong biological underpinnings"** Martin Seligman, *Flourish: A Visionary New Understanding of Health and Well-Being* (New York: Atria Paperback, 2011), pp. 51–52.

220 **In the words of former Twitter CEO** Jennifer Aaker and Naomi Bagdonas, *Humor, Seriously: Why Humor is a Secret Weapon at Work and in Life* (New York: Currency, 2020), p. 29.

222 **In her book,** *Bossypants* Tina Fey, *Bossypants* (New York: Little, Brown and Company, 2011), p. 84.

226 **For example, you could experiment** René T. Proyer et al., "Can Playfulness be Stimulated? A Randomised Placebo-Controlled On-line Playfulness Intervention Study on Effects on Trait Playfulness, Well-Being, and Depression," *Applied Psychology: Health and Well-Being* 13, no. 1 (2021): 129–51.

227 **The first exercise** Martin Seligman, *Flourish: A Visionary New Understanding of Health and Well-Being* (New York: Atria Paperback, 2011), p. 38.

227 **In the traditional version** "Three Good Things," Greater Good in Action (website associated with the Greater Good Science Center at UC Berkeley).

Martin Seligman, in *Flourish* on page 33, just calls this "What-Went-Well" and describes it as "write down three things that went well today and why they went well" Then next to each positive event answer the question "Why did this happen?"

228 **In the study about playfulness** René T. Proyer et al., "Can Playfulness be Stimulated?"

229 **When we look down at our phones** Gillian M. Sandstrom, "Social Interactions and Well-Being: The Surprising Power of Weak Ties," PhD diss., University of British Columbia, Vancouver (2013).

229 **In one experiment that proves this point** Kostadin Kushlev et al., "Smartphones Reduce Smiles Between Strangers," *Computers in Human Behavior* 91 (February 2019): 12–16.

230 **"Smiling is a really powerful social lubricant"** Jill Suttie, "How Phones Compromise Our Ability to Connect," *Greater Good Magazine* (website), January 30, 2019.

230 **"What play signals do"** Stuart Brown, *Play: How it Shapes the Brain, Opens the Imagination, and Invigorates the Soul,* with Christopher Vaughan (New York: Avery, 2010), p. 161.

231 **As one paper put it** Jordi Quoidbach et al, "Positive Emotion Regulation and Well-Being: Comparing the Impact of Eight Savoring and Dampening Strategies," *Personality and Individual Differences* 49, no. 5 (October 2010): 368–73.

231 **The title of another research paper** Matthew A. Killingsworth and Daniel T. Gilbert, "A Wandering Mind Is an Unhappy Mind," *Science* 330 (2010): 932.

231 *The Book of Delights* Ross Gay, *The Book of Delights* (Chapel Hill, N.C.: Algonquin Books, 2019).

232 **As Jennifer Aaker** Jennifer Aaker and Naomi Bagdonas, *Humor, Seriously,* p. 38.

234 **Fred Bryant, a social psychologist** Stacey Kennelly, "10 Steps to Savoring the Good Things in Life," *Greater Good Magazine,* July 23, 2012.

235 **Positive psychologists have also found** Jordi Quoidbach et al, "Positive emotion regulation and well-being."

236 **"The idea is that you can stay"** Anne Marie Conte, "Wearable Sleeping Bags: the Height of COVID Function and Fashion," *The New York Times* (website), February 16, 2021.

239   **These structures are helpful** Miguel Sicart, *Play Matters* (Cambridge, Mass: The MIT Press, 2017), p. 7-8.

239   **As Johan Huizinga explains** Johan Huizinga, *Homo Ludens* (Mansfield Center, Conn: Martino Fine Books, 2014), p. 9.

241   **Pie Madness also illustrates** Priya Parker, *The Art of Gathering: How We Meet and Why It Matters* (New York: Penguin Business, 2019), p. 120.

242   **In the words of Priya Parker** Ibid., p. x.

242   **Instead, she writes** Ibid., p. xiv.

242   **As Miguel Sicart writes** Miguel Sicart, *Play Matters*, p. 7.

243   **"Making music bears at the outset"** Johan Huizinga, *Homo Ludens*, p. 42.

244   **Traditions can be particularly potent playgrounds** Ibid., p. 12.

245   **"Of course, not every game"** Ibid., p. 12.

245   **"We all have an inclination"** Ingrid Fetell Lee, *Joyful: The Surprising Power of Ordinary Things to Create Extraordinary Happiness* (New York: Little, Brown Spark, 2018), pp. 5–6.

246   **And you should never underestimate** The initial version of this sentence read, "Never underestimate the fun-generating potential of balls." But then several friends who apparently are just as immature as I am told me that they laughed out loud upon reading that sentence and found its testicular implications to be distracting. I ended up changing it in the main text, but am including the original version here, in an endnote, as a juvenile reward for anyone who bothers to read citations.

248   **As Huizinga explains it** Johan Huizinga, *Homo Ludens*, p. 11.

249   **As bestselling author Michael Lewis** Jennifer Aaker and Naomi Bagdonas, *Humor, Seriously*, p. 233.

CHAPTER 9: REBEL

250   **"The need of feeling responsible"** William James, *Talks to Teachers on Psychology: And to Students on Some of Life's Ideals* (New York: Henry Holt and Company, 1899), pp. 199–28.

253   **As play expert Stuart Brown writes** Stuart Brown, *Play: How it Shapes the Brain, Opens the Imagination, and Invigorates the Soul*, with Christopher Vaughan (New York: Avery, 2010), p. 193.

253   **Similarly, Johan Huizinga wrote that** Johan Huizinga, *Homo Ludens* (Mansfield Center, Conn.: Martino Fine Books, 2014), p. 8.

253   **As journalist Jennifer Senior puts it** Jennifer Senior, *All Joy and No Fun: The Paradox of Modern Parenthood* (New York: Ecco, 2015), p. 99.

254   **Doing so will help you** Ibid., p. 98.

255   **William James described this** William James, *Principles of Psychology* (New York: Henry Holt and Company, 1890), p. 625.

256   **"a treasure to be retained"** Johan Huizinga, *Homo Ludens*, p. 8.

259   **4,000 participants in New York** "The No Pants Subway Ride," Improv Everywhere (website).

259   **happy means fun** *This American Life*, "Mind Games," episode 286, first aired April 8, 2005.

261   **It creates a fundamental characteristic** Johan Huizinga, *Homo Ludens*, p. 12.

261   **"to be playful is to"** Miguel Sicart, *Play Matters* (Cambridge, Mass: The MIT Press, 2017), p. 2.

CHAPTER 10: KEEP AT IT

270   **"Rest is not something that the world gives us"** Alex Soojung-Kim Pang, *Rest: Why You Get More Done When You Work Less* (New York: Basic Books, 2018), p. 10.

272   **this size is particularly conducive** Priya Parker, *The Art of Gathering: How We Meet and Why It Matters* (New York: Penguin Business, 2019), p. 51.

274   **"anticipatory savoring"** Caroline Adams Miller, *Creating Your Best Life: The Ultimate Life List Guide* (New York: Sterling, 2011), p. 205.

276   **as Caroline Adams Miller explains** Ibid.

277   **But doing so is worth it** Leaf Van Boven, "Experientialism, Materialism, and the Pursuit of Happiness," *Review of General Psychology* 9, no. 2 (2005): 132–42.

277   **Leaf Van Boven** Ibid.

281   **In fact, Google itself** Julie H. Aranda and Safia Baig, "Toward 'JOMO': The Joy of Missing Out and the Freedom of Disconnecting," *MobileHCI '18: Proceedings of the 20th International Conference on*

Human-Computer Interaction with Mobile Devices and Services 19 (September 2018): 1–8.

283 **"Some of the really transforming acts"** Stuart Brown, *Play: How it Shapes the Brain, Opens the Imagination, and Invigorates the Soul*, with Christopher Vaughan (New York: Avery, 2010), p. 213.

284 **as Ashley Whillans explains** Ashley Whillans, *Time Smart: How to Reclaim Your Time and Live a Happier Life* (Cambridge, Mass: Harvard Business Review Press, 2020), p. 87.

INDEX

Page numbers of illustrations appear in italics.

ABOUT THE AUTHOR

Dubbed "the Marie Kondo of Brains" by *The New York Times*, CATHERINE PRICE is an award-winning science journalist and speaker and the author of books, including *How to Break Up with Your Phone* and *Vitamania: How Vitamins Revolutionized the Way We Think About Food*. She is also the creator and founder of ScreenLifeBalance.com, a resource hub dedicated to helping people learn how to scroll less and live more. Her work has appeared in *The Best American Science Writing*, *The New York Times*, *Popular Science*, *O: The Oprah Magazine*, *Los Angeles Times*, *Time* magazine, *San Francisco Chronicle*, *The Washington Post Magazine*, *Slate*, *Men's Journal*, *Self*, and *Outside*, among others.

HowToHaveFun.com
catherineprice.com, screenlifebalance.com
Twitter: @catherine_price, @screenlifeblnce
Instagram: @_catherineprice, @screenlifebalance

WANT MORE FUN?

First off, thank you for taking time from everything else going on in your world to read this book. I truly appreciate it, and hope that prioritizing fun will have the same transformative effect on your life that it's had on mine. To make this more likely—and to thank you for reading the book and spreading the word—I've put together a collection of bonus resources, including quizzes and worksheets, that are designed to help you put the ideas in this book into action and to spark interesting conversations with the other people in your life. To get them, just sign up for my newsletter at HowToHaveFun. com and I'll send you an email with links.

And please, stay in touch! I love hearing from readers. You can always write to me at hello@screenlifebalance.com or reach out via @Catherine_Price (Twitter) or @_CatherinePrice (Instagram) or the contact form on CatherinePrice.com.

Watch Catherine Price take to the TED main stage to explain why having fun is the secret to a healthier life.

Photo © TED

Visit the link below to watch Catherine explain her definition of fun – what she calls 'true fun' – and share easy, evidence-backed ways to weave playfulness, flow and connection into your everyday life. A daily dose of fun is not just enjoyable; it's also essential for your health and happiness.

www.screenlifebalance.com/fun

IF YOU LIKED *THE POWER OF FUN*, YOU'LL LOVE

HOW TO

BREAK UP

WITH YOUR

PHONE

CATHERINE PRICE

'Price's book is an invaluable guide of how – in the author's own words – to turn your phone back into a tool, not a temptation. In these dopamine-drenched days of the smartphone era, hours can be lost to the mindless scroll. Price's easily digestible tome is practical, not preachy, and a must-have for even the worst phubber.'
PANDORA SYKES

'By the time I was halfway through following Price's system, I was a convert.'
New Statesman

'Entertaining (and also terrifying), this is a book that should be available on the NHS.'
Emerald Street

'This book should be number one!'
CHRIS EVANS, *The Chris Evans Breakfast Show*, BBC Radio 2